PeRRY

Other books by Dave Thompson

Red Hot Chili Peppers
Depeche Mode: Some Great Reward
Never Fade Away: The Kurt Cobain Story
Beyond the Velvet Underground
The Cure: In Their Own Words

PeRRY FARRELL

The Saga of a HYPeSTER

by DAVE THOMPSON

st. martin's griffin ⚝ new york

To Jo-Ann—
You and your great ideas!

AUTHOR'S NOTE

It should be noted that for dramatic purposes I
have occasionally taken the liberty of constructing
scenes and dialogue based on previously published
statements by or about Perry Farrell.

Photo collages on pages 18 and 176 by Hoboken Works

Library of Congress Cataloging-in-Publication Data
Thompson, Dave.
    Perry Farrell : (Pe-'rif-[e]rel) : the saga of a
hypester / Dave Thompson.
       p. cm.
    ISBN 0-312-13585-8
    1. Farrell, Perry—Biography. 2. Rock musicians—
United States—Biography. I. Title.
ML419.F375T5 1995
    781.66'092—dc20
[B]   95-21610
                                                  CIP
                                                   MN

First St. Martin's Griffin Edition: October 1995
10 9 8 7 6 5 4 3 2 1

CONTENTS

PeRRY FARRELL

The Monsters Take Off Their Masks

1

t was hell, Passchendaele with a PA system; and above the mud-drenched trenches of miserable, huddled moshers, the music echoed like mortar fire.

"Where's Perry?" howls the kid outside the artists' enclosure.

"Where the fuck's Perry?"

A few people look round, but nobody pays much attention. A quarter of a century ago, it was the brown acid that did everyone's head in. Today it's anything and everything.

Doug Coupland would be proud of him. Lank hair, flannel shirt, a stained Nirvana T-shirt, the kid *is* Generation X, or at least a very twisted approximation thereof. A tousled dirty goatee gives him a look of disheveled mischief. His eyes: a burned-out television set.

He starts spinning, arms outstretched like a heli-copter, and he's still hollering, *"Where's Perry?"* The weird thing is, Perry's on the North Stage right now, and if the kid would just stop whirling long enough to look in that direction, he'd see him, cavorting topless in mud-spattered denims through a carnival gathering of fishnet-clad fire-eaters.

There's not much chance of that, though. Losing his balance, the kid cartwheels into the small knot of kids who stand watching him, sending them flying as he lurches into the mud, and now he's lying on his back with the slime squelched in his hair, and his lips are still moving in dumb dismay. "Where's Perry?" And, maybe more important, "What the fuck's he doing here anyway?"

Before it even began, Woodstock 1994 was a con-tradiction in terms. Perry Farrell at Woodstock '94—well, now you're being ridiculous. In the quarter century that had elapsed since Woodstock's mud-spattered shroud first rose from the grave of an official upstate disaster area, Perry Far-rell did more to exorcise the lingering ghosts of the festival than anyone else in recent rock history.

Lollapalooza, the traveling circus Perry inaugurated four years before, which was rampaging through the American South during Woodstock weekend itself, was nothing if not the final proof that the age of the corporate festival was over.

No giant Pepsi banners draped the Lollapalooza stage, nobody could claim that theirs was the official sneaker/sandwich/condom of the Lollapalooza Generation, and when somebody did try to leap aboard the festival bandwagon, slip-ping its name into a television commercial, Perry was on to them like a shot.

"You're standing on the stage at the Lollapalooza," ran the proposed Ford Escort commercial, "plugging in on your Marshall amps, the fans are going wild . . . and that's just second gear."

Perry's lawyer, Eric Greenspan, told *Q* magazine that while not disparaging Ford, "Lollapalooza had no inten-tion of looking for a commercial tie-in with anybody, and if we were, I don't think the Escort would be the right car to associate Lollapalooza with."

It wasn't only the conflict of naked commerce and alternative altruism that Lollapalooza resolved. It ended the age of the static festival, too. Nobody needed to haul their cookies halfway across the country any longer. Now the show came to them, and the welter of mini-paloozas that blossomed in the footsteps of the original festival only confirmed the demise of the old ways. Lollapalooza '94 sold 90 percent of its available tickets, most of them weeks in advance. Even as Woodstock '94 got under way, it had yet to pass 60 percent; even as the gates opened on the first morning, Woodstock augered forebodingly.

Michael Lang, John Roberts, and Joel Rosenman, three of the original festival's organizers, spent five years and $30 million on putting the thing together, calling on the cream of modern rock and Woodstock survivors alike to perform.

But still everyone said that it couldn't be done, that trying to rekindle the twenty-five-year-old flames of a sensation that wasn't that sensational to begin with was a pipe dream at best, a perversion at worst, a disaster area waiting to happen. The show's own participants acknowledged that the only thing Woodstock '94 had in common with its historical counterpart was the fact that neither show was actually held in Woodstock. That, and an absolutely stellar lineup.

The team pulled off some sensational coups. They persuaded Bob Dylan to perform at the festival he had so famously snubbed twenty-five years earlier. Peter Gabriel, the Red Hot Chili Peppers, Blind Melon, Primus, Green Day, the Rollins Band—the list of attractions encompassed the musical spectrum. Joe Cocker, Country Joe McDonald, Aerosmith, the Band . . . and Perry Farrell's Porno for Pyros.

Roberts, the Block Drugs pharmaceutical heir who bankrolled the 1969 Woodstock, had worked with Perry in the past, promoting a few Jane's Addiction shows. "He's a nice guy," Perry affirmed. "So we did it."

The first day, Friday, August 12, continued un-eventful, unexciting. All across the campsite, there was a stilted sense of overachievement, and in the press tent, you could hear the first murmurings of that most ghastly question, born of sluggish ticket sales but reinforced by the rigors of actually reaching the festival site. . . . What if they threw a Woodstock and nobody came? It wouldn't be the first time, after all. Five years earlier, the twentieth anniversary of this venerable granddaddy of American festivals also passed off unnoticed, unremembered.

Would 1994 suffer the same sorry fate, memorialized only in a landfill full of undrunk commemorative Pepsi cans, unsold $135 tickets, unwanted concert recordings and video souvenirs? With Live and James the best-known bands on the first day's bill, and Blues Traveler eclipsing even the Spin Doctors' challenge for the luckless role of the new order's Sha Na Na, what loss would it have been?

Saturday brought the rain, and with it the crowds. Around 190,000 paying customers witnessed the first out-sized droplets of rain which fell, just as Ireland's Cranberries came out onstage. Almost twice that many, most of whom cheerfully bucked the exorbitant ticket prices and simply crashed their way in to the festival grounds, remained to witness Sunday's incandescent conclusion. Throughout it all, wallowing in a mire that clung to hair and clothes with the urgency of a virus, they put their entire lives on hold, as though simply being there, amidst the muck, mud, and music, was enough.

Suddenly Woodstock took on a new meaning for them all, soaring out of the dust of a tired, ancient touch-stone, shaking off the shackles of its disreputable hippie past, and dancing anew, celebrating afresh. As the slime caked their bodies, it obscured the memories, too, of the twelve-hour queues and deep-sixed bathrooms, the blanket ban on bringing even the bare essentials of life into the camp-ground, all the petty rules and regulations that were foisted upon the weekend, until all that remained was the music.

The music, the mayhem, and the appalling odor of several hundred thousand very wet, largely unwashed people crammed together into one seething mass.

Woodstock '94 worked for the same reasons Woodstock '69 worked. Because the people who were there made sure it did, and for one weekend spent rolling in mud, they would have a lifetime of memories to keep in their trunk.

Sunday began much as Saturday ended, with the sheets of rain that transformed the air itself into a shimmering haze, barely even breathable without an Aqua-Lung to hand. Saugerties was on the verge of being redefined as a lake. If the audience—already rechristened a bunch of "miserable muddy fuckheads" by a miserable, muddy Trent Reznor—even noticed, only a handful of early departures appeared to show it. They were only leaving because they needed to get to work the next morning, "and it's a helluva long way home, to . . ." Texas, Florida, Washington State.

Nineteen ninety–four may not have built upon the same peace and love tenets as its forebear, but it fulfilled them better. In the preshow haze that greeted the omnipresent MTV cameras, Perry Farrell leaned back and played his part to the hilt. "I just got to meet Carlos Santana," he said, grinning. "That was pretty heavy."

Porno for Pyros played a great show, an explosion of vivid activity, a carnival whose brilliance was only accentuated by the leaden skies above it, the muddy seas in front. A clutch of new songs ricocheted from the stage, interrupting the steady slow of now-familiar first-album favorites, and Perry, always animated, but today positively radiant, ricocheted with them. "Porno for Pyros," the self-mythologizing epic that would eventually appear on the *Woodstock II* soundtrack album, was one highlight; "Pets," pulled from the band's year-old debut album as their biggest hit single yet, was another. A tale of aliens coming to earth and making domestic playthings of the human race, Perry prefaced it with a preamble about crop circles, the mysterious markings that superstition insists were not made by earthly hand.

Even Perry's opponents acknowledge that "Pets" is a great song, and live, it transcended every accolade. Porno for Pyros had never really received their due as a live band, but at Woodstock, even the pay-per-view television audience agreed—they wadded up every past disappointment, and dumped them in the trash.

In the post-Woodstock aftermath, as the reviews rolled in from around the globe, Porno for Pyros appeared barely to have been a bit player. The band was ranked fourth on the final day's billing, before the closing triumvirate of Gabriel, Dylan, and the Red Hot Chili Peppers, but their performance was completely ignored by what were arguably the most important reviews of all, *Rolling Stone* in America, *Vox* in the U.K. The ground seemed doomed to mortality, a mere footnote in the annals of the greatest show on earth.

Perhaps it was simply an oversight, Porno for Pyros lost in the scramble to fit every name in without the page turning into a simple superstar shopping list. Other fine names, too, were omitted. Considering the fuss with which Perry's very name was once synonymous, the fuss and the media's baying overkill, was that really all it was?

Or was it, as the vultures who gather over every superstar's media demise now asserted, a sign that arch-prankster Perry had been rumbled at last, had his mask stripped away after one nightmare too many, and been revealed not as the bogeyman of rock's post-eighties hangover, which we'd always thought he could be, but as just another cosmic buffoon who'd sold us down the river?

It wouldn't be the first time.

Alice Cooper was not the first band to use horror as a pop prop. Screamin' Jay Hawkins did much the same ten years before him, Arthur Brown even more recently than that. Both of them were good as well. But Alice was better, and certainly the most realistic.

Everything about Alice Cooper was calculated to outrage, beginning with that name. What was disturbing about Alice, though, was not the fact that he was a man—which was, in any case, only evident when you wiped away the makeup from that hook-nosed birdlike face—but the fact that Alice Cooper was originally five men, and all of them, on first hearing, certifiable Grade A psychos and fruitcakes.

Then there was the stage act. Live snakes and dead babies, gang war and street fights, straitjackets and electric chairs. Today, two decades on from Alice Cooper's 1974 breakup, it all resembles so much hammy theater; entertainment has grown so much more sophisticated since Cooper's heyday, and no one would be fooled by the fake blood today.

How did it become so sophisticated in the first place? Because of Alice Cooper. At a time when "rock choreography" still meant simply knowing which foot to put in front of the other, and costuming meant changing your trousers before the first encore, Alice Cooper orchestrated extravaganzas that would put Busby Berkeley to shame, were Busby Berkeley to have choreographed snuff movies: vast, sprawling epics that didn't so much reflect, as drive a stake through the heart of, the nighttime neuroses of Middle America.

Alice Cooper ruled America through fear: fear of schizophrenia and lunacy ("The Ballad of Dwight Frye"); fear of child abuse and suicide ("Dead Babies"); fear of rebellion, and the threat of wild youth ("Eighteen," "School's Out," "Elected," monster hits one and all); but most of all, fear of the darkness that lurks in every man's soul.

"The only performance that really counts," Mick Jagger told James Fox in the 1970 movie *Performance*, "is the one that achieves madness." Alice came close to that, closer than anyone before or since. Believable *and* believed, showmen and shamans, Alice Cooper liberated American rock not only from the earnest shackles of the multi-instrumentalist supergroups that still overflowed from the recently interred 1960s, they paved the way for so much more: Kiss, later in the seventies; punk, toward the decade's end; goth and death rock in the early 1980s.

Even more than that, though, Alice Cooper confirmed what is most unique about rock 'n' roll—its ability to demolish the barriers between what is real and what is make-believe. In other media, the audience suspends its belief, accepting that the people onstage are simply playing a part, then accepting the ensuing characters under *those* terms. But what a rock star does, a rock star is, which meant that Mick Jagger could never stop being Mick Jagger, even when he was acting Ned Kelly or Turner; David Bowie was always David Bowie, no matter which mask he sang behind this time; and Alice Cooper—now personified by singer Vince Furnier—was always Alice Cooper, which meant that the things he did . . . were the things people believed he *really* did.

Alice Cooper backed down in the end, from the potential of holding office (in 1972, he sang of being "Elected," and probably could have been, too), and from the next stage of his cabaret of the grotesque. He'd taken his trip to its logical extreme, raising specters that America simply wasn't ready for; he didn't need to take it to its *il*logical one, and really unleash the madness. The next thing anyone knew, he was an all-around entertainer, playing golf with Bob Hope and finally confessing, "I Never Wrote Those Songs." The dream was over, but more important, so was the nightmare.

No one ever came close to recapturing either the intensity or the intensity of belief that Alice Cooper conjured from the disease of early-seventies America. There were pretenders to his throne, of course, and a handful of performers who even eclipsed Alice Cooper's embodiment of the all-American psycho-nut lunatic. None of them ever crossed over, not one could straddle the divide between the suspension of belief (which is what such smacked-out regional cults as the Germs' Darby Crash, and the infamous G.G. Allin, achieved) and the suspension of *dis*belief, which is what Alice Cooper traded upon.

Comparing Perry Farrell to Alice Cooper is a fascinating if fraught exercise. No less than Alice, Perry's reality is utterly indistinguishable from his fantasy. The success of the video movie *Gift*, which he produced and performed with his then girlfriend, filmmaker Casey Niccoli, proves that. Staged, at least in part, as a documentary, the Santerian marriage ceremony the couple celebrate in the movie's centerpiece was still believed by many people to be real; many people believe, too, in the narcotic-soaked world through which the celluloid Perry so easily moves.

But it is Casey who carries the bruises on her arms and thighs, not Perry; it is Casey who is shown tying off with a telephone cord (while talking to a friend of her mother's—that's cool!), Casey who shoots up, and Casey who spends most of the movie lying overdosed and dead in the apartment. Perry only fucks her corpse in the shower, then drapes it with flowers on the bed, and now there are people running around convinced that he's a necrophile as well.

Perry knows this, but he carries on regardless. "Name something degrading and I've done it," he once boasted, and though he refused to proffer details, the mere suggestion was more than enough. Whether by raising topics of conversation that society has tried so hard to bury, or by flying in the face of censorship and "Just Say No," Perry Farrell confronts taboo, and in so doing, he appeals to precisely the same public mind-set as Alice Cooper did—the need not to defy *authority*, which is, after all, what rock 'n' roll has always strived to accomplish, but to defy society itself.

The difference is, whereas Alice eventually kicked his mythology away, revealing himself as a simple, beer-drinking all-American boy, Perry has not afforded his public that relief. Through Jane's Addiction, through Lollapalooza, through Porno for Pyros, through everything, it seems, that he does, his legend remains immense, certainly larger than the body of work he has produced—larger, possibly, than life itself. While he hasn't always told the truth to the media, the media hasn't always told the truth about him.

It has often been said, of sportsmen and spokesmen, politicians and, of course, pop stars, that if they had not existed, then society would have invented them. So it is with Perry Farrell.

The world is smaller today than it has ever been in the past. We invent our own monsters, write our own myths, dream our own dreams, and out of that comes the alternate reality within which the icons of the modern age are at their most powerful. It is no coincidence that among the earliest press notices Jane's Addiction attracted, the terms that were most frequently applied to Perry were those that conjured up an otherworldliness, a sense that witnesses to his performance were witnesses to something primal, primitive, striking, stark: the flailing medicine man, the whirling dervish, the canting shaman. He tapped energies that rock 'n' roll had forgotten how to tap, and in so doing, reminded it of all it had lost . . . reminded it, and helped restore it.

Though for every acolyte there was another disbeliever, who heard the howls and dismissed them as hype, who wiped the writing from the wall the moment it appeared, the spell remained unbroken, the dreamers did not waken.

Like Johnny Rotten a decade before, Bob Dylan ten years before him, Elvis a decade earlier still, and Alice Cooper over them all, Perry lifted himself above the mundane not by virtue of his own merits, considerable though they were, but on the virtues of the people around him, the fans who stretched out their arms and gave him their hands, who laid down their souls and gave him their hearts. They suspended their disbelief. Perry is just taking it from there.

Just a Lot of Hectic Things

2

T he old woman smiled and squeezed the boy's cheeks. She called him charming, and a few other things as well, mumbled Yiddish endearments that he didn't understand, but that made him glow with embarrassment anyway. He couldn't have been more than four or five, standing with his father in that cluttered parlor full of faded tchotchkes, but even at that age, he knew why he was there.

Perry has not talked much about his childhood, but one can imagine him accompanying his father on buying trips.

On those trips he might well have met an old woman who needed money. There was rent to pay, food to buy, cats to care for, all those petty necessities she once took for granted but were so hard to come by these days. Not even in her vilest dreams could she ever have imagined, this sad old lady whose red, wrinkled eyes still danced with the vitality of youth and beauty in the photographs that lay on the mantel, that one day she would have to start selling her past just to barter for her future.

She came to America years ago, aboard one of the steamers that once crossed the oceans so effortlessly, bringing whatever she'd been able to carry: photographs in ornate frames; heavy furniture that creaked and groaned in the hold of the leviathan liners; and the family jewels, the diamonds and gold that were handed down for generations and were worth their weight in . . . There was a joke one of his father's friends once told, at one of those family dinners that went on forever, that the only thing on earth not worth its weight in gold was gold itself, particularly old gold, from the Old Country.

The boy never really understood what the Old Country was until he started accompanying his father on these little field trips. Now he knew its odor a mile away, and when he himself went there, much later in life, that odor still hung in his nostrils.

"Coming to Europe is like going to your grandma's house," he would mock. "It's full of all these pictures and knickknacks, and it's kind of dark and musty-smelling. You don't want your grandma ever to die, but you don't want to hang out at her house much, either."

The boy's father was a jeweler, with a bustling store on 47th Street, in the commercial heart of Manhattan. In many ways, the shop ran itself—upper midtown had long since inherited the Lower East Side's Jewish diamond trade, and the very sidewalks seemed to glitter from the sparklers in the windows. Customers came from all over to buy jewelry there.

Mr. Bernstein spent time far from the hustle and bustle of New York's diamond district, in houses perhaps like this one, with old ladies like this one, waiting patiently while they wondered one last time, were they doing the right thing?

"See this one, *bubeleh*?" The crone held out a brooch, painstakingly crafted, glistening even in the faded half-light of the room. "That was my mother. Wasn't she beautiful?" Her eyes were moist as she turned them toward the boy's father. "Mr. Bernstein? You wouldn't mind if I . . ."

"Keep the photograph? No, of course not. I was going to suggest that very same thing myself." The boy blinked back a tear of his own. His mother had died just a year before, and already her face was fading in his memory. He touched the brooch. It was so lovely. He wished he had something like it himself, to keep a picture of his own mom in, just like this old lady, and bring out to look at whenever he wanted to.

"The boy . . . he's so quiet. He's a thinker. You have a thinker there, Mr. Bernstein. What's his name?" She looked at the boy while she spoke, but her questions were directed over the shoulder that his father now squeezed affectionately.

"Simon."

"My boy, he was a Simon as well. It means 'to listen,' you know. My Simon, he never listened. He stayed behind, he thought everything would be all right in the end. You make sure that your one does listen, Mr. Bernstein."

She made a strange sad clucking noise at the back of her throat, and though he was far too young to have been taught about the Holocaust and the inhuman horrors that one race of people inflicted upon another, perhaps Simon would have known what she was talking about, though her words had been cloudy and vague.

In so many of the families he knew there were the people who got out, from Germany, Holland, France, everywhere the Nazi jackboot fell, and those who didn't, who had thought, like this other Simon had thought, that "everything would be all right in the end."

That was another thing he would carry with him into the future, the knowledge that many people had perished, but many more had survived, saved by their own wits, or the wits of the people around them. "If it weren't for you people," he would tell a Dutch audience many years later, "I wouldn't be here right now. Thanks for hiding my ancestors during the war."

The old woman spoke, and Simon felt the pressure of his father's hand increase just a little. "Oh well, I suppose we'd better . . ." It was time for the adults to get down to business, and Simon had been charming once again. He could have charmed the birds from the trees if he'd wanted.

Perched at the northern fringe of the modern borough of Queens, Flushing was full of houses like that, and days like that.

Flushing is one of New York's oldest neighborhoods, although it was not the Dutchmen of New Amsterdam who named it after one of their own homeland's most important naval stations. Instead, it was first settled by Englishmen, religious nonconformists who had themselves first settled around there. They came to the New World in 1644, and the influence of their religious freedom was to remain strong in the region. In 1672 the founder of the Quakers, George Fox, stayed in Flushing during his mission to the Americas, and a century later, while the rest of the country boiled with prerevolutionary fever, Flushing was a genteel backwater of Anglican calm, the county seat for the richest English colonial officers.

Flushing continued exploding with bright ethnicity, so that by the turn of the nineteenth century, when the borough of Queens was finally consolidated into New York City, its suburban character had already been determined long before.

When Simon's sisters were given dolls to play with, they came in every color of the human spectrum, just like the children they would play with at school. East Indians and Koreans arrived in such numbers that outsiders rechristened the subway "the Orient Express." Others joked about the church, which boasted so many different nationalities in attendance that it held services in four different languages, all of them Asian tongues.

New York's Jews began arriving during the first decades of the present century, erupting out of the squalid alleyways of Manhattan, among which they originally settled, and into the tidy ranch-style neighborhoods through which the Grand Central Parkway would subsequently scythe, during Robert Moses's highway-building boom of the mid-1930s.

The New York World's Fair of 1939–40, the last international exhibition to be staged before World War II, brought an estimated forty-five million people flooding into the fairgrounds on Flushing Meadow, many of them flying into the town's newly opened North Beach (now La Guardia) Airport.

As many again, or so the beleagured residents felt, would descend a quarter of a century later, when the Beatles became the first pop group to play the year-old Shea Stadium in August 1965, and even the fenced-in basketball courts that pockmarked the streets fell silent as first a Beatles blimp sailed overhead, then the Fab Four themselves passed by in the back of a Wells Fargo security van. Nobody went to bed early that evening, the keening of 56,000 hysterical teenagers jammed into the biggest pop concert in the world made certain of that.

Flushing's Jewish community was close-knit, and that made Mr. Bernstein's job much easier. When Simon was old enough to accompany him on his field trips, the warm economic opulence of the 1950s had long since exploded into the white-hot commercialism of the 1960s, with its skyrocketing prices for the commodities the television insisted you needed.

It was heartbreaking that people needed to sell their personal treasures just to keep up with the fast pace of life, mementos they'd hung on to through Stalinist purge and Hitlerite genocide. It was even more heartbreaking to think what might happen if they couldn't sell them, or if the money they collected was far less than they deserved. There were a lot of con men in the jewelry trade, so people turned to the tradesmen they knew they could trust.

"Mrs. Rubens said I should call you; I hope you don't mind, but times are so hard, and I've got a few trinkets you might want to buy. . . ." Mr. Bernstein would arrange a time to visit the house, dress Simon up in his Sabbath-best clothes, and be there punctual and pleasant.

His wife's death, in 1962, when Simon was three, shook Mr. Bernstein to the core. She left him with seven children, of whom Simon, born on March 29, 1959, was the fourth, and Bernstein did his best to ensure that, contrary to the popular saying, the middle one was not always neglected.

Perhaps he wasn't always successful. In years to come, the grown-up Simon would reflect that he barely remembered his family being around him, that for much of his childhood he existed in his own mind alone, jerked back to reality only when his older brother would pin him to the floor and force him to slap his own face.

Even a casual day out in the city with his father was not what it seemed. Nobody who saw the two of them sitting on the subway or walking hand in hand on the street would ever have guessed that the little boy's pockets were stuffed with diamonds, which of course was the whole idea. "I carried diamonds for my father, so he wouldn't get the shit kicked out of him. That's how I got all my courage."

The boy seemed destined for a career in the jewelry trade. Ask him what he wanted to do, and that's what he would reply: either a jeweler, like his dad, or a lawyer. Good professions, responsible professions, and "really Jewish shit," as Simon later laughed. What other options were there back then for a chubby little Jewish kid from Flushing, New York? Not too many.

When Simon was seven, he was designing jewelry that his father would display in the shop. His creativity came from his mother, people said; strangers might have thought it terrible as she walked home proudly hauling the bagfuls of junk which she picked up during her day's travels, but a few days later, the discarded odds and ends would be transformed.

Mrs. Bernstein had been an accomplished antique restorer, and the more restoration the antique demanded, the happier she would be. So broken chairs became as good as new, scuffed furniture shone like it was fresh from the workshop, and hideous objects were transformed into beautiful art.

Her death stole from Simon the best teacher he'd ever have, but her influence lived on, in his mind if not his art.

Creating things from silver for his father to show in his shop, that was okay, but what did it prove? Creating things from rubbish, though, something from nothing as his mother had done, that was something else entirely. That was something he could throw himself into. The careers that were already mapped out ahead of him suddenly lost their appeal. "I considered [them] for a while, but as I got older . . . by the time I was twelve years old, the idea [had] pretty much disappeared."

Looking back, a lot of things disappeared by the time Simon was twelve years old. "I used to draw bombs and naked women," he himself recollected. "They had to hide the stuff I brought home."

In 1971, when Simon was thirteen, the Bernstein family left Flushing and drove down the coast to Miami, Florida. "My father wanted to get out to a warmer climate." Simon didn't want to move. It was, he later snapped, "fucked."

He dates his departure from the sports scores. "Everywhere I move, the teams do incredibly," he mused. Between 1969 and 1970, New York City carried all before it as the Knicks won the NBA, the Jets took the Super Bowl, and just down the road from the Bernstein home, the Mets won the World Series!

Three years later, with the family happily living among the transplanted blue-rinsed harpies of Miami, it was that city's turn, and the Dolphins swept to two successive Super Bowl victories, in 1973 and 1974. "It's me, I'm the charm!" laughed Simon fifteen years later. He'd moved to Los Angeles, "and now, as you know, L.A. is totally ripping!"

Miami wasn't everything that New York was, muggy summers and frigid winters. Simon himself could barely remember the decaying landmarks of his hometown. It didn't even matter that half the voices he heard were pure, native Queens. Bellowing out over the sun-drenched boulevards and

beaches, even they were affected by the abrupt change of pace. Compared with New York City, everything was slower, lazier, warmer; even the gangs, just beginning to blossom within the first lapping breakers of what would become a tidal wave of Cuban immigrants, looked healthier, happier.

On the beach every moment he could be, Simon learned first how to surf, then how to make surfboards, for sale to the battalions of tourists and college kids who descended upon Miami in droves every year and never seemed to go away.

"There were a lot of kids like that on the beach," remembers Marky, a Pittsburgh student who joined the traditional spring-break exodus religiously every year. "They would attach themselves to a group, join in a game of beach volleyball, share a joint with someone, pick up one of the girls, become part of the scenery. They were like little tour guides, they knew all the best places to score, the best bars to get loaded in, the best clubs to get laid at . . . ."

You could spot them a mile off as well, because they were the ones who could so easily do all the things that the visitors tried so hard to do. The best surfers, the best swimmers, were always the kids who'd spent all year on the beach, with nothing better to do than swim and surf. Sixteen-year-old Simon knew every wave in Miami.

The beach wasn't Simon's only distraction, though. After Eric Clapton brought Derek and the Dominos down to Criteria Studios in August 1970 and emerged with *Layla and Other Assorted Love Songs*, Miami became a must-stop spot on every touring band's itinerary. Clapton himself was back there in 1974, recording at Criteria and hanging out at the Spanish-style house that he immortalized in his next album title, *461 Ocean Boulevard*.

For the month or so that Clapton and his band were in town, Ocean Boulevard was a teenage magnet. It was the same when Rod Stewart blew into Criteria for his groundbreaking *Atlantic Crossing* album. Rock 'n' roll's star system was in full cry through the pre-punk 1970s, and the untidy knots of curious kids who might hang round a musician's hotel today would have been a small army encampment two decades ago.

Simon's own musical taste was dictated exclusively by peer pressure, what the kids he went to high school with were into, "and whatever I heard on the radio." He was fifteen, sixteen, seventeen years old, sneaking into the Sportatorium to see whichever superstars were passing through, but it was strange. There was always that aching sense of unfulfillment to deal with, settling in his belly halfway through the drum solo; bilious in his throat when the audience held up burning Bics. Rock 'n' roll was the music of rebellious teens, and he'd always thought of himself as both a teen and a rebel. But somehow it wasn't connecting. Somehow, "Free Bird" didn't make him want to smash the system. It just made him want to break his radio.

The mid-seventies was the age of Alice Cooper slipping into the era of Kiss, theater rock turning into glitter. And the volume kept increasing. Jim Dandy's Black Oak Arkansas was one of the biggest live bands in the country, Led Zeppelin the biggest in the world.

Peter Frampton was breaking out everywhere, proclaiming, "(I Want You to) Show Me the Way," and Captain Fantastic himself, Elton John, was breaking hearts and dropping jaws with every new extravagant stage suit. Radio stations programmed him constantly, describing themselves as "your number-one Elton John station," priding themselves that they played more Elton than their competitors, more Elton than the human brain could take.

Suddenly punk arrived and pushed an entire generation of rock 'n' roll bands into premature retirement. It would be years before the old order recovered, years during which a new order would erupt, and hopefully, hatefully, keep the old one in check. Won't get fooled again? You bet we won't. Unless, of course, we happen to live in Florida.

Punk hit America in dribs and drabs, isolated outbreaks that shuddered through the biggest cities and left a few weird-looking kids on the streets of the smaller ones. By mid-1977, though, most everyone knew what was happening and was bringing it into their own backyard. New York and Los Angeles bristled with homegrown psychosis, San Francisco and Boston weren't far behind; even Seattle, up in the middle of nowhere, had the Fastbacks, just setting off on a musical journey that, in 1995, is still going strong.

Down in sunny Miami, though, the waves still crashed, and out on the boardwalk, the bath chairs still creaked. The leather-clad, three-chorded Ramones, then the play-anywhere-anytime-anyplace Ramones, played fucking Finland before they hit Florida. When the state's first indigenous punk band, Roach Motel, kicked out their own ode to their homeland, the treasonous "I Hate the Sunshine State," it was already too late for the in-crowd. They'd upped and split the place ages before. Simon watched them leaving, and he vowed he'd follow them out.

Falling back on the profession his father once mapped out for him, Simon picked up some jewelry-making equipment, making pendants and earrings he would take into town and hawk around at the jewelers'. "There's always a cool silver shop in every town," he recalls. "I'd try to get work just designing jewelry."

He earned money every way he could. Although he had no academic training, "I was doing graphic arts. I just sort of picked it up." Eventually, though, his interest started to fade, and Simon only kept at it because it helped pay the bills, and helped toward his Greyhound fare, too. Once he'd bought the ticket, he barely had twenty-five dollars to his name. The day Simon left home, his father had a heart attack.

They say that the best way, the only way, to see America is from the window of a moving vehicle, a train or a bus. You can probably blame Simon and Garfunkel for that; they recorded "America" in 1968, and promptly enshrined the romance of Greyhound in the cultural memory of a nation.

Simon's bus was bound for California, where he had a friend in Hemet, a city out beyond the Los Angeles suburbs. He figured he'd crash there for a while at first, then see what happened.

The only time you ever read of Hemet in California tourist guides is in April and May, when the entire area is given over to the outdoor play *Ramona*. There wasn't even a Greyhound terminal there; the nearest station was in Perris, and as Simon stood on the station forecourt, waiting while the driver rooted through the luggage compartment in search of the only piece of luggage he had, Simon wondered why he'd even bothered bringing it. It was his surfboard—and the ocean was over sixty miles away.

Work was easier to come by in California than it had been in Miami. He worked for a while in a vitamin factory, then moved to Oceanside, halfway between Los Angeles and San Diego. Here, at least, he'd be able to surf.

It was weird, though. Oceanside is the gateway to the U.S. Marine base at Camp Pendleton, and the military dominates the city, off-duty and on. On the beach, Simon would find himself surfing alongside the camp's prize athletes; in the bars, he'd be drinking with the prize knuckleheads, and occasionally, Simon would drop into conversation with one of them, to try and figure out what went on inside their little shaven skulls.

Tensions were high at the base at the tail end of the 1970s. Half a planet away, Soviet troops had spent Christmas 1979 marching into Afghanistan, and nobody knew what was coming next: A move into the already critically unstable infant republic of postrevolutionary Iran? An invasion of India? A ruthless drive to the Persian Gulf, to secure the oil upon which the Western world depended? The possibility that American forces might finally be marshaled against the communist foe that had haunted U.S. dreams through a never-ending Cold War was never far from anybody's mind, and the Marines were almost rabidly gung ho. Why? Simon wanted to know. Why?

He enrolled himself in an art course at Oceanside College, but according to his own mythology, a nervous breakdown sent him reeling out of class, and out of work. He was twenty-one, living in Orange County, and he didn't have much choice in his life. He was only an hour or so outside of Los Angeles, but sometimes it felt like an eternity away. So did reality.

Orange County bored him, he quickly discovered, with its "shitty K-Marts and strip malls," its eager-to-please-you plasticity, its garrulous, soul-crushing greed, the studied superficiality that oozed from every corner. Nothing about the place appeared genuine, not the gaiety of the Disney Kingdom, nor the bronzed-beach-boy-and-babe parade you could see on every beach, every day.

He started kicking northward, then, reaching into the sleazy soul of the city itself, the city of lost angels: L.A. You found all the same filth there, but at least you could scrape the glitter away, and beneath it, bathe in good, honest filth.

There's a tension that cuts through L.A. like a switchblade, the knowledge that around every corner, off the most opulent streets, poverty, pain, and paranoia lurk, waiting to embrace even the most careful passerby.

Years later, Simon would try to explain the city to an Englishman. "It's just not the same as living in London. It's a lot more violent. In L.A. there are drive-by shootings every day, you can't even tell a fourteen-year-old to fuck off 'cause he might blow you away." All the shit that you can step in on the streets of New York, Chicago, of any major city, Los Angeles has in abundance and then some. But like Simon said when someone asked him why he even stayed there, "It's a helluva lot nicer having it going on in a temperate climate."

What initially caught Simon's attention was the punk scene. It was as if youth as a whole had risen up in violent rebellion; all it needed now was to work out precisely what it was rebelling against. Its past, the bitter butt of too many Linda Ronstadt jokes? Its present, the smog-choked asshole of a million splintered Hollywood dreams? Or its future, mapped out by daddys who heard you sing along with the Clash's "Brand New Cadillac" and offered to buy you one of your own? Good thing you weren't singing "White Riot" instead.

With this new city came a new life; Simon demanded a new identity. First, he picked Perry, because that was his older brother's name; then he tacked on Farrell, because when you put the two together and said them really fast . . . perry-farrell became: peripheral. It means something that remains on the outside, an observer, watching and winking, but never really getting involved. That was how Simon always wanted to be; that was how Perry would forever remain. He would encourage, he might even give directions, but he would never, ever, get involved.

In his first movie, *Gift*, Perry would script in a piece of dialogue that encapsulated his new identity better than anything else ever could. For close to an hour, the viewer would have watched his character progress through life with hedonistic abandon, scoring drugs and screwing stiffs, but when the cops come around and ask him if he's ever been arrested, he can honestly look them full in the face and say no. And even the cop can't believe it. "Never?"

Newly named Perry started hanging out at the suburban clubs, the redneck biker bars that had either surrendered voluntarily or simply been seconded by the local punk community. The bands they staged were usually mediocre, second-generation hardcore thrash merchants who gave nothing more to their audience than an excuse to go completely crazy: breakneck guitar breaks with plenty of yelling, a lot of foul language, herniated hedonism. The audience impressed Perry more than the music, and it was the audiences that kept him going back.

There was also a new sense of kinship there, a sense that even with a switchblade at your throat and a broken bottle in your fist, and the violence so heavy you could taste it on your tongue, everybody was in it together, and they'd better help one another out. Because no one else was going to.

Perry learned to slam, the insanely violent dance that spread out of Huntington Beach's own rabid hardcore punk scene, and made headlines in the *Los Angeles Times*. The dance was painful as hell. It was true what people said about ambulances parking outside punk concerts before the show even started, waiting for the first battered slam casualties to come out. Perry delighted in it anyway, the physical contact, the energy, the sheer sense of invulnerability you felt when you merged with the seething mob and crashed the night away on pure, naked adrenaline. "And if you fell, they picked you up and everybody was your friend."

Naked aggression was what fired punk in the first place; naked aggression was the only thing that could keep it going into the future. That and the belief that no matter how fucked up things were, by directing that aggression in whichever direction it demanded, maybe things could change for the better. When someone asked Perry his ambition, it was frighteningly pure: "I want to feel like I can walk down the street in a pair of goofy underwear, and a weird haircut, and a tattoo that says 'mom' that was done by my friend, and it's really ugly, and nobody's gonna go, 'Hey, fuck you, asshole!'"

That wasn't going to happen; not yet, anyway. Punk paranoia spread through Los Angeles like brushfire. The clubs that hadn't banned punk had either closed down or been busted. There was the great "Nazi Surf Punk Killer" scare, when every unsolved murder was blamed on the punk-rock psychos who were allegedly hanging out on beaches in the hope of becoming some stranger's vilest nightmare. There were the cops out on Huntington Beach, who rated punk bands as dangerous as street gangs, and reacted to them accordingly. Walk down the street in a Circle Jerks T-shirt then, and you could be spending the night in a cell.

Punk's nihilism was contagious. If the music insisted that nothing really mattered, it was easy, so easy, to start believing that yourself, especially when you found that the only things you did care for either ended up dead or ended up buried.

Darby Crash, the mercurial frontman with the legendary Germs, jammed a needleful of smack through his vein, then stretched out his arms in mock crucifixion, to overdose on drugs and raw Christian symbolism. The Masque, the only club the punks could call home, was padlocked shut by the LAPD. Everywhere it was the same, everywhere it was the end. Twice, Perry would later remark, he himself was brought back from the brink of death, and both times he'd curse when he discovered how close he had come. He'd wanted to die because living was too much hard work.

He spent some time living in his car, and endured another spell on the beach, with his surfboard and some art supplies. All that he wanted to do was draw and surf. "I was pretty aimless, and at that age, aimless means nothing because you don't know you're supposed to be aiming for anything."

When he did set about looking for real work again, his father stepped in to help him. He had a friend who was president of a liquor company, "and he told me he could put me to work."

The job sounded great, even if Perry would have to wear a suit and tie. He'd be on the road all day, making deliveries and taking orders; essentially he'd be his own boss. He could even dump the jacket and tie while he drove.

It's one thing, though, to see liquor in bars, sparkling in the bottles, to enjoy a shot or three of the stuff on your way to getting drunk. It's quite another "when you see rows and rows of this fluid, this weird clear, brownish fluid in bottles. It freaks you out that they're selling this to people. Most people are screwed up anyway, then when you put that down their throats, what'll happen?" Perry wasn't a prude, but there was something about peddling poison that scared him. Was that what he'd come to Los Angeles for? To become a pusher, with the only thing between him and a full-blown smack dealer the thin moral line between hard drink and hard drugs?

He ended up hating the job. He was a great salesman, but a lousy liquor merchant. Every trip he made, he vowed it would be his last, but when he tried to explain how he felt to his father, his old man just couldn't understand. The last time he called his father and new stepmother, it was a bitter exchange.

"We got into a big fight and I told them both to fuck off, that I never wanted to see them again or speak to them." That very day, Mr. Bernstein suffered his second heart attack.

One afternoon as he made his rounds, Perry noticed a stop he'd never had before, a nightclub out in the boaters' paradise of Newport Beach.

The club boasted its own modeling troupe, a team of models, dancers, and actors who staged a nightly cabaret, and while Perry stood around waiting, he watched the video of the previous week's show, which flickered on a television by the bar.

Maybe it was something on his face, a supercilious smirk stretching those rubbery features into a mocking grimace perhaps, or maybe it was something *about* his face, but he'd only been watching for a few moments when a woman walked over. Perry nodded hello; he recognized her from the video. By the time he said good-bye, he was a member of the dance troupe.

"I kind of bluffed my way in. I told her I was a model and she asked me what else I did. They did all these things. They modeled and they had dancers and they put on shows, so I told 'em I did everything. I was a model, and I sang and danced and did impersonations."

In fact, he'd done none of these things, although he was hanging out with people who had. "I was into the idea of acting and modeling when I was really too stupid to realize how stupid the idea was. I liked the idea of modeling because I was really vain."

He had been along to a handful of auditions, but he lost interest very quickly. It was simply too dispiriting "waiting in line with guys that were six-four and really gorgeous." The only thing he got out of the auditions, he later laughed, were a lot of offers to sleep with people. Usually fat, ugly little men who knew someone who knew someone. . . .

The casting couch was alive and well, but Perry wasn't about to climb aboard.

This nightclub thing, though, this was different. For a start, they'd come to him, and he'd just led them on a little. He'd seen the video and he'd been to enough other clubs to know what was expected from him.

"It took me about two weeks," he says, and he was onstage every night, sometimes clad in nothing but the skimpiest of g-strings, other times encased in full-blown pop-star drag, miming whoever was hot or hysterical at the time, throwing in impersonations he'd make up on the spot, putting everything he could into his little performance.

Studying photographs and, in those days before the newborn MTV had reached its tentacles into Southern California, television appearances, Perry discovered that he was a natural mimic. Mick Jagger's pout and stadium stomp-dancing, Bowie's cool indifference, Rotten's stooped sneer—he could carry them all off, and in rehearsal he'd mix and match his impressions, until the audience could almost hear him thinking, If *I* were a rock star, this is what I'd be.

"And people reacted to me like I was really singing!" Perry was incredulous. "People were asking for my autograph! People liked it real fast!"

His newfound success surprised him. He had never practiced singing when he was younger, hadn't even entertained the rock-star dreams that amuse so many other teens. He had just watched. "I felt real comfortable doing it. It was just kind of a natural thing. It just came out of nowhere." He truly believed that fate, eventually, makes sure that "you get pushed into going where you belong, and I just kind of went with the flow.

"I put a lot of hard work into it once I said, 'Hey, this is happening and I'm having a great time.'" People were already under the impression that he was singing when he was onstage. Now he wondered what would happen if he really did sing.

Hanging around his apartment, Perry would put on his headphones, stack a pile of records beside the deck, and

DEATH CULT

blast away entire evenings just singing to himself, flinging himself as far as the cord would allow. "I spent a lot of time singing with headphones on . . . to train myself," he remembers.

He kept his eyes closed throughout these performances. "That way you don't feel bummed out, and you can give the exact same feeling as if there were a zillion people there. You just go into your own head."

He wasn't one hundred percent happy with the sound of his own voice. It had range, it had power, but he learned from his mimickry that there is still only so much that you can do with the human voice. So he started to "mess around with electronics and stuff," developing sound effects that he could apply to his vocals.

Then he started writing songs, something else he'd never tried before. It wasn't easy; his first efforts, he readily admits, were childish, fixating around being homeless and having rich men steal his girlfriends from him. "Just a lot of hectic things."

At long last he was ready. The way he looked at it, "I've had a lot of time to do things besides music. I think I've paid my dues." He bought himself a PA system and moved up to the city. He'd spent "probably a year just singing alone. . . . I didn't look for a band for a long time." While the rejections came fast and furious, once he'd started, he didn't give up. The sound was already locked in his head. All he needed to find were the musicians who could unlock it.

The British group Bauhaus released "Bela Lugosi's Dead" in mid-1979, nine and a half minutes of spectral clanking; intense, insistent, inspiring. Though the song started as a joke, it spawned an entire genre; an art-school arty project that clicked and clacked and rattled its chains, then spread them across a 12-inch single that hit the independent stores like a plague and blew the seventies off like a hurricane.

There never had been a musical movement like goth. Other forms had dipped into theater, combining performance with art, then layering the soundtrack over it, but from the moment goth started to seep from the closed coffin of punk, there was no questioning its uniqueness. Nor its precociousness.

It was a movement that opened with the Damned's Dave Vanian's vampire-chic stage and the cold metallic Poe-like scars of the first Siouxsie and the Banshees album; peaked with the rise of Joy Division, the post-punk Mancunians whose two-album career was cut short on the eve of a sold-out trip to America by the suicide of their vocalist, Ian Curtis; and exploded overground with the Cure and the rain-soaked cathedral of shadows of *Faith* the following year.

Goth influences were Roxy Music, David Bowie, T. Rex, Alice Cooper, a twisted sexuality, and lashings of black humor. The Banshees' Steve Severin recalls of his band's gothic heyday, "We'd say, 'Make it a cross between the Velvet Underground and the [shower] scene from *Psycho*.'"

Dyed black hair, deep black makeup, Sunday shroud costumes, and faces white as driven death—by 1982, goth was breaking out everywhere, and in every guise: oozing leather across the Top 40 sleaze joints of London, the Birthday Party allying Nick Cave's horror vocals to some of the gothiest song titles ever ("Release the Bats"—how could you resist?); the Cocteau Twins twisting sideways through cobwebs and strange—even the Lords of the New Church pounding to a "World Without End," Red Lorry Yellow Lorry . . . No less than punk's easy absorption of everything from the Clash to Costello, goth's confidence knew no bounds.

The heart of the goth scene was the Batcave, the club that opened in London's Dean Street in the spring of 1982. Nik Fiend, vocalist with primal goths Alien Sex Fiend, remembers, "The Batcave really was an alternative to whatever else was happening at the time, an alternative independent. It was the perfect outlet for doing something that made no sense. I was always into Alice Cooper, but I was also into Salvador Dali, so for me it was an opportunity to do something that was visually exciting, to an audience that was equally visually exciting."

He continues, "The people that we knew at the inception of the Batcave really were a diverse group, which is something Mrs. Fiend [Nik's intriguingly named wife] and I often commented upon. It was this mental idea of loads of people, photographers, clothes designers, musicians, artists, people from all different walks of life all thrown in together, everybody helps everybody through. Other people, the media, just shut that out because they didn't want to hear it. They wanted goth to be—goth. But the Batcave exploded into a thousand million fragments."

A few of these fragments embedded themselves into Los Angeles. There were no specific goth clubs in town, just a handful of venues that entertained the morbid masses: the Anti-Club on Melrose, the Roxy on Sunset, the Music Machine, and so on. There, basking in the half-light of the funereal freak show, Perry heard the closest thing to the music he had dreamed up for himself.

Christian Death was the first of the American goth bands to stir, toward the end of the 1970s. Led by the teenaged transvestite outrage of Rozz Williams, powered by the shattered riffing of former Adolescents guitarist Rikk Agnew, in terms of future influence, Christian Death would essentially become America's answer to the Banshees, Bauhaus, and the Batcave all rolled into one.

"People categorized us because of the theatrics, the stage sets, and how we were dressed," reflects vocalist Williams, "although I never really considered Christian Death a goth group. It came from a punk-rock attitude. To me, the musical style was combining punk with the stuff I grew up with: the whole English Glitter thing, David Bowie, Roxy Music."

Rapidly following in Christian Death's footprints, 45 Grave was formed in Los Angeles in 1981, by ex–Germs drummer Don Bolles, Gun Club bassist Rob Graves, and the Phoenix duo Paul B. Cutler and Dinah Cancer. Their roots, too, were unquestionably punk, but Graves's musical background alone demanded a darker edge, a macabre melding of campy heavy metal and horror-movie thrash.

Los Angeles audiences, which were once distinguished by their disparity, suddenly became a sea of black-caped conformity, draping funeral processions from the doors of the Anti-Club, and as they moved, so the bands they followed moved with them, physically and emotionally.

The defining moment in the development of American gothic was the release, in November 1981, of *Hell Comes to Your House*, a compilation album that led off with Christian Death, 45 Grave, and Eva O's Super Heroines, then exploded with the remainder of the Los Angeles/Orange County goth scene as it metamorphosized from its stark punk homebase after one bumpy ride on the bandwagoning plague cart: the Conservatives, Modern Warfare, Secret Hate, and a very early incarnation of Social Distortion. For a short time, even without a Batcave-like home base to call its own, goth gelled even in the brilliant sunshine of California.

Perry's vision gelled with it. Christian Death, 45 Grave, the Super Heroines—all those other bands approached their art from a pure Hollywood punk stance. Perry dreamed of excising the punk middleman altogether. The bands he listened to most were those that haunted the fringes of mainstream goth but had sidestepped the most obvious connotations, concentrating instead on its intensity and purpose: the Cure, the Banshees, the Cocteaus, and Joy Division—four faces of the phoenix which rose from the ashes of punk's cremation of the old art-school rock regime.

There was the Irish band U2, in 1982 still poised at the precipice between alternative cult heroism and all-out stadium-packing superstardom. There were the Psychedelic Furs, arguably the most brilliant British band of the early to mid-1980s. Maybe, Perry mused, maybe there was no way that anybody could improve on the Psychedelic Furs' wall of bellowing sound. If only a band could combine it with the intensity of Joy Division and the commitment of U2, they could have a damned good try.

Los Angeles, as 1982 rolled into 1983, was a good time to be having such visions as well. Beyond even the wild experimentation of goth, the city was locked into a flux in which anything, or anyone, could become what the local press was euphemistically calling "the next big thing." The Red Hot Chili Peppers were feeding the city a new diet of frenzied funk. By the time they were six months old, they were signing a seven-album deal with EMI. What Is This, spiritual kin to the Red Hots, but infinitely more convoluted and arty, were on the verge of signing to MCA.

From the spiraling punk-based flamboyance of the Minutemen and Savage Republic, to the seething Afrobeat of the Bonedaddys; from the histrionic metal guitars of Disaster and Road Crew, to the convoluted firestorm of punk's last gleaming, melting into the twisted speed-metal roar of hardcore; the city's music raced feverishly toward the cleavage of the decade. Perry was racing as fast as anyone.

When he finally made the decision to move into the city, Los Angeles still hit Perry like a gang of hoodlums. Literally. His first day there, he was set upon by a gang of twenty punks who didn't like the way he looked or the way he dressed. They thought he didn't belong. The next morning, he went out and got a Mohawk haircut. No one ever made that same mistake again.

B o o, m !
There's a
Guy on My
W i n d -
s h i e l d

3

T he classified ad in the *Recycler,* Los Angeles's premier free weekly, looked promising, even if the job it offered wasn't. Perry wasn't a drummer, never wanted to be a drummer, and that's what the ad was after. WANTED: DRUMMER.

The band sounded cool, though, and the groups it cited as influences sounded even cooler: U2, Joy Division, even the Furs. They wanted a drummer; Perry wondered how would they react if they were offered a messiah. As he dialed the number at the bottom of the *Recycler* ad, he'd convinced himself that he would be singing with the band before they even knew what hit them.

"I was in luck," he laughed later, because the guy who answered the phone, Rich, "hated" the singer the band was already rehearsing with, and complained he couldn't sing. Perry was invited down to try out while the other guy wasn't around, and even though they only jammed, they were sure that something clicked. "Okay, you're in."

Psi Com was only a couple of months old when they placed the *Recycler* ad, pieced together around guitarist Vince Duran, an *L.A. Times* writer remembered only by his Christian name, Terry, and the drum machine they'd been hoping Perry would supplant. Their vision grew with the lineup: the husband-and-wife team of Rich and Marisca joined first, followed by a singer who couldn't sing.

It would be Perry, however, who made the whole band coalesce, who visualized the music Psi Com wanted to play as something that reached far beyond simple bars, chords, and a collection of post-punk import albums. He even turned up for his audition with an armful of lyrics, because he wasn't the only one who was going on trial. They were as well, and if they didn't like his writing, then that would be the end of it. Perry was the only band member who was writing much.

The group carried on rehearsing with the drum machine. Perry hated it; there were enough bands out there already, trying to copy the Sisters of Mercy, the three-piece that was two singles old who were already redefining the sound of English goth. The last thing he wanted to do was throw himself onto that same clicking scrapheap. Psi Com kept the DRUMMER WANTED ad running.

Terry left and wasn't replaced; shortly after, Rich and Marisca quit, too. Even though he'd brought him into the group, Rich never seemed to have time for Perry. Tempers flared constantly, the slightest thing setting one or the other of them off. But while Rich kept his own counsel, never letting on what it was about Perry that so rubbed him the wrong way, Perry had no doubts whatsoever. "He hated me," he still insists today, "because I started doing flyers."

Psi Com weren't gigging very often, but when they did, Rich would design the advertising posters that would then be gummed all over Hollywood, working into the night at a table covered with clippings. "Science logos, dinosaurs, and shit like that." Rich and Marisca had a massive library, and even Perry agreed that what Rich did was "cool!"

What Perry was dreaming of was cooler. "I just don't think he liked me doing paste-up art. He was Mr. Paste-Up Man."

Perry wouldn't let up, though. Working just as hard, just as late, as Rich did, he would turn up at rehearsals, bubbling over with enthusiasm: "Hey! Check this out!" Rich would quietly seethe while the others gasped and gabbled. He never said a word. "He couldn't tell you what was on his mind," Perry mourned, "so he held it in and his head just kept getting bigger and bigger and bigger. You could tell something was bugging him."

When Rich finally announced he was quitting, and that Marisca would be going with him, Perry's first response was total panic.

"But why? Why do you want to quit?"

Rich looked down. "I just do."

"Don't you think we're any good? Don't you think Psi Com will make it?"

"I don't know." Rich wouldn't commit himself, he just wanted out. The way Perry reasoned things out, if "he wouldn't say he didn't think we would make it," there really was only one alternative possibility, completely absurd though it was. "I swear to God, I think he just wanted to be the only one doing the flyers."

Rich and Marisca left around the same time the *Recycler* ads finally paid off, and a real drummer, Aaron Sherer, called up. Perry answered the phone.

"What music are you into?"

Sherer told him. "The kind of groups you say in the ad."

Perry probed some more. "What clothes are you into, then?"

Sherer said he had a Mohawk, a roosterlike explosion of brightly dyed hair which erupted from a strip along his otherwise clean-shaven head. And Perry said, "Cool, me too."

"And, I've got a feather in my ear. . . ."

"That's good enough for me!"

Newly reconstituted, with Sherer's powerful drumming at last giving the group's sound the kind of resonance the drum machine was never capable of, Psi Com resumed their sporadic gigging schedule, airing the swooping atmospherics that fought their shadowy duels in the combination of Duran's effects-laden guitar, and Perry's equally echo-drenched voice. He picked up an Ibanez EM1000 echo box, and though he was still coming to grips with it, already Psi Com had a distinctive sound. Now they had to figure out what to do with it.

Perry was working for a commercial artist, operating the stationary camera. It was the perfect life. "I would go into the darkroom," he remembers, "and I would just sit there writing poetry." Then someone would start banging on the door, demanding, "'What the fuck's wrong with the stat?' and I'd say, 'It's coming, it's coming!'"

Perry's early flyers for Psi Com were simple, graffitied images cut from magazines mostly, but, like the lyrics he was spewing so frantically, they abounded with jokes, puns, and twisted common sense.

One, advertising a show at Al's Bar, depicts a beggar, denounced both in Perry's childlike script—*Greedy was the beggar*—and punningly, with the numeral 23 inscribed on the man's open hand—P(s)alm 23: "The Lord is my Shepherd, I shall not want." The riddle did not end there, though. *Psi*, in the band's name, is the twenty-third letter in the Greek alphabet.

Perry's songwriting showed this same gift for the incisive absurdity, even if he has since claimed, "I used to just pull out the thesaurus and wing it." He certainly took it seriously then, so seriously that whichever job he was holding down at the time swiftly took second billing to the band until finally he'd be fired.

"I just wanted to concentrate on the band," he pleads in self-defense. Psi Com meant so much to him, how could he ever concentrate on the mundanities of the nine-to-five life? Or the mundanities of everyday life in general?

One evening, Perry told *Hypno*, "I was driving along, listening to the rehearsal demos, thinking about what-the-fuck . . . just spacing out. I'm like, 'La lala lala . . .' and suddenly, Boom!" Perry dramatized. "There's a guy on my windshield.

"I have this sickness about me where I just can't stop writing or thinking," Perry explained. "There's no end. You know the feeling when someone tells you that you gotta move, like no one will let you settle?"

In August 1984, Psi Com opened for Ian Astbury's fast-rising Cult, playing their Los Angeles debut at the Music Machine. Born amidst the clammy trappings of the British goth scene, but pursuing a vision that reached way beyond even those generous confines, the Cult was still only slowly moving from the pounding tribalisms that characterized the band's original Southern Death Cult identity, to the white-hot metal that the Cult would eventually perfect.

"Moya," the original group's thunderous first single, had been a Los Angeles club favorite from the moment it hit the import racks in December 1982, and Psi Com was just one of many bands that had sensed the sheer primitive power of the song's percussive backdrop; sensed it, and then incorporated it into their own sound. Certainly its shattering percussion drove "Ho Ka Hey" through the splintered attack of Vince Duran's guitar, providing Perry himself with a musical signature that would ultimately even outlive Psi Com.

The Cult's newly unleashed "Resurrection Joe" was soaring to the same heights as its predecessor, and to coincide with its release, the group was making its American debut with a handful of shows split between the two coasts. At a time when the Cure and the Sisters of Mercy were yet to break out of the cozy confines of regional acclaim, the Cult's sights were set squarely on becoming the first British goth band to make serious inroads into the American market.

"We'd only heard the records," remembers Kerry Tamm, one of the hundreds of black-frocked kids who seethed at the lip of the stage from the moment the club doors opened. "So everybody was expecting them to come out in gothic makeup and dresses. Instead, Ian Astbury was totally into the tribal rock 'n' roll gypsy look, and it just blew people away. Leather pants, frilled shirt, the lot.

"Psi Com looked good," Kerry continues, "with Perry shaking his Mohawk around, but they dressed very normal. After the Cult show, though, Perry really started to put on a show with his clothing, and there was a definite Ian Astbury influence, even if Perry didn't go in for the bandanna. He left that for Guns N' Roses!"

The Cult show seems to have marked a turning point in Psi Com's development. Perry began allowing his Mohawk to grow out, until it sprouted the long bell-tipped braid from which would eventually tumble Perry's trademark dreadlocks. He talked with increasing enthusiasm about body-piercing—at that time a statement the public mind reserved purely for sexual deviants and all-purpose perverts. One night he turned up at a show wearing a homemade mask.

The idea, Perry explained as the band waited backstage, was for him to perform the early part of the set wearing his mask, but keeping his back to the audience. It was a trick he'd learned from John Cale, who once performed entire shows like that. Perry, of course, would take the routine even further.

When Perry finally turned around, Aaron remembered, the band would hit his head and the mask would crack. The effect from the first rows of the audience would be as if his face had shattered, while behind him, the backdrop would erupt into a kaleidoscope of colored slides.

It was a very physical performance.

At one venue, "One of the club owners was a real schmuck who had ripped off other bands," Perry remembers. Furious that Psi Com was even booked into the place, but determined that they would never return there, Perry decided to take matters into his own hands.

When Psi Com's set was reaching its conclusion, Perry measured the space between stage and bar, then launched himself skyward.

His aim was perfect. He came down on the bar, sliding on his ass from one end to the other, sending drinks and drinkers everywhere. It was carnage personified, and even as he slid, Perry cackled with glee. No one likes to have their bar trashed, and so what if the schmuck kept the band's payment back? He probably wasn't intending to pay them anyway.

The stunt simply looked too good. With the show at an end, the club owner walked up to the band with a smile and their money and asked them when they'd be back. He thought they were great.

As Psi Com's Los Angeles following grew, so their confidence followed it skyward. They needed, the band members decided, to start looking out of town for work, to expand their fan base. San Francisco, San Diego, Victorville all beckoned.

Victorville has few claims to rock 'n' roll immortality. Christian Death's Rozz Williams was born there, and spent his early adolescence stalking the streets in dresses and makeup, "getting beaten up by rednecks, then going out the next day to show I didn't care."

Even so, Rozz's patent outrage caused little more than a ripple in the heat-hazed calm of Victorville. The city's biggest draw is the Roy Rogers Museum, the ultimate Hollywood cowboy experience, with its studiously stuffed body of the faithful horse Trigger, and an African safari scene populated with the bodies of all the wild things Roy has killed. If a teenage transvestite couldn't disturb the city's equilibrium, how could a bunch of painted L.A. freaks hope to compete with that?

Psi Com played their Victorville show to the usual out-of-town smattering of curious onlookers, then headed down to a nearby AM/PM convenience store for beer. As

they piled out of their van, a watching passerby saun-
tered over.

"You guys are freaks! You guys are weirdos!"

Psi Com looked at one another and smirked. Then
they saw the knife. And the passerby's friends.

It was, Perry later said, as if "the whole town went
to AM/PM to get beer. It turned into this big brawl. The whole
AM/PM parking lot was like, 'What the hell?' It resembled a
real bad Kung Fu movie starring a bunch of inbreds from Victorville." The band beat a hasty retreat.

Such events never deterred them, though. Rather,
the more uncontrollable a situation became, the more Perry
professed to enjoy it and even encourage it. One night at the
Anti-Club, Psi Com were hanging around on the street when
suddenly they noticed a trail of people cantering out of the
liquor store across the road, closely pursued by a guy with a
gun. "Everyone was trying to outrun [him] and not be the
person he was going to pick on and hold up," Perry described.
He thought it was hysterical.

Hustling the scene, local club owners, other bands,
Psi Com would play anywhere and everywhere. Legend has it
that they played as many free shows in people's lofts as they
did paying gigs on the Southern California circuit. They were
ready for anything, Perry would boast; even a return trip to
the desert.

One hundred fifteen miles out from Los Angeles,
in the heart of the Mojave Desert, the Mojave National Mon-
ument is a bona fide rock 'n' roll Lourdes. When Gram
Parsons died in 1972, friends body-napped his corpse and cre-
mated it under the yuccas in the Mojave. The Eagles shot an
album sleeve out there, and later, in the 1980s, U2 would
wrap their *Joshua Tree* album in a similar image. Stuart
Swezey, the head of the specialist underground booking
agency, Desolation Center, organized a series of concerts in
the desert which remain legends in Los Angeles punk lore.

Desolation Center was never a conventional agency.
One promotion incorporated a ferocious set by the Minutemen

on a shipboard cruise around San Pedro Harbor. Another packed Savage Republic and, once again, the Minutemen out to the desert, for a show that, simply in terms of the attendance, lived up to its billing as the Mojave Exodus.

The Exodus was followed by the Mojave Auszug, headlined by the incendiary German industrialists Einsturzende Neubauten, exiled to the desert by the arsenal of high explosives that might have been intrinsic to their performance, but were hardly the kind of thing that would endear the band to in-town promoters.

Desolation Center was now planning a third desert concert, the Gila Monster Jamboree, and Psi Com were invited to play. Also on this January 5, 1985, bill were Hawthorne-based garage brats Redd Kross, Arizona's Meat Puppets, and, making their West Coast debut, the outré experimental group Sonic Youth.

"They were really different and interesting," Perry reflected on Desolation Center; and with just a hint of irony, he continued, "Those guys really mixed and matched [the bands on their bills]."

Although they'd been around in one form or another since the late 1970s, Sonic Youth was yet to fully emerge from the chrysalis of self-released cassette albums that hallmarked their earliest days. A clutch of recent domestic releases, spread across the spectrum of independent labels, revealed little more than the further adventures of their same brooding dissonance and cacophony.

In an interview with the *Los Angeles Times* just a few days before the Gila Monster Jamboree, Sonic Youth acknowledged their own profound debt to the West Coast—the "jangly guitars" of the Byrds, the all-American purity of San Franciscans Creedence Clearwater Revival. Not for nothing was their latest album, *Bad Moon Rising*, named for one of that band's biggest hits.

Southern California was putting its swagger to the test, pitting these hellacious East Coasters against the Meat Puppets, another bunch of out-of-state imports, but infinitely more in tune with what Los Angeles had come to expect from its heroes.

The Meat Puppets came hurtling out of their native Phoenix, Arizona, in 1980. When they first appeared, they looked like a conventional hardcore punk group, and for a couple of years, they sounded like one, too. They even signed to Black Flag's independent SST label (what higher hardcore recommendation could there have been?) and played Southern California's hardcore circuit for over a year, says bassist Curt Kirkwood, until "we discovered that most punks are just rednecks in disguise. By changing styles with every new album, we eliminated most of the idiots who might come to our shows."

Most of the idiots is right, but not all of the punks. It would be another decade before the Meat Puppets would acquire the Fame by Association which came from Nirvana and Kurt Cobain's "MTV Unplugged" championing of their now-classic second album. These earlier community links would continue to serve the Meat Puppets well. Their presence at the Gila Monster Jamboree raised it high above the status of a simple outdoor festival. It now all but amounted to a battle of the bands, East meets West, and may the biggest noise win.

The Gila Monster Jamboree sparked the local imagination in other ways, too. Retaining the same spirit of extra-metropolitan liberation as the Desolation Center's earlier shows, the venue itself wasn't actually announced to the public. Instead, ticket buyers were handed a map, directing them to Victorville. When they got there they would be given further directions, a ploy guaranteed to capture the imagination. Psi Com just needed to prove that they were ready to grab their own share of this fuss.

For almost a year now, Psi Com had worked as a bass guitar–less trio of Perry, Aaron, and Vince. It was an unusual lineup, particularly for a band that still operated within the typically bass-heavy confines of goth; indeed, in terms of simple dissonance, it placed the band closer to the kind of territory Sonic Youth was mapping out, when they claimed that their influences included "a lot of jazz musicians. . . . They see sound as color, and we're really into that."

Psi Com shared that vision, shared that taste. For all their affectations, Sonic Youth still remained within the loosest parameters of rock 'n' roll. Unhindered by the rhythmic conventions of a bass guitar, Psi Com's sound paintings couldn't always claim even that, and their showing at a gig like the Gila Monster Jamboree couldn't be left to chance. With all the nervous enthusiasm of a society debutante, Psi Com began casting around for the last link in their musical chain: a bassist.

Kelly Wheeler was a friend, a musician, and a bassist to boot. He was a Psi Com fan, too, around for every show they played, and as familiar with their music as anybody could be. His only problem was, he didn't actually own an instrument. Psi Com wanted him badly, though; so badly that they pooled whatever resources they could and bought him the bass of his dreams, a solid-body Ibanez. Then Perry cut all Kelly's hair off.

It was a ritual, he explained. Before every Psi Com gig, Perry would cut his bandmates' hair, whether they needed it trimmed or not. With the Sonic Youth show looming, Psi Com needed to present at least a visually coherent, maybe even—by the standards of the Los Angeles underground—conventional face to the largest audience they'd ever played before.

"Kelly didn't have time to learn the parts," recalls Perry. He simply hoped "it would work out all right." As Perry came offstage at the end of Psi Com's set, he doubted it had.

The entire show whirled around Perry's mind like some kind of nightmare. The only thing he could remember about his performance was getting stuck "in this pocket onstage, having all this sand kick up around us, [and] spouting off like an idiot."

It was Psi Com's big chance, a big bill, a bigger crowd . . . "and we blew it." Unable to control himself any longer, Perry fled the arena, hid behind a convenient rock, and burst into inconsolable tears. It was only later that he learned that "it didn't matter what I'd done, because *everyone* in the crowd was on acid." The drug was being given away free to whoever wanted to take it.

With Wheeler's distinctive bass an increasingly integral part of the Psi Com sound, the band's horizons began expanding. They rehearsed hard, five nights a week sometimes, and for the first time, the amalgamation of musical influences that first appeared in Perry's mind from the pages of the *Recycler* suddenly were within reach.

Kelly and Perry together moved into one of the ramshackle Victorian-type houses that pock the area around the University of Southern California.

It was a chaotic house, shared by so many other people, hippies and artists as Kelly recalls, that every day you'd see someone new in the place. You'd never be sure: Do they live here? Are they visitors? Or are they burglars? Perry continues, "There were between eight and thirteen kids there, depending upon who broke up with his girlfriend and whose band was practicing in the garage at the time."

The neighborhood was even more chaotic. The house sat in the heart of Los Angeles's gangland. Gunfire echoed on the street nightly.

Psi Com continued to play the freebie shows that had been their bread and butter in the past: parties, weddings, Mexican restaurants, anyplace where they could grab something to eat between sets. In the meantime they continued making serious inroads into the Los Angeles club circuit.

On February 15, 1985, less than six weeks after the Gila Monster Jamboree, Psi Com landed another plum performance, on the bill with Kommunity FK, one of the great lost treasures of the L.A. goth scene, at Al's Bar in downtown Los Angeles. For Psi Com, the show was simply another indication of their own burgeoning power. So was the next big date in their calendar, Psi Com's first headlining appearance at the Troubadour on Santa Monica Boulevard.

Simply being offered the show was a genuine coup. Throughout the 1970s, after all, the Troubadour had been the most influential club in town. Elton John made his American debut there in 1970, and seven years later, the Troubadour was one of the first establishment barricades to be overrun by Los Angeles' burgeoning punk scene, an occupation that only ended—in an ignominious blanket ban on punk—following a typically raucous performance by the Bags. Since then, the Troubadour had devoted itself over almost exclusively to hard rock and heavy metal; those bands might have been rowdy, may even have been crude, but they didn't overturn tables like the punk rockers did, and they certainly didn't provoke the waitressing staff to turn in a petition demanding, "Either the bands go, or we do," like the punk rockers had. Guns N' Roses played their first gig at the Troubadour, shortly after Psi Com, one Thursday in June 1985. It was there, too, that they would be "discovered." The Troubadour was a valuable showcase, and Perry was intent that Psi Com would not disgrace themselves there.

The Troubadour performance was, says Perry, the height of Psi Com's "weird and spiritual" stage. Still trading his vocal effects with Vince Duran's guitar, with his songwriting moving ever deeper into the soul of mystic philosophy, Perry describes their sound as pure "Cure, Siouxsie, Cocteau Twins stuff," a debt most evident on the eerie, Banshees-esque "Xiola," penned for artist Xiola Blue. If the dark imprimatur of those groups was already firmly in place, then how could it hurt if Psi Com simply expanded on the gothic vision, and carried it back to its own roots of inspiration?

The occult had always fascinated Perry. "Don't you think it's the most delicious temptation?" he teased. "To cheat on your life and kick the shit out of fate?"

He'd already experimented with it in the past, conjuring little charms and spells from the tomes he picked up on his travels around Los Angeles's arcane bookstore community. He thought he understood the pitfalls as well, remembering the occasion when he performed one ceremony, "with all the shit that entails, and suddenly, within a fraction of a second, this huge bank of noise, so high-pitched, manifested itself in my head. You cannot start to imagine how much it hurt. I thought my head was literally going to blow up with all the sound that was pouring into it. So I shouted for it to go away, and I was just lucky that it did."

Now he reserved his magic for occasions that demanded it, and the Troubadour show was one such. The night before the show, "I opened a book and did some little thing with candles and prayers."

The following evening, Psi Com walked out onstage, plugged in—and Kelly's bass amplifier promptly exploded. Perry never touched that book again.

The band had its first set of promotional photographs taken at a Sears department store. It was "Picture Day," and the Sears staff was expecting nothing more than the customary shower of grade-schoolers to be dragged unwillingly along by their determined mothers. Psi Com turned up in their best stage threads. The photographs they had taken were then mailed to everyone they could think of—friends, club managers, record-industry types, you name it.

They also took on a manager—a prostitute, says Perry, who turned up at one of the band's shows, enjoyed what she saw, and offered to invest. She "didn't know what the hell she was doing in the music business," Perry reckons, "but she could get us money, fast." The group liked her a lot. "She was a real doll. Managing a band was the easiest way she knew to make money. She loved music and she loved men." After managing Psi Com she ended up moving to London and becoming a financial consultant.

The biggest decision that Psi Com took during the summer of 1985 was to make a record.

Nineteen eighty-five was a weird time in rock 'n' roll history. It was the year in which the entire Western world locked itself into the private dance of self-retribution which would culminate in Live Aid, on the one hand; and on the other the blind moral fascism of the PMRC (Parents' Music Resource Center), the Washington Wives, headed by Tipper Gore, who united so vehemently against what they perceived as the creeping tide of moral obscenity in rock.

The biggest casualties of the new wave of conservatism that was sweeping the industry were the unsigned bands who, under earlier regimes, would have been regarded as the next generation of rock 'n' roll. Instead, they became the lost generation.

An industry-wide recession was in full swing in 1985 as well. Labels were cutting back in every department, at least so far as young bands were concerned. Why, the thinking appeared to be, should they invest vast amounts of money developing new talent that might never recoup its advance, when for a fraction of the effort, the old warhorses like Phil Collins and the Live Aid crowd could simply carry on cranking out their multi-platinum monsters?

On the street, bands repaid the record companies for their lack of interest with a similar lack of concern. You won't sign us? Fine—we'll sign ourselves. There were times when it was impossible to even enter a local Los Angeles record store without tripping over another band selling their singles from the back of a borrowed station wagon.

What singles these were! In the few years since Black Flag set the entire independent scene reeling with the first release on their own SST label, 1978's *Nervous Breakdown* EP, the city had exploded with pop entrepreneurs. SST itself unleashed everything from future Sugar frontman Bob Mould's Hüsker Dü to the corrosive Saccharine Trust, the Minutemen to the Meat Puppets, and was now preparing to reissue Sonic Youth's first screeching slabs of sound bites.

The ground SST broke proved more fruitful than anyone could have imagined. Establishing itself as the template for just about every independent label operating in America, SST enjoyed the kind of success—temporal, if not commercial—that made it so bands whom geography alone placed within Black Flag's shadow really had no alternative but to follow the SST lead.

Bad Religion, a pure-roots punk band who stayed true to their course long after it fell from fashion, and would still be burning brightly when it came back in again, had their Epitaph label off and running. Posh Boy, Dangerhouse, Slash—at a time when major labels were a dirty word on the street, when true credibility could be garnered only from maintaining firm control of one's own destiny, and the free-spiritedness of punk's Do It Yourself ethic was that genre's last bequest to its mutant children, Los Angeles bubbled with homemade revolution.

"It wasn't a question of getting signed to a label, because that wasn't even a possibility," Perry confirms. It would be several years more, in the ironic wake of Guns N' Roses, before the locusts descended again upon the Los Angeles club scene.

What was important instead, Perry insisted, was that Psi Com earn the recognition of their peers. He knew already that slowly, they were getting there. One day he spotted the band's name in *L.A. Weekly*, ranked among "the best new bands in the city."

"I was completely thrilled. I'd tune in to the college radio stations just to hear our name get mentioned in the club listings!"

Releasing their own EP would confirm the group's burgeoning status.

In March 1985, a month after the Al's Bar show, Psi Com set about getting the logistics together of releasing their own 12-inch EP. It would comprise five of their most popular live songs: "Ho Ka Hey," "Human Condition," "City of Nine Gates," "Winds," and "Xiola," titled after one of Perry's closest friends, Xiola Blue. Recording time was booked at Venice's Radio Tokyo studios, and Psi Com linked up with engineer/producer Ethan James for one frenzied weekend of all-day and -night recording sessions.

These sessions turned up little that Psi Com had not already assumed they possessed. They simply enhanced the band's already confident roar.

Perry, at the time, was entertaining his own visions of vinyl immortality. This was Psi Com's first record, it needed to be something special, to go beyond what the fans could hear onstage when the group played. As he recorded the vocals on "Xiola," for the first time on record—for the first time, he says, in his life—Perry's familiarly dark voice rose to an unearthly shriek . . . and kept rising.

"I'd never really sung the way I did on that one before," he told *Musician* magazine almost a decade later. "I thought that, for the sake of the recorded version, I'd scream as loud and hard as I could." Pumping everything he had into his performance, feeding it through his trusty Ibanez echo box, "I started screeching on some high notes, and that's where you can actually hear my real voice being born." The result, closer in impact to Siouxsie and the Banshees' *Scream* album than any band had ever aspired to, still retains its impact today.

Perry designed the sleeve, lettering it in the same distinctive mock-Oriental style that he'd already adapted for the band's posters and flyers. The cover picture was clipped from a newspaper photograph that Perry found depicting a horrifically emaciated young woman lying dead in the streets of "Africa or Afghanistan." Cutting away the ground around the corpse, Perry explains, "I made her stand up and she looks like she's dancing." Affectionately, Psi Com nicknamed the corpse "the dancing anorexic," and laughed when people asked if it was a picture of Vince.

Psi Com set up its own label; digging deep into his library of legend, Perry named it Mohini, for the supreme seductress of Hindu mythology, noting also that Mohini also gave her name to a slow, gentle, undulating dance that enjoyed a lengthy popularity in India, among both respectable society women and, it was noted with increasing distaste, prostitutes, who used it to attract clients. Such sordid associations quickly led to the dance's decline.

In July, Psi Com took delivery of fifteen hundred copies of their baby. That, they deemed, would be more than sufficient for friends, fans, and anybody else who cared. It was also all they could afford to manufacture at the time.

It was a disaster.

More than half of the total pressing was totally unplayable, warped like saucers and not even good for a Frisbee.

Psi Com staged a record-release party at Club Lingerie and, with copies of the EP being sold out of the back of their van at shows, as well as snaking into a handful of area record stores, they launched into an intensive spate of live shows throughout the remainder of the summer.

"We had some of our best gigs after [the record]," Kelly Wheeler confirms. "But by September, there was no more band."

The problems that contributed to Psi Com's demise were not wholly internal. Quite simply, it was as though everything was falling apart, the entire Los Angeles scene grinding to a standstill as it girded its loins for its next mutation.

In short succession, as 1985 inexorably wound down, Savage Republic, Black Flag, and Kommunity FK each shattered and broke up. Touring in Europe, Christian Death was rapidly approaching meltdown, as Rozz Williams and Valor locked horns over the band's future direction. The Red Hot Chili Peppers, for so long the Los Angeles band that seemed most likely to make it, were dealing with a spiral of self-abuse and debasement that would finally culminate in the death of guitarist Hillel Slovak, a smack OD at the age of twenty-five.

Three days before Christmas 1985, the Minutemen's guitarist and vocalist, Dennis Dale "D." Boon, died in a motor accident in the Arizona desert.

Even Psi Com, peripheral players on the wider screen, felt the enormity of the strain. Their closest friends on

the local musical scene were numbered among those imminent casualties, the maverick ranks of independents that were
cast in, then developed from, the Southern California hardcore culture; for as long as those bands existed, Perry felt,
then Psi Com had a reason to exist alongside them. "I just
wanted to keep up with them," he admits. With them gone,
what was there left to aspire to?

In later years, Perry would play down Psi Com's
role in his past, would write off their nearly three-year existence with the terse complaint that while he got into Satanism,
his bandmates became Hare Krishnas and forced a theological
breakdown which even the strength of the band's music could
not repair.

In truth—although almost a decade of deception
would pass before Duran, Sherer, and Wheeler got to tell their
side of the story—the four musicians simply drifted apart. The
Krishna story was completely untrue, was simply Perry trying
to write off his past while rewriting his present, as a pat explanation for one of the last songs he came up with before Psi
Com's demise, "Pigs in Zen."

It upset him, he explained, that the other guys in
the band, the so-called Krishna fiends, seemed so sure of
themselves. So Perry decided to check out all the religions,
reading everything he could. "I read the Gita, I read Black
Magic Crowley, the Bible, anything I could get my hands on."

His reading led him to just one conclusion. "If you
want to talk about reaching nirvana, reaching Zen, well, the
pig is closer than we are because the pig doesn't have material
possessions. He fucks when he wants to, he eats when he's
hungry, and he sleeps when he's tired. That's the whole point
of Zen. That's exactly what pigs do . . . so, 'Pigs in Zen.'"

It was not the first time that Perry changed the
facts of life to suit his frisson; neither would it be the last, and
Psi Com were to become the butt of more than one private
joke in the future.

One thing that Perry could not change, however,
and which he gladly admitted when the band's sole vinyl

legacy was repackaged for release nine years later, was how much the group really meant to him.

"We were a smash success as far as I'm concerned," Perry enthused in 1994. He even acknowledged that there was an inevitability to Psi Com's demise. "The end of our chapter was right around the end of the scene we were part of."

Jenny's Addiction

4

t was the Sex Pistols' fault. The Sex Pistols and a handful of other bands, screeching out of the no-man's-land of the latest marginal pop fad and sweeping the headlines clean. If they'd been ignored, they'd have just gone away, because rock 'n' roll is like that. You can be the greatest band on the planet, have the most important message on earth, but if the kids won't dance, or at least twitch rhythmically, you're finished, done for, dead in the water.

It comes down to hype. It's an emotive term, and one that has rung down through the annals of pop and caused more fuss, scuppered more careers, crippled more newcomers than any other word in rock. Who remembers Brynsley Schwarz today? The Doctors of Madness? Even the New York

Dolls? A few vinyl fetishists, the odd archaeologist, the occasional journeyman hoarder.

But the Man in the Street, the Voice of the People, he doesn't know and he doesn't care either, and though punk changed the world, it might just as well have been jazz. The people will buy what they're told to, and the only exception to that rule is when they're told not to buy it.

They were told not to buy the Sex Pistols. The group's first British single, "Anarchy in the UK," faltered when the women at the EMI pressing plant refused to print any more copies after they saw the group on prime-time TV, swearing like dockers and looking like dogs.

The Sex Pistols' second single, "God Save the Queen," was destroyed when the band was slung off their record label, A&M, before the disc was even released, and their third, a reprise/reprieve of that same disrespectful anthem, made Number 1 because it trumpeted subversion when the world was submissive.

Banned from the radio, banned even from having its name mentioned on daytime pop-radio broadcasts, "God Save the Queen" hit the top of the British charts in the very same week Queen Elizabeth II was celebrating her Silver Jubilee. In a perfect world the Sex Pistols would have broken up the very next day. There was no way they could top what they'd already accomplished.

They carried on regardless, and rock 'n' roll carried on all around them. It was older now, though, and wiser as well. The lessons of the past, of the Pistols and their ilk, had been learned. In the past, rock 'n' roll had been considered a childish diversion; now it had proved it was armed and dangerous.

In 1984, a studio band called Frankie Goes to Hollywood released its first single, "Relax." A throbbing slab of computerized funk, rendered vaguely controversial by vocalist Holly Johnson's outspoken homosexuality, "Relax" became the biggest-selling British single of the year, *not* because it was danceable, but because a daytime disc jockey took exception to the way Johnson sang the word *come*. The record was banned from the airwaves. Frankie became a byword for hype, hype itself became an art form.

The first time people outside of Los Angeles heard of Jane's Addiction, they were sensitive about the hype. Another senseless night out with another faceless band. So what if there's a buzz about this one, and a roaring whisper on the street? The defenses went up regardless: It's all hype, they thought.

A record-company bidding war and a self-released live album simply added up to more shop-window schmaltz. Somebody said, "They sound like Led Zeppelin," and suddenly that name, too, was on every lip and every page of every paper. The world had been waiting for a new Zep to take flight, and as the *L.A. Weekly*'s Sportscar Frank left a Jane's Addiction gig, he remembered, "I heard more than one person mumble, 'This is the best band in L.A.' But I wouldn't place such limitations on them."

Hype is only effective when people fall for it. There still needs to be something there that's worth falling for to begin with, be it mood, music, or simply an indefinable moment or form. Beginning in the spring of 1986, Los Angeles was in the grip of one such indefinable moment.

Psi Com's disintegration was cemented when one of Perry's housemates introduced him to a new bass player, Eric Avery. Perry was still living in the house he once shared with Kelly, and it was still a rambling free-for-all. "One day," he remembers, "this girl Jane appeared. I think she was a friend of someone else's. Anyway, she ended up living in the room next to mine, and we became close."

Eric was one of Jane's friends, and Perry took to him immediately. Like Perry, he was a musician; like Perry, he was between bands; and like Perry, he was bored with all the bands that were already out there. That's what clinched their friendship, really, the way the five-year divide between their ages—Perry was twenty-seven, Eric twenty-two—

simply melted in the face of Eric's loathing of all he saw around him.

In March 1986 Geffen Records snagged Guns N' Roses for a bargain $75,000. It was a typically audacious move on the part of a record label that had forged its reputation on audacity, and no one doubted that it would pay off. Most things David Geffen put his mind to did.

Unrecorded and comparatively untried, Guns N' Roses enjoyed success that sent shock waves through the Hollywood underbelly, *not*, as a few cynics suggested, because the band members were able to remain sober enough to sign the contracts (according to Danny Sugarman's biography *Appetite for Destruction*, a large chunk of their advance "went to drugs and drug dealers"), but because Guns N' Roses got to where they were as virtual outsiders.

The individual band members all boasted local experience, of course. Izzy Stradlin and Axl Rose were former members of glam kittens L.A. Guns, guitarist Slash played with Road Crew. But those bands had really been outside the loop, running with their own sleazoid metal pack.

Guns N' Roses, Perry complained—and Eric agreed —were just "too obvious." They possessed a certain "chemistry," he acknowledged, but it was a look, a mood, a stance, that was already well established and borrowed wholesale from a thousand shots of Keith Richards nodding out in his snakeskin boots, a scarf draped over the table lamp, cigarette ash spilling from the butt in his mouth.

"They know how to dress," Perry conceded, and they knew "what licks to play." They took it all from the past, tried-and-trusted teen-rebellion touchstones that had worked for everyone from the Rolling Stones through Aerosmith. "In that respect," Perry continued, "they're smart, but *how* smart is that? They've only stolen the most clichéd ideas." As he and Eric talked over their new project's ideals, just one phrase kept coming to mind, sledge-hammering itself into the consciousness over and over again. Think of something different! THINK OF SOMETHING DIFFERENT!

Perry was adamant. You didn't have to "dress up in leathers" to be a rock band or play Hollywood tourist traps. "Just put on cool shows."

Perry's first rehearsal with Eric only confirmed the instinct that initially brought them together. According to Perry, the temperature hit a hundred degrees inside, but Eric just put his head down and locked in to something. "He played the same groove over and over for about forty-five minutes." When it was over, Perry just looked at him and smiled. "You wanna do a gig together?"

With Perry on vocals and effects, and Eric armed with a collection of old chemical-storage drums, the duo played their first show sometime around March 1986, in front of a handful of friends, including Jane, Perry's girlfriend Casey Niccoli, and a roomful of very straight onlookers.

The venue was a Top 40 club, Perry vaguely recalls, somewhere in Orange County, and they were opening, of course, for a Top 40 cover band. It was unfortunate that the Top 40 was even less exciting than usual back then, all Mr. Mister and Miami Sound Machine, Sting and Survivor mixed, blended, and shaken together. There was nothing within earshot that could possibly have prepared the audience for what Perry and Eric had in mind.

Plugging in and letting rip, they emptied the room in record time.

"We went into this like a pair of art-damaged kids," Eric recalls. "I remember playing to try to get a grant from this art school downtown. I just played on these chemical drums, and he sang."

Soon after, Eric returned to playing bass, but still Perry acknowledges that the duo possessed only the loosest notions of precisely what they were trying to accomplish with their latest project—that it was all very well trying to think of something different, but another thing entirely to actually pull it off. The only thing Perry felt certain of was the new band's name. He called it Jane's Addiction.

In later years, Perry would claim Jane herself as the inspiration for the name. "When you invite someone like her out, and you come to get her and she's dancing in front of the mirror with a wig on, and there's nobody there . . . you just gotta name a band after her."

Throughout the group's formative days, though, there was another story going around, one that is just as likely as this tale of Jane, and maybe even more compelling.

When Perry and Eric first started rehearsing together, they only knew one song, the Velvet Underground's "Rock & Roll." It was an appropriate choice regardless. The song's lyric itself spelled out their manifesto, the story of a girl named Jane, and how she switched on the radio, "couldn't believe what she heard at all," and had her very life saved by rock 'n' roll.

"Rock & Roll" was a song whose meaning went way beyond its message, striking not the cliché-ridden cult of Music Is My Life-rs, who use rock 'n' roll as an excuse for the way they live their lives, but something far deeper, far more spiritual than that—the people for whom rock 'n' roll surpasses mere entertainment and becomes a religion with an intensity to match the music.

It would be some years more before Lou Reed would publish his own lyrics for the song, in the 1991 collection *Between Thought and Expression*, and reveal that for twenty years people had been singing the wrong name; it was Jenny, not Jane, who flicked that fatal dial, by which time it was too late. Jane's Addiction it was.

"When I first named the band," Perry affirms, "I used the name Jane rather than, say, John, because it was a very anti-macho thing to do, like calling yourself Sue (or Alice!). We weren't afraid to play softly, with tenderness, which is a word men tend to cringe over."

The word *addiction*, on the other hand, sounded hard, harsh, and violent. It is unlikely that Perry missed the fact that Guns N' Roses' name, too, conjured up those same yin/yang shades of feelings. Before either group was even recorded, the scene was being set for one helluva battle of the bands.

Describing their music as improvisational bass poetry, the two-piece Jane's Addiction began performing in the loft-party circuit that had sustained Psi Com through so much of its early career. Occasionally the pair would be joined by a drummer or guitarist, friends dropping by just to fill out the sound, but the basic nature of their performance didn't change. Building up his collection of effects boxes, Perry "would supply what the guitar does, your musical wash, while Eric held down a rhythm, and then I would just . . . be singing poetry. I had a big wealth of my own poetry intermittently through the course of his jam." Some of it, he remembers, "was really good."

Perry's former Psi Com bandmates agree. Since their band's demise, the rest of the group had all fallen into their own projects. Kelly linked up with Dino Paredes, the bassist with the Red Temple Spirits (coincidentally, Paredes would be credited as the art director on the 1994 reissue of Psi Com's EP), before linking up with ex-Berlin vocalist Terri Nunn. Aaron and Vince, meanwhile, concentrated on simple home recording and part-time bands. Every so often they would drop by to see what Perry was up to.

Kelly often came down to check Jane's Addiction out, and he vividly remembers when Perry "was still trying to figure out" who the rest of the group was going to be.

No matter how high Jane's Addiction's stock might rise on the art circuit, the lack of a drummer and a guitar player remained the one flaw in the group's master plan.

Perry and Eric knew that what they were doing was simply a stopgap, something to hone their own relationship while they worked to fill in the gaps on the stage all around them. It was a difficult procedure, though. Neither Perry nor Eric enjoyed the prospect of holding formal auditions; the musicians they would work with, they determined, would have to be ones with whom they felt comfortable as people, long before the musical aspects of their relationship could be brought into play. When Eric introduced him to a couple of old school friends, Stephen Perkins and Dave Navarro, at a loft party, Perry knew right away that their search was at an end.

Both eight years Perry's junior, Perkins, a drummer, and guitarist Navarro were, at the time, members of Disaster, a metal band which the now-defunct rock monthly *Creem* summed up as members of "that generation of metal players that acknowledged little musical history beyond Led Zeppelin and . . . Eddie Van Halen."

For that reason alone, the duo's tastes and credentials would scarcely have warranted a second glance from Perry if he'd come across them through a MUSICIANS WANTED ad.

When he discussed their recruitment in later years, Perry concocted such a ridiculous background for Perkins that any further questioning—Navarro's love of Metallica, for instance—tended to end there and then. Perry's tale would begin with a mythical first drummer "[who] had a business smuggling canaries into the country from Tahiti. He would drug them and then swallow them. He overdosed on the canaries and died on the plane." Stephen Perkins, the fable continued, was the deceased man's twin brother, and a former boyfriend of actress Jodie Foster. He had taken his sibling's place in the band, "[and] also started dating his girlfriend, who happened to be Eric's little sister."

The age difference between Perry and his bandmates was crucial to his dream; more than anything else, it contributed to his reluctance to work with many of the musicians who were his own age.

At twenty-seven, Perry was a late starter. A good four or five years older than Guns N' Roses and the Red Hot Chili Peppers, close to a decade older than a lot of the kids playing the club scene, he didn't see his age as a disadvantage. He felt it gave him a head start on his peers—not only the knowledge that he had "paid his dues" and got a lot of shit out of his system, but that he had already lived through three generations of rock 'n' roll.

It infuriated him to meet kids whose musical knowledge dated back no farther than punk, and who could not see back in time beyond it. It excited him as well. To understand rock 'n' roll's future, you had to come to grips with its past. Relying on nothing more than the strength of his own experience, Perry knew he could meld the most musically naive unit into something fresh and strong. With Jane's Addiction's lineup now complete, that is what he set about doing.

Journalist Gina Arnold, contemplating the band's earliest rehearsals, likens what happened next to "a rape of sorts." Perry "practically forced" his bandmates to sow the "barren ground" of their own musical tastes with "the fertile seed of punk and rhythm." It was to become a potent mix.

In April, Jane's Addiction opened for Gene Loves Jezebel at the Roxy.

Having traveled the same route through the British goth underground as the Cult, Gene Loves Jezebel—featuring the Welsh-born twins Jay and Michael Aston, and former Chelsea guitarist James Stevenson—were now nipping ferociously at that other band's well-stacked heels, with a similar blend of gritty guitar-powered glam rock tacked to catchy pop histrionics. "Desire," the first fruits of their newly inked pact with Geffen Records, was already poised to crash both the record and video charts; *Discover*, their major-label debut, would also spawn the crashing club hit "Heartache."

"A girl we knew told us about Jane's Addiction," James Stevenson recalls, "said that they were a great band, and that we had to make sure we saw them. As it turned out, we missed their show, but their name always stuck with me, because it was so great!"

Had the Jezebels seen Jane's Addiction, they would have understood immediately where the Los Angeles group was coming from. The Aston brothers' vocal trademark, like that which Perry was still developing, was an effects-laden battery of yelps, squeals, and screeches, the similarity of the twins' own voices dueling in constant competition with each other, creating much the same ambience as Perry's beloved echo boxes.

Musically, however, Jane's Addiction was already moving away from such blatant archetypes. What they played, Perry explained, was essentially ". . . freestyle, with everybody going for what they wanted. It didn't seem that there were any limitations for what anybody was doing. There wasn't a formula like, 'Okay, this is for four measures, this is for eight.' It was just like, 'Go for it, let's feel it out.'"

It was refreshing to Perry, a step back to the raw, primitive roots of rock 'n' roll, before musicianship and high conceptual art stepped into the picture. "I was really happy to get back to that."

Dave Navarro, his past-the-shoulder-length hair framing a perfect, near-equine face, the consummate Los Angeles guitar-slinger look, continued, "When I hear music, I see colors, and I think we're a real colorful band, even though there aren't a lot of instruments." In one interview, he likened Jane's Addiction to a sandwich. "You've got the ham and cheese—Eric and Steve—and then Perry and myself would be like the lettuce and tomato, mustard and mayonnaise."

It was this combination of elements, Perry's often surreal lyrics meshing with the rest of the group's musical storm, and the collision between old values and new, that set the scene for what was simultaneously the greatest compliment and the biggest albatross of Jane's Addiction's early career—the incessant comparisons to Led Zeppelin. No matter where a journalist's reference points started, sooner or later they would arrive at Led Zeppelin. Even *Music Connection*, one of the band's staunchest supporters, admitted, "Let's call this band the Led Hot Zeppelin Peppers."

As far back as their first album in 1969, and with increasingly strident versatility over the seven that followed before the band's demise in 1980, Led Zeppelin never balked at eclecticism. Their reputation, of course, was as a heavy metal band, probably the most important band ever to work in that genre. Yet no more than a handful of Led Zeppelin recordings even remotely conform to the traditional strictures of heavy metal, and of those that do, the majority are contained on the band's second album, *Led Zeppelin II*, rush-recorded during a period of almost constant gigging.

Led Zeppelin constructed a melting pot of influences from which bands are still extracting new notions today. While anyone (as a host of subsequent Zeppelin imitators have proven) can isolate some of the elements of the band's complex brew, it was something else entirely to accurately harness all of the elements, the driving hard rock and gentle plainsong, the questing ballad and the down 'n' dirty dirge. To accomplish that would be to possess a genius that rivals Led Zeppelin's own.

Jane's Addiction did not have that particular genius. What they did have was the courage that opened the way for that genius to emerge. Long before worldbeat became a passionate watchword for anybody with a couple of tablas and a worn-out copy of the fourth Peter Gabriel album, Jane's Addiction was stepping outside of traditional "rock" song structures and imbibing their performance with whatever took their fancy—whatever its musical provenance.

A lot of it was secondhand; the ghosts of Southern Death Cult and Gene Loves Jezebel would continue haunting Perry's musical imaginings for some time still to come. But while it was easy to dissect Jane's Addiction's sound from behind the keys of a typewriter, it was damn near impossible to do the same thing from the floor of a club.

The very collision of sound, Navarro's guitar and Perry's vocals, conjured up a wild otherworldliness. Concerts often ended with wild tribal celebrations, the band members pounding upon anything that resonated, and if they could—as their earliest reviews insisted—invoke images as disparate as a Hopi rain dance and urban funk, they did so without the barest hint of self-consciousness. Then, at the end of the evening, they would be compared with Led Zeppelin because, in terms of the sheer magnitude of a Jane's Addiction performance, there simply wasn't anybody else to compare them to.

The band members themselves reveled in the freedom that their music, brought together in the melting pot of their earliest rehearsals, allowed them, then marveled as Perry's ambitiously ambiguous lyrics liberated them even further.

Within weeks of coming together the linchpins of Jane's Addiction's future live set, "Pigs in Zen," "One Percent," and "Whores," were already in place. "Jane Says," the dazzling acoustic drive-by which would be established as the band's anthem long before the year's end, followed. If the casual listener marveled at the ease with which the band could slip from the dense roar of "Trip Away" to the wide-open breeziness of "Ocean Size," Perry already had an answer for them. The only restriction the group set itself, he bragged, "was that there would be no restrictions." Two years later, he would look back and congratulate himself. "In that respect, we've held true from the very first day."

By Perry's side was Casey Niccoli, who shared much of his musical vision. Casey came to Los Angeles from Bakersfield. Casey was a skinny, dark-haired woman whose head was filled with the kind of cinematic visions that her lazy hometown could never fulfill.

When she first met Perry, he was still struggling through the dog days of Psi Com. It was art, not music, that brought them together, and while Jane's Addiction's earliest supporters remember Casey as a seemingly omnipresent fixture at the band's live shows, "you never felt like she was muscling in on the action. She was more like a sounding board for Perry, someone for him to bounce ideas off. She never involved herself in band politics."

What Casey and Perry shared was the fervent belief that there were no boundaries to what the human imagination could achieve through art; none, that is, beyond those that society itself imposed.

Visiting Bakersfield once, for her mother and stepfather's marriage, Casey and Perry made a movie about the wedding, out in the backyard in their underwear, eating little bits of paper at four in the morning. The neighbor who watched them over the fence, Perry laughed, thought they were members of a cult.

Late into the night, with and without Casey's movie cameras, the pair would sit together debating censorship and its free-speaking corollary, and the point at which personal creativity and the public well-being finally drew each other's blood. Dately everywhere you looked, censorship had taken rock 'n' roll by the balls, and no amount of squirming had forced it to release its crushing grip. What would happen, Perry and Casey wondered, if you forced it to let go?—not by squirming, or even by pulling away sharply. Censorship was a grasping hand . . . so let's cut off its fingers.

It had been done before, they knew that. In Britain, gay-rights campaigners still acknowledge that the Tom Robinson Band achieved more with one song, 1977's pink punk anthem "Glad to Be Gay," than any amount of conventional propaganda ever achieved. Five years before that, David Bowie set the same ball rolling with this flirtatious wardrobe of dresses; five years later, Boy George would propel the concept of bisexuality into even the most uptight of households. Less than a generation before, homosexuality had barely even been acknowledged, let alone openly tolerated.

Art was cyclical, that was undeniable, but rock 'n' roll was even more so. Elvis, Dylan, Jagger, Bowie, Rotten, Boy George—every five years, regular as clockwork, another revolution rolled around; every five years, that invisible line was shoved back just a little farther.

How much farther could it go? The intervention of the PMRC into the world of rock did more than enforce the age-old divide—the generation gap, if you will—between what the kids listened to and what their parents thought they ought to be listening to; it cemented it into place. The fact that the so-called "older" generation of today was on the front line of

'Retailers Find Jane's Album 'Shocking'

that same debate during their own adolescence did not make an iota of difference.

During the Senate committee hearings that were convened to discuss the Washington Wives' complaints, Susan Baker, one of the PMRC's founders (and the wife of then Treasury Secretary James), admitted that she listened to Fats Domino and Chuck Berry when she was a youth. Yet by the standards of the time, neither Berry nor Domino was the kind of role model any "responsible" parent would want their teenage daughter listening to.

In 1956, for example, a Fats Domino concert at the Rhode Island navy base turned into a genuine rock 'n' roll riot. Five years later, Berry began a two-year sentence for violating the Mann Act, transporting a minor over state lines for immoral purposes. Yet no one at the hearings asked Mrs. Baker what kind of moral damage that music had inflicted upon her impressionable teenage mind.

None of the PMRC's complaints were new, then, but they drew a line in the sand all the same; and all across the board, rock 'n' roll was falling meekly into place behind it. Perry and Casey knew what the other was thinking before either of them opened their mouth to speak. It was probably time for another revolution. "We'll start it next year, though," Perry laughed. It was, after all, only four years since 1982, the year when Culture Club unleashed their armies of transvestite storm troopers upon America. "We have to stick to the five-year rotation plan."

Jane's Addiction's reputation had already long outgrown the loft-party circuit. Perry and Casey schemed ever greater stage extravaganzas for the band. The pair talked of filling the stage with performing midgets, with fire eaters and sword swallowers, of turning every concert into a carnival freak show, a wealth of visual insanity that would explode with the music.

When they took their ideas to the line of club owners who were so desperate to book Jane's Addiction, though, their enthusiasm swiftly turned to outrage.

"What is wrong with these people? They want us to put on a show, but when we try to give them a real show, they tell us we can't do that onstage."

Fire regulations, safety precautions, everywhere the pair turned, there was another local ordinance to be conjured up against them. It was then that Perry remembered Desolation Center. When they wanted to put on a show, they just went ahead and did it. If they couldn't do it in a club, they'd just find somewhere else where they could. Cutting Jane's Addiction out of the traditional rock-club loop, Perry and Casey began promoting the band's concerts themselves.

"It was much cooler than doing them at a venue where they're choosing the bill for you," Perry reasoned— venues whose own resident lighting engineer and sound engineer "could care less about you, where they've got their Monday through Sunday setup and it doesn't change."

Warehouses, lofts, vacant lots, Jane's Addiction set up wherever they could, and did whatever they wanted— "strange shows," as Perry put it, each one awash with as many artistic alternatives as Perry and Casey could muster. Jane's Addiction's own show would be sandwiched amid carnival turns, poets, performance artists, anything and anyone who could "entertain" for a while.

The ambition didn't halt there. One night, Jane's Addiction played its set amidst a gathering of classic motorcycles, with exotic lights and slide shows projected onto every available surface.

It was exciting, but it still wasn't satisfactory, simply recreating the spirit behind that most apropos of Perry's pet imageries, the Velvet Underground. They, too, had begun life as just one artistic sideshow among a roomful of others . . . "but look what happened to them," Perry would laugh. Cult heroes at best throughout their five-year life span, the Velvet Underground had long since hung up their shiny boots of leather before they began to reap the acclaim they deserved.

THINK OF SOMETHING DIFFERENT!

Aerosmith
on Acid

5

he first sign that the balance of American pop power was shifting came in the months immediately following Live Aid in July 1985. The smugness of Live Aid, and the subservience with which the industry acknowledged the PRMC's demands for self-regulation just three months later, were not the frontline maneuvers of teenaged rebellion. They were the rear-guard manipulations of a self-made fifth column. It was only after the fact that the industry realized what its compliance had wrought. Now it was eager to upset the balance.

Although appearances remain deceptive, Guns N' Roses were the first of what would, in later years, be termed "alternative" bands. Think what you wanted about their appeal, Guns N' Roses did not represent the safe pop options that hitherto became accepted as the norm. At a time when the term AIDS was sweeping into the heart of even straight Republican white-bread territory, Guns N' Roses' very attitude glorified promiscuity. Sex and drugs and rock 'n' roll; dispatched into battle with Phil Collins and Springsteen, *of course* Guns N' Roses was then considered "alternative."

But it wasn't the only one. The Replacements, according to legend, got their name after an earlier incarnation, the Impediments, turned up drunk for their first-ever gig, an Alcoholics Anonymous coffee morning. "With a pedigree like that," Britain's *Melody Maker* asked, "how could they go wrong?"

Blasting out of home-base Minneapolis, juvenile punks whose attitude showed on early album titles like *Sorry Ma, Forgot to Take Out the Trash* and *The Replacements Stink*, the band was well on course for nothing more notable than a place in hardcore heaven. When they delivered 1984's *Let It Be*, their third album and possibly the most raggedly majestic record to emerge from early-eighties America, the new decade's *Exile on Main Street*, people began to take note.

Within months, the band's independent status was behind them, as America's major labels stampeded to greet them. *Tim*, the Replacements' debut album for Warner Brothers' subsidiary Sire, was produced by Tommy ex-Ramone, and earned fresh accolades from an alternative press that simply couldn't believe that at last, someone had made the transition from independent credibility to major label artistry. Before Hüsker Dü, before R.E.M., and long before the majors built a shopping mall upon the independent underground, the Replacements were setting the stage for the future.

Things did not change overnight, however.

History, and the history of the 1980s in particular, is littered with the bones of bands who couldn't make the transition, who had everything dropped into their lap by a major record-label deal, only to have the whole glittering platter snatched back the moment their sales dipped below the break-even point.

The Suicide Commandos, Romeo Void, Pere Ubu, Hüsker Dü, X—all were bands that started out promising, then bummed out or burned out. The higher the expectations when a band was signed, the louder the thud when it fell apart.

Salutary lessons cried out from every corner. Around the same time as Seymour Stein's Sire label was courting the Replacements, in 1985, Elektra was sinking close to a quarter of a million dollars into the Unforgiven, a Los Angeles metal band that prompted the most frenetic bidding war in recent memory, yet would be dropped by their proud owners after just one album.

Across the Atlantic in Britain, the natives were tearing their hair out over Sigue Sigue Sputnik. They looked great, thrift-store castoffs in multicolored mayhem, platform-booted wasps'-nest hairdos. They were computerized Hanoi Rocks who'd spent too long playing Nintendo. Their manifesto said it all: "I'm desperately looking," said leader Tony James, "for something that's a bit exciting, or dangerous, or subversive—*and I can't find anything.*" So he did it himself.

Front-page news before they even played a live show, Sigue Sigue Sputnik swiftly became Britain's most sought-after new band. As the offers increased, though, so did the ante. Sigue Sigue Sputnik joined EMI for a rumored million British pounds, but all that really meant was that they were going to have to make their record label an awful lot of money before they earned any more for themselves. The sad fact is, after all the hype and the hullabaloo, Sigue Sigue Sputnik, like the unfortunate Unforgiven, simply couldn't, and didn't, follow through.

After the kind of buildup both bands had enjoyed, the kids wanted more than that, and all eyes were out for hype's rightful successor. Meanwhile back in Los Angeles, Jane's Addiction knew that most of those eyes were on them.

The group was playing the club circuit again, weaving its way through the rabbit's warren of fire and safety regulations that forced Perry to strip the stage show back down from its customary extravagance. He had begun substituting visual bombast for its aural equivalent. If Jane's Addiction was going to make it, if the group was even going to try and make it, it would be, it almost had to be, on musical terms.

In August, Jane's Addiction opened for Dream Syndicate at the Roxy on Sunset Boulevard. It was a weird billing, even if it did make sense on paper. Up there with the Red Hot Chili Peppers, Dream Syndicate was the undisputed king of local psychedelia; Jane's Addiction was the surly young upstarts taking their first tentative steps toward nirvana.

Musically, the two bands had blossomed from a very similar branch. There were distinct elements of swirling psychedelia wrapped up in Jane's Addiction's brew. Stylistically, however, there was no common ground whatsoever. Jane's Addiction was still to hit their powerhouse stride, was still tentative, informal, searching. Journalist Kurt Hueg pointed that out when he compared their Roxy show with another one six months later. At least he remembered them. For a support band in Los Angeles, even that was high praise.

Jane's Addiction supported Peter Murphy at one show; at another, they opened for Australian Nick Cave, carving through their now-customary smog of dry ice with the opening chords to the Rolling Stones' "Sympathy for the Devil," and leaving even Cave's fiercely partisan audience agape and aghast. It took an awful lot to upstage Nick Cave, but riding on the back of an increasingly vocal crowd of supporters, Jane's Addiction came very close.

Perry was not at a loss to explain how such a young band had, within a matter of months, developed one of Los Angeles's most rabid live followings. "Our shows are like really good sexual adventures," he bragged. "It's like spending the night with the very best prostitute you could find. It's pretty above the law. Whatever happens happens. There's nothing that's staged out. We try to push the limits of reality."

Push them, and shatter them. "I bet you girls never liked a guy in a dress as much as you like me tonight," Perry would habitually tease his audiences. "I bet you guys never did, either. But don't worry, I won't tell your dads. I think your dad kinda likes me as well!" "His talent for cross-dressing rivals that of early David Bowie!" enthused one journalist.

The group continued playing throughout the early fall, turning up anywhere that would take them. Perry and Casey were no longer even trying to book the shows anymore; instead they turned the reins over to one of the multitude of would-be management companies that were already sniffing around Jane's Addiction.

Triple X management started keeping tabs on the band some weeks before they finally made their move. "Seeing Jane's Addiction then was just great," Peter Heur, one of the three partners in the company, recalls. "It was just like nothing you've ever seen or heard before. They were so aggressive, so in your face, and so intense. Not everyone got it, but those who did were blown away."

While Heur and Dean Naleway took over Jane's Addiction's ever-increasing office workload, the third partner, Charley Brown, set about establishing a personal reputation no less uncompromising than the band's. A hard-talking hustler who stuck to the group like glue, already he saw Jane's Addiction as superstars. Now he made it his business to make sure that other people treated them as such. Years later, when Perry immortalized a glimpse of the band's early days in his film *Gift*, he recollected the occasion when Charley turned down a photo shoot because there wasn't a limo to take the band down there.

With Triple X behind them, developing a name that would swiftly become synonymous with an unprecedented form of musical mayhem, Jane's Addiction now entered the second phase of its development, the point whereby they didn't even need to advertise their concerts. A traveling audience that could fill any space simply spread the news among itself, and all Jane's Addiction needed to do was turn up. When the band hit the club Scream on November 8, 1986, it was as if half the city was turning out to greet them.

Scream dominated downtown Los Angeles like no other club. Originally based at the Ebony Theater on Washington, Scream moved to the basement of the Embassy Hotel on Ninth and Grand after just a handful of shows. There, it spread out to become a veritable labyrinth; the regulars reckoned it was impossible to even count how many rooms Scream spread into, and one evening would never be enough to sample the delights each one offered.

Bands played in one, videos flickered in another. There was a rehearsal space, with a fifty-piece piccolo marching band from Watts in apparently permanent residence, and a tatoo parlor which was only open to people who had already had themselves tattooed. "It keeps out the idiots who only want a teardrop," one of the guys on the door would growl.

Another room offered to shave your legs for fifty cents a limb, and another contained nothing but an enormous white skull. Scattered throughout, performance artists, actors, painters, sculptors, and musicians teemed together in one seething cauldron of creativity. Many visitors described it as little more than a secondhand Batcave, a sun 'n' sand recreation of that early-eighties cradle of avant-garde art; for others, the locals, it was the only gig in town.

Scream, Perry recalls affectionately, was "the only club to book bands purely on the basis of whether they were a good group or not, while Sunset Strip was being ruined by commercialism." The Red Hot Chili Peppers were an occasional headliner. Members of Gene Loves Jezebel played a memorable impromptu show there one evening, ad-libbing four of their most dynamic songs; the Cult and the Lords of the New Church were regulars, both onstage and in the audience. Even Guns N' Roses and L.A. Guns made a play for the Scream crowd, during that period when each aspired most heavily toward the local glam-metal scene.

Jane's Addiction was the first band to play Scream while it was still at the Ebony, and following its move, as Perry proudly recalls, they were "one of the bands that generated [what became the] Scream scene." They were "the club band, the biggest drawing band," and they played Scream at least once a month. Scream became Jane's Addiction's scene-by-default, and they responded with some of the greatest shows of their career. The very stage welcomed them, the roar that would ricochet bad-temperedly around their Hollywood rehearsal space walls suddenly sounding bigger, brighter, and more expansive than ever.

Those feelings only increased during soundcheck; even from behind the squealing monitors, with Perry wrestling with his arsenal of effects; even amidst the offstage clatter of bar being set up, Jane's Addiction could sense that the music they heard in their heads, that they *thought* they'd recaptured but could never be sure of, was finally going to break through. They also knew that if it didn't work at Scream, it might never succeed.

Later in the year, people would point to the fact that, with three major local reviews in the space of one month (in the *L.A. Weekly* for the Scream show; *Music Connection* for the Roxy, days before; and *BAM* for the Pyramid five days later), Jane's Addiction had already received the sort of head start other local bands could only dream of.

That was true. Such observations overlooked one final, intrinsic fact, however, the knowledge that Jane's Addiction actively merited the response they received—for the sound that was indisputably their own, for the songs that their raging embedded in your skull, and for their sheer devotion to their performance, a devotion that ensured that every show was more packed than the one before, that every performance more intense than that.

Club Lingerie is one of Hollywood's longest-established rock venues. Back in 1960, it was radio station KRLA's "Teen Night Club," hosting a succession of clean-cut balladeering heartthrobs. Renamed Red Velvet later in the decade, it was the first port of call for a host of visiting out-of-towners, from the Kinks to the Righteous Brothers. During the early 1970s, with the old Motown offices just up the road, it was transformed into that label's unofficial hangout. In the next decade, it became the responsibility of Brendan Mullen, the transplanted Scotsman who did so much to pioneer the local punk scene when he was booking bands into the Masque. There was a lot of history within those walls, but as Jane's Addiction played their set one night, there was a lot of negative energy, too.

According to Perry, "the club owners really pissed us off . . . lied to us about a bunch of stuff, so I said, 'I know what I'm gonna do . . .'"

The band was blasting into "Ocean Size," "just rocking," says Perry, "as hard as they can." Suddenly Perry leaped onto the railing that divided the stage from the dance floor, and hurled himself toward someone's table.

"I smashed their drinks off, the table goes flying over, the couple goes falling on the floor." Pushing the on-lookers aside, Perry jumped onto the bar and started drop-kicking everything he saw. "The lemons were going left, the cherries were going right." Then he drop-kicked the cherries about fifty feet, planting them neatly on the head of a watching Bono.

"He said he liked us after that," Perry said with a smile. "Maybe because he likes soccer," or maybe because he enjoyed the show. People who might ordinarily have over-looked even the most promising young band were suddenly paying attention to Jane's Addiction: metalheads drawn by the comparisons with Led Zeppelin, punks pulled in by the promise of onstage anarchy, even a smattering of goths, the Lost Tribe of the Alternative Nation, sensing that in Jane's Addiction, like Psi Com, their own cult of the disenfranchised lost had found a new voice. They heard it every time Perry opened his mouth to sing.

"Driven by pulsating rhythms and a . . . psychotic tempo, Jane's Addiction take its audience into a whirling, drug-induced state of (un)consciousness." *Music Connection* had mentioned Jane's Addiction one issue before; now here they were devoting half a page to the group.

Journalist Steve Kozak caught Jane's Addiction at the Roxy and came out reeling. "Aerosmith on acid," he wrote, and Perry smiled as he read those words. "Reminiscent of early Pink Floyd. . . ." Piled on top of the Led Zeppelin comparisons, Perry chuckled to himself; if Jane's Addiction weren't careful, they'd be re-creating the seventies all by themselves.

Jane's Addiction understood the dilemma of the state of current music. More important than that, they also understood how to change it. After months of planning, Perry finally voiced in public the dream that he had nurtured for so long. "We're actually making an attempt to change things around in a major way, like the Sex Pistols did. Popular music has gotten really stagnant, it needs someone to come in and knock down the walls."

Dreadlocked, down and dirty, a virtual tornado clad only in his underwear and a sneer, Perry reckoned he was the guy to do the knocking. "The world goes so fast these days [that] people don't have the time to ponder so much. Our stuff is easy to understand, but at the same time it has a lot of depth. We're trying to be as direct as possible, getting to the heart of the feeling we're trying to convey.

From a mainstream-sales point of view, the hopefulness with which the Replacements emerged had not been justified. The band topped the alternative charts and burned their way through the college listings. But in the real world of facts and figures, on the *Billboard* charts to which every executive turned, it was business as usual. For one solid month in the heart of 1986, the three top-selling albums in America were exactly the same—Whitney Houston, Janet Jackson, Patti Labelle. Behind them, Journey, Genesis, Van Halen . . . Those were the people behind the walls that Perry was threatening to burst through.

Los Angeles had blazed with punk rock. Not the art-crafted punk of Europe, the young-and-broke-and-on-the-dole maxim that fired the original spirit of 1977; Los Angeles punk burned instead with the contradictions of its own self, the agonizing conflict between the established order of California rock—the soporifics of the Eagles, Jackson Browne, and Linda Ronstadt—and the new: the passion of the Germs, Black Flag, and X.

No one ever expected to make a million bucks from punk; groups could rise in the critics' estimation, even establish themselves on a cult circuit outside of their immediate environment and join spiritual forces with the indigenous scenes that erupted elsewhere across America, so that from the outside looking in, punk was indeed a coalition of chaos, bent on the destruction of all that stood in its way. In marketing terms, punk remained a musical no-man's-land. Too harsh for the cultural wastelands of Middle America, too limited for the wider demographics of the coasts, as a commercial commodity, punk was a demilitarized zone at best, a musical snipers' gallery at worst.

In the mid-1960's, at the London Palladium, John Lennon scorned his well-heeled charity audience by telling them to rattle their jewelry in time to the music. Now the bands were rattling as loud as their listeners, but it wasn't their jewels that shook to the beat. It was their bones, the skeletal remnants of rocking rebellion clunking around in designer bags of skin. The Replacements were the exception that proved that cadaverous rule. Jane's Addiction wanted to help them become that rule, and they wanted to do it quickly.

Two years before, Jane's Addiction's peers had been the Minutemen and Kommunity FK. Now they were Poison and Jet Boy. Only Scream defied the strictures of conformity; only from that venue could Jane's Addiction explode the narrow categorization of rock 'n' roll.

"Los Angeles is the easiest city in the world to make it in if you're a rock band," Perry once protested. Musicians came from all over America to try and make it, until it seemed as though "working in the music business in Los Angeles is like being in a big corporation, only the work clothes are different. Instead of wearing a suit and tie, people go to work in a shag [haircut] and spandex."

When you bucked that system things became interesting. Jane's Addiction didn't have shag haircuts. "Guns N' Roses might be the bad boys of town," Scream deejay Mio Vukovic remarked at the time, "[but] Jane's Addiction are the smartest, the most intellectually and artistically extreme"—the offspring, as Perry himself would put it, of the city's other smart bands: "the Minutemen, the Red Hot Chili Peppers, and Fishbone."

"Our taste goes from funk, hip hop, reggae, anything that's really bassy," Perry once remarked, and that much was true, that much was noticeable. There was more to it, though. Comparisons with the modern, mid-nineties concept of "world music" bear inspection, that Jane's Addiction incorporated these elements because they belonged in the brew. Not, as would so often become the desperate case, simply because they tasted good.

"We're a reasonably eclectic group of guys," Eric mused. "None of us, with the possible exception of Stephen, really listens to rock 'n' roll. So it's such a collection of disparate parts, anything from fifties kind of cheesy salsa music or Germanic marching or drinking songs, all the way to the other side, things like Joy Division or Siouxsie and the Banshees."

The other thing that separated Jane's Addiction from other bands was Dave Navarro.

Although Eric insisted that "most of [the songs] came out of a bass line first, then parts put on top of it," it was Navarro's guitar that gave Jane's Addiction's music its inherent physicality, the sense of pure power that was evident whether the band was playing hard or soft, ugly or beautiful. By the end of 1986, the group was proving its dexterity by alternating their live sets between the two, one night acoustic, the next night electric. Both evenings were cut through with raging psychopathy.

"There's nothing better than mixing things," Perry said of the band's total disregard for the tidy generic captioning into which Jane's Addiction was so loudly refusing to be drawn. "We're forcing heavy-metal dudes and Mohawk dudes and young girls and blacks to all get in the same room and actually open up, and it's really great. I love looking out and seeing the Mohawk guy in the pit with the skinhead and some guy wearing a Joy Division T-shirt hanging out with some older guy who's maybe in college. It's a really healthy eclectic crowd."

It was that mix that Mio Vukovic conveyed to Geffen Records when that label first began investigating the Scream scene, and that he would endeavor to capture once the label gave him the go-ahead to document the scene for an eventual album release.

The original idea was to tape an entire album live at Scream itself, recreating the same raw, cinema verité feel of the decade-old London punk showcase album *Live at the Roxy, WC2*. The sheer logistics of the project defied belief, everything from safeguarding the recording equipment from a clubful of frenzied fans, to actually twisting a high enough–quality sound from the in-house PA. It would be easier simply to give each band a budget and set them loose in the studio.

As executive producer of the project, Vukovic himself would supervise a few of the contributions, from Francis X and the Bushmen to Tender Fury, the band formed earlier that year by T.S.O.L. frontman Jack Grisham and drummer Todd Barnes. (The latest incarnation of T.S.O.L., featuring no original members whatsoever, also turned up on the album.)

Jane's Addiction, however, would be going it alone. In December 1986, Perry returned to Radio Tokyo to slam down four songs: "Jane Says," a roaring barrage of sound far superior to any they would subsequently tape, "Had a Dad," "I Would for You," and a raucous "Pigs in Zen." The first three, the band would use for their first demo tape. The fourth would be included on *Scream*.

There's a hint of that mysterious ambivalence embedded deep in "Pigs in Zen," a sense that the band isn't taking the recording process too seriously—they are battling to preserve the *feel* of Jane's Addiction, not the sound of it.

Scream: The Compilation was scheduled for release early in the new year. Within twelve months, there would scarcely be a Scream regular that had not garnered a major deal. While Caterwaul singer Betsy Martin achieved many of the same vocal effects as Perry (*she* didn't need the electronics to do it) and went to IRS, and Human Drama joined RCA, Jane's Addiction went to the auction block.

Once, the band had been simply a talking point. Now they were a selling point, too. As the first track on *Scream: The Compilation*, "Pigs in Zen" would launch the album with a high to which it would never truly return.

More future anthems rolled into the set, "Mountain Song" and "My Time," and witnesses to Psi Com's last dazed days could not help but wonder where this new inspiration had been hiding. Because even before *Music Connection* published its annual "Pick of the Players" poll toward the end of 1986, Jane's Addiction's dominance of the listings was a foregone conclusion.

"Pick of the Players" is one of the Los Angeles underground's most eagerly anticipated musical events. Rather than throw opinion over to the public or critics, as is the formula at most publications, *Music Connection* allowed the bands to be judged by their peers, with the 1986 listings being opened to representatives (two per band) of ninety-nine different local groups.

The criteria were that participants could not vote for their own band, nor for any group that had landed a major label deal. Hard luck indeed for Jet Boy, who would have placed eighth were it not for the small matter of an Elektra recording contract. Hard luck, too, for Guns N' Roses, whose own campaign to reassert their street credibility saw them release a live EP on their own independent label, nine months *after* they signed with Geffen. Years later, their move would have serious consequences on the industry as a whole, as major labels shunted their latest "alternative" signings off onto

their own pseudo-independent subsidiaries. For now, though, it didn't fool anyone.

Success in the *Music Connection* poll did not, of course, auger success in the outside world, or even in Los Angeles itself. Leatherwolf, the 1985 winners, would not even make the Top 20 the following year, while previous years threw up their own fair share of future obscurities. Even in 1987, who remembered VVSI? Or the Fibonaccis? Both had been triumphant in past *Music Connection* polls.

Jane's Addiction's victory, however, boded for far greater things than a multiple-choice answer in some future rock trivia quiz. While Guns N' Roses' *Live?!*@ *Like a Suicide* sold ten thousand copies in less than a month, Jane's Addiction was presenting itself as an alternative to them, an alternative to all the ham glam-metal bands that now tarted it up in Axl n' Slash's tat-bedraggled wake.

Beyond the obvious geographical connotations, the things that tied Jane's Addiction to Guns N' Roses were obscure at best. It was pure coincidence that the two groups had emerged from the same city at the same time. Musically they were planets apart, even if Axl Rose, too, possessed a voice that could tap almost preternaturally high notes. The very polarization of Jane's Addiction and Guns N' Roses meant, as British journalist Jonh Wilde discovered, that "wherever you go in L.A., people will tell you [about] Guns N' Roses or Jane's Addiction, the two far ends of the city's current rock renaissance." Because the far ends, the extremes, were what Angelenos thrived upon.

It didn't matter if Perry denied that Jane's Addiction "fit into any part of the Los Angeles scene." As Mio Vukovic remarked at the time, "You experience a whole lot in L.A., the highest peaks of life to the very bottom of things. Jane's music reflects those extremes better than any band in town."

Vukovic also conceded that "those extremes exist in all cities," but where else, Perry asked, could they be discovered so close together? Stumble into the heart of Hollywood, and it is but a few blocks from the affluent shoppers' paradise of Melrose to the sordid no-man's-land of Santa Monica Boulevard; from the downtrodden anorexia of Fairfax to the bloated corpulence of Beverly Hills. The music in a way echoed the terrain.

Guns N' Roses also mirrored those extremes, but they did so from a strangely dualist viewpoint. Whether you believed that they reflected the Saturday-night slumming of the moneyed yuppie or the sadness of the true social outcast, it was still the passion of the fashion dilettante that characterized their stance; the sleazy grandeur of Keith Richards erecting his own Porta-Slum in the swankiest hotel room. It was not real. Axl Rose sang for people who lit their rooms with candles because they wanted to make a place look mysterious. Perry Farrell sang for those who couldn't afford anything else.

The end of 1986 brought the first serious bid for Jane's Addiction's signatures—from Slash, a local independent label that was distributed by Warner Brothers. Triple X turned them away. They knew they could do better elsewhere.

At the same time, though, there was something beguiling about going with an independent first; the same thing, perhaps, as Guns N' Roses had so belatedly realized.

Released on the group's own Uzi Suicide label, the *Live?!*@ Like a Suicide* EP was produced and marketed without any noticeable input from Geffen, and launched with none of the ballyhoo that would ordinarily have attended the band's debut recording. It allowed the band to find its own level in the alternative marketplace, before the big guns were brought to bear on the mainstream. That was a major consideration, and most likely a marketing ploy.

"We need to get something out there before anyone else gets to us," Perry explained. "We have to establish our style." That way, "record companies would know what we were," and what they would be getting into if they signed the band.

Scream: The Compilation would play a part in that process, of course, but it was still only a shop window. Perry wanted any potential purchasers to sample all his wares before they made their decision; a decision, he knew, that would affect his life as much as theirs.

There was another reason for wanting to beat the big boys to the punch and get a Jane's Addiction record onto the streets before a major label could.

For all its latter-day sophistication, rock 'n' roll still demands that its adherents pay their dues. Perry had done that already, he believed, and so had Jane's Addiction. But L.A. is a tiny place, comparatively. Beyond its limits, Jane's Addiction remained unknown. Unknown bands simply don't get major-label deals. Not unless there's something very fishy about them, anyway, something that bellows "Hype!" Perry needed to divert those bellows before they were even uttered. Does the band have any worries? he was asked by one journalist, and he replied with astonishing candor: "Just drive about three hours outside Los Angeles. That's *our* worry."

I   Wanna
Raise Your
Kid   for
Y o   u .
I'll Give
Him   Back
When I'm
D o n e .

ane's Addiction rang in the new year of 1987 with two
nights at the Roxy, on January 2 and 3. The shows were
billed as a showcase, with every label that had expressed
a glimmer of interest in the band invited.

   To add to the sense of occasion, the two shows
would be very different from each other; the first, a full-
fledged rock 'n' roll extravaganza, Jane's Addiction at their
volatile electric peak; the second, a more controlled, if not
sedate, semi-acoustic bash. Such shows years later would be
called "unplugged," and everyone would be playing them, but
for now, the uniqueness of the second outing was one of Jane's
Addiction's greatest selling points. The other was the sheer
dynamism of the performance.

It was that dynamism, that tension, upon which Jane's Addiction thrived, musically and personally. Perry later claimed that within two months of getting together, "the guys in Jane's hated each other." They remained together simply because "we didn't want to break up whatever chemistry we had."

He was exaggerating, but only a little. Onstage and off, there was a tangible tension between the band members, especially between the band members and Perry. "Why is it that whenever you guys get your picture in the papers, the only one they ever show is Perry?" someone asked Dave Navarro once.

"I dunno. You'd better ask Perry," was the guitarist's reply.

"Eighty percent of our material thrives [on tension]," Perry once remarked, "putting together elements that might not seem to fit"—musically and personally. Both ways, the blend packed an emotional punch. "What we try to do is create something close to the heartbeat, maybe some kind of fucked-up heartbeat. We aim for the center of the chest."

The Roxy shows were never intended to be simple music business schmoozes. It looked as if Jane's Addiction entire fan base, milling among the besuited bigwigs, had turned out to see them. In the face of so much passion, those same bigwigs simply reeled at the power of Jane's Addiction, and at the manipulation power with which they themselves were being courted.

A traditional record company showcase is usually sedate. The guests are courted at the bar with free drinks and warm handshakes. If seating is available, it will already be reserved. The guests, in other words, are *attended* to.

Triple X didn't give a shit about the traditional record company showcase. Instead, they pulled out all the stops to transport their guests into the very heart of Jane's Addiction's world. There was no high-budget buffet, no free bar, and no comfy chairs. The executives were left to fend for themselves, almost as though Charley Brown, Triple X's delegated "bad guy" frontman, was smirking, "You want this band? Show us how much you want them."

Jane's Addiction turned in a furious set, one of the finest, many people said, that they ever saw the group perform. Perry was like a madman, tense and threatening, a banshee blur of aggression that hurled itself across the stage while the rest of the band put their heads down and blasted. They knew Perry had something planned, they were just waiting for him to reveal it to the masses.

They did not have to wait very long. Of all the legends that have sprung up around Jane's Addiction, the most endearing still dates from that moment at the Roxy when Perry coiled himself up as tight as he could, then sprung into the air with a roar that could be felt at the other end of Sunset.

"Fuck you, assholes! We're gonna make our own record!"

If his fans hadn't been making so much noise, you probably could have heard a checkbook drop after that; might even have heard it on the live album that the band was recording those same two nights for their own record. A live album, Stephen Perkins later explained, "was the best description of what we were." A live album taped in front of the corporate chiefs of American music only compounded the gesture. "We just went for it."

The first night, the electric night, would dominate the album, supplying seven of the eventual ten tracks, but it was the three songs from the second, acoustic night that remain the most intense: the melting "I Would for You," the blues-driven "My Time," and the song that had long since been adopted by band and supporters alike as the group's anthem, "Jane Says." Ten lines tell us that nobody cares. "Jane's addicted." It was as simple, as unequivocal, as that.

Lou Reed's "Rock & Roll" was another of the album's highlights, powered by Navarro's fluid guitar playing and backed with a liquid percussive track that bled almost seamlessly into another song that Jane's Addiction had adopted as their own, the Rolling Stones' "Sympathy for the Devil." While "Rock & Roll" howled with the exuberance of the Jane's Addiction experience, "Sympathy" (to which the song's original title was abridged on the album jacket) reveled in the *other* side of the band's appeal, the brooding hedonism through which Jane's Addiction connected with the streets that "bred and spread" them.

The *L.A. Times* made that connection shortly after the album was released. "What these songs show is a gritty street reality as seen through the haze of troubled adolescence. So it's a bit surprising to find that Farrell is not an adolescent at all." It was also to the *L.A. Times* that he offered that now-famous boast, "Name something degrading and I've done it. I'm not going to be explicit about it, just anything degrading I've done so I could eat."

The Roxy shows were a turning point for Jane's Addiction. They announced the commencement of what would become a furious record-company bidding war; announced, too, a press scramble that even Triple X would acknowledge was getting out of hand.

Jane's Addiction's performance at the Cooperage in late January was greeted by writer Kurt Hueg as "new with a capital N . . . the best new sound in Los Angeles." Elsewhere, journalist Jon Matsumoto continued, "this ambitious quartet is just about the most-talked-about new outfit in Tinsel Town," and even the *Los Angeles Times* weighed in, invoking what would become one of the decade's most trusted clichés when it announced that Jane's Addiction were "habit-forming," and informing its readership, "If you've ever wondered what Led Zeppelin would've sounded like without that mystic twerp singing lead, the answer might be . . . Jane's Addiction."

On Valentine's Day 1987, Scream hosted the Los Angeles Fashion Show. Jane's Addiction, now the epitome of local fashion, headlined the evening, glorying in an audience that mixed club regulars with what the *L.A. Weekly* described as "Thanksgiving at Bob Guccione's—gorgeous gloomsters displaying fur, feathers, thighs, and breasts."

At the end of February, *BAM* was describing Jane's Addiction as "a quartet who've been inked and hyped to the point of saturation." The magazine confirmed that "every year produces a gaggle of local Next Big Thangs, and right at the front of the pack in '87 is Jane's Addiction."

The following month, the group was a headline attraction at the *L.A. Weekly*'s own newly instituted Rock Music Awards, at the Variety Arts Center on March 5; two months after that, they were *the* main attraction when Scream rang down the curtain on its residency at the Embassy on May 30, 1987.

Thirty minutes after Scream's normal closing time, Jane's Addiction were still playing. Tonight was their night, tonight was their audience's night, and when the show did finally wind down, Perry, shirtless and sweat-soaked, his mascara'ed eyes bleeding black down his face, reminded them of that. Reminded himself as well. Raising one first in the air, he stood impassive for a moment, staring into the crowd. Then he bellowed the words with which he cautioned himself every night—"Whatever happens, don't sell out!"

When he later was asked what he would tell any new bands wanting to emulate Jane's Addiction's success *so far*, he remarked: "My advice . . . would be, sit down and really think about what you're [doing]. Think how you want to present it to people. Seriously think about what you're saying." The alternative was unimaginable. If what you do sucks, "[then that's] how you're gonna go down in history, and you're gonna lay on your deathbed going, 'Man, I'm a damn sell-out and what I had to say was shit. Now I'm gonna be lumped in there with Peter Frampton and the Bay City Rollers.'"

"The most important thing a label has to understand is that we want to go against the grain of what's being done. Nothing new is going to come out if you don't try to change [what's already been done]."

Perry outlined Jane's Addiction's immediate plans. When band members dropped by the Triple X offices at 6715

Hollywood Boulevard and climbed the stairs to Suite 282, there was another sheaf of offers on the table every day.

Before Triple X took over, Perry asserted, the band had nobody to promote them. So they did it themselves, starting from the street and working their way up. "There was no parent figure behind us. The only person who'd say 'Fuck this shit, we're happening' was us." Now there was someone to act as a buffer, not only between the band and the shit, but also between the band and the bullshit. There was a lot of that flying around, as the label offers piled in.

Elektra, the company that passed on Guns N' Roses because it had already signed Mötley Crüe, started chasing Jane's Addiction after one of their A&R men stumbled upon them at the Music Machine. With *Scream: The Compilation* about to hit the shops, Geffen was still interested, describing Jane's Addiction as potentially the next Guns N' Roses, and maybe even bigger. Even Motown, seriously considering updating its classic soul image by expanding its roster into rock 'n' roll, was showing some cautious interest, and for a moment, Perry pondered the possibilities that linkup would raise.

Motown had always nurtured its subversive streak: Four years before, the label's U.K. wing came very close to signing Southern Death Cult. Plus, Perry figured, a band could have one helluva worse bunch of labelmates than Diana Ross, Smokey Robinson, and the late Marvin Gaye. "Yeah, you could have Lionel Ritchie," someone reminded him, and promptly ducked. Perry was still smarting from something his father had recently asked him, about why *he* couldn't sing nicely . . . like the silk-voiced Lionel Ritchie.

Perry returned to reality. "What we're going to do is . . . blow people away. When we get out there, we're going to do things no one else has ever done. Musically," he warned Jane's Addiction's peers, "we're already light-years ahead."

One journalist, the *L.A. Times*'s Steve Hochman, reminded Perry of his earlier prophecy, that Jane's Addiction was going to do to Los Angeles what the Sex Pistols did to Britain: smash it down, then rebuild from the rubble. Perry simply sneered. Jane's Addiction was now so far ahead of the Sex Pistols that it was barely worth considering anymore.

The Sex Pistols, he snarled, "were just a fashion band." Jane's Addiction was the real thing. The only thing they needed to do now was make sure that all interested parties knew that, and if that meant exploding their hype, so fucking be it.

The fanfare that surrounded the group gratified but simultaneously mystified Jane's Addiction. "If anybody started a hype," Perry reasoned, "it's the people who hate us," for they knew that "the first thing that kills a band is to listen to what other people say about you. Don't listen to anybody. If you do, you're a fool." He denied that he even paid attention to the band's press, good *or* bad. Perry Farrell was just about the only person in Los Angeles who *could* say that.

As Jane's Addiction made the rounds of interested labels, Perry's spiel for each one was always exactly the same. "If you're gonna sign this band, you're gonna sign the band for how the band is right now. If you think you can even begin to change us—sign another band."

It was an uncompromising stance and, coupled with the increasingly vast sums of money being waved in Jane's Addiction's direction, it doubtless did much to scare a few would-be suitors away. That was the point. "Do you want to hear about the bidding wars?" Perry teased later. "We had them all kissing our feet." In fact, for as many labels that kissed the band's feet, there were more that simply took to their own and withdrew from the contest forthwith.

In the end, it came down to a straight contest between three companies: Geffen, whose *Scream: The Compilation* was just reaching the stores; Capitol, on whose roster were the other major players on the Los Angeles scene, the Red Hot Chili Peppers; and Warner Brothers.

All three had their attractions, and all three were prepared to dig deep into their pockets. Before a deal was finally concluded, for a rumored, but apparently highly overexaggerated $300,000, the Los Angeles grapevine was rustling with reports of one company offering to drop twice that into Jane's

Ritual De Lo Habitual

Addiction's open lap. Perry turned them down. To his mind, there were commodities at stake far more important than cash.

Jane's Addiction signed to Warner Brothers in early spring 1987. In many ways, Warner's had been their best option all along. The Warner Brothers group, which also included the Sire, Elektra, Atlantic, and soon-to-be-reborn Reprise imprints, was already known to be hungry for what it—almost alone among the majors—perceived to be the Next Big Thing: the "alternative" scene which was now breaking out all across the American map.

Around the same time as Warner's chairman Mo Ostin was okaying Jane's Addiction's recruitment to the label, with all the outspoken heartache Perry was already promising, he was also giving his approval to the proposed jacket for Prince's latest album, *LoveSexy*, a portrait of the naked, prone performer. He could already hear the screams of protest.

According to a former Warner Brothers employee (one of Jane's Addiction's many admirers within the company compound), the first time Perry met the label's art department to discuss Jane's Addiction's own artistic requirements, the chief topic of conversation was the number of Warner Brothers acts that had been condemned for their album jackets. "It was as if they were daring him to try and go one better than them." Mo Ostin intuitively understood the value of controversy. His staff simply followed his lead. As he left the company's expansive Burbank headquarters, Perry knew he could fulfill his label's wildest dreams.

According to Perry, the key to Warner Brothers' offer was the amount of control it placed in the band's own hands. It was not only the group's advance that was compromised by that concession, however. In every other way, Warner Brothers appeared to have the upper hand.

Charley Brown remained stoic. "We have no illusions about being [this being] a big deal. We just have someone who'll pay to support our act until they can quit their day jobs. We still have a lot to prove."

Perry laughed, "We love being exploited."

From the outside, it looked as though they already were.

Perry had always protested his involvement in rock 'n' roll, loudly proclaiming that there was no way he would remain a musician forever. "I don't look at it like David Bowie, big career man." He reckoned he didn't even listen to rock 'n' roll anymore, didn't "get off on hearing that same rock 'n' roll riff. It's boring. I like Cajun music."

Yet the Warner Brothers contract demanded that, including options, Jane's Addiction supply a staggering seven albums, and now Perry was backpedaling furiously. He even admitted, "I might just end up really loving this. Who doesn't want to be liked?"

There were more conditions.

Warner Brothers was not bound to offer the group any tour support, which meant that any live expenses came from their own initial advance. The company pledged backing for just one video, at a time when MTV would barely look twice at an unknown band's debut offering.

The contract did grant Jane's Addiction complete artistic control over all that they did, but that control would only be surrendered once every other option was exhausted. The band discovered this when they announced that they wanted to produce their next album, their major-label debut album, themselves.

Warner Brothers' own idea was to line up their investment with one of several big-name commercial producers. "You boys need time to learn your way around a recording studio," the band was told, and when they argued that they already had, the corporate jaws went into overtime. "Recording a studio album is not the same as mixing a live record," and when Perry opened his mouth again, "Recording a studio album for Warner Brothers is not the same as recording an EP for your own independent"—or anything else he had done in the past.

Jane's Addiction remained adamant, however. No matter who Warner Brothers suggested pairing them with, they turned them down. "Why give somebody else the reins when we've worked to get this sound?" Perry demanded. "It's like if you had a baby and somebody said, 'I wanna raise your kid for you. I'll give him back when I'm done.'"

Warner's laughed. "You'll be in the studio with him. You'll still have the final say."

Eric spoke up. "A band that goes into the studio with a producer who has his own track record is there to make it in the music business, not to create their own art in its purest form." Perry agreed. For some bands, the producer was "the Moses of rock 'n' roll who'll lead them to the fucking mountaintop." For others, he was someone who would hold their hands, because they "simply don't know what they want."

Jane's Addiction did not fit into either of those categories, but the wrangling still didn't end. "It's beginning to make me feel like it's not fun anymore," Dave Navarro complained. Suddenly, Warner Brothers was "starting to have all this input, things that might not go with us creatively." These demands were not in the contract. It was time for Jane's Addiction to take matters into their own hands.

It wasn't, after all, as though their request was particularly unique, in the world of rock or even in the world of Warner Brothers. Ten years earlier, in 1977, the label had been locked into a similar impasse with Prince. He, too, was a brand-new signing; he, too, wanted to produce himself, against the better judgment of the label chiefs. They finally agreed to a compromise. Prince would submit to a studio audition and record a few songs for the label to hear. If they liked what he did, he'd be given what he asked for. If they didn't . . . well, it never came to that. Prince would never have to contemplate external producers again.

Jane's Addiction took the same route. Dipping into the Warner Brothers advance, Triple X booked the band into a small local studio to record and self-produce a demo of "Ocean Size," perhaps the most musically ambitious song within their entire canon. Then Charley Brown extracted the same promise from Warner Brothers as Prince had wrung out:

"If you like what they do, Jane's Addiction can go ahead and do the entire album their way. If you don't, and you can show us how it could be done better, well, then maybe we can talk."

The label heads smiled indulgently. It wasn't their money—what did it matter what Jane's Addiction did with it? When the band returned to the boardroom, the response to "Ocean Size," Charley Brown said, was "smiles" from the people who'd believed in the group in the first place, "and grimaces" from everybody else. Jane's Addiction got their own way. They were booked into the studio, on their own.

In July 1987 Jane's Addiction flew to New York to appear at the annual New Music Seminar, the four-day celebration of "alternative" music which would dominate the city's nightlife between July 12 and 15. The group knew that if they were to make any headway beyond their California stronghold, New York was the place to start.

Was New York even interested in them? A couple of weeks before the New Music Seminar got under way, *Billboard* magazine published its "Top Ten Guide to the Class of '87," a breakdown of the bands most likely to break through within the next year or so. The list determined Concrete Blonde and Suicidal Tendencies to be the cream of the recent Los Angeles crop. Then came World Party, Soul Asylum, Mission U.K., the Housemartins, Hipsway, Australia's Go-Betweens, and two bands that still remain essentially unknown, Fire Town and the Other Ones. Jane's Addiction was not listed at all.

The group dropped $7,000 on the trip to New York, out of their Warner Brothers advance. It was a total waste of money; the group returned to Los Angeles with little more to show for their pains than the bemused disdain of their first New York audience.

"I didn't know there wasn't gonna be kids there," Perry spat as he described the weeklong all-industry schmooze into which Jane's Addiction had unwittingly catapulted themselves. Instead of potential fans, they were confronted with critics and journalists who flew in from all over the country to hang out with their buddies and snag freebies from the record companies.

Perry admitted that he had a really bad attitude that night. "I just insulted the audience, because I knew they were all New Music Seminar people."

The highlight of his tirade remains legendary on the rock epithets circuit—"This song," Perry announced from the lip of the stage, "is for the fat record-company executives with hairy bellies that fuck little boys." Looking back, Perry could not help but reflect, "I was just totally rude."

Jane's Addiction played a second show the following night, away from the Seminar at what Perry describes as "a biker rock 'n' roll club." He simply asked the owners to let Jane's Addiction play the following evening, "and they said okay."

This time, the band did find the audience of kids they'd been seeking, but again the show was haphazard. "I just kind of felt things out," Perry recalled ruefully, but then brightened up. Good shows, bad shows, what did it matter? That was the magic of Jane's Addiction. "It's not predictable. You never know what we're gonna do."

The New Music Seminar was Jane's Addiction's first public appearance since May; it would be their last until mid-August. After the hectic pace of the past twelve months, the band members were exhausted. Perry wanted some time out to concentrate on his writing; the others just needed to get away from the group for a while. The media would have to find somebody else to blitz for a couple of months.

Triple X, according to many accounts, did not necessarily agree with the group's resolution. Shortly after Jane's Addiction's Warner Brothers deal was concluded, they were approached by one of the biggest public-relations companies in Los Angeles, with an offer that was as tempting as it was straightforward.

The company wanted Jane's Addiction on its books, and it wanted them badly. "Give us a few months, we'll represent you free of charge. A trial period. If you like what we do for you, fine. If you don't—well, that's fine as well." No amount of cajoling could convince Jane's Addiction to accept the offer. Why did they even need a press office? They only had to break wind, and someone would review it.

Jane's Addiction had already achieved its first objective by grabbing a lucrative record deal. Now it was time to let things calm down a little. "We don't want the people to overdose on us, do we?" Perry smiled in explanation. "They're probably sick to death of our name by now."

He was right to be cautious. When Jane's Addiction was still an unsigned band, they were hot property, local heroes into whom everyone could stake a discovery claim. Now, though . . . they were still a hot property, but *so what*? So were . . . And out came the exhaustive list of past hot properties, over and over until finally Perry snapped. "All I can say is, if you could *possibly* compare us to the Unforgiven, you're a moron!"

Wrapped in a self-depicting sleeve that Perry, of course, designed, working late at the West L.A. Graphics print shop, the band's live album, *Jane's Addiction*, was released in August 1987 on Triple X's own, self-named record label.

It was, of course, serviced to every radio station that might remotely have an interest in the group, but band and management alike were well aware that the album was intended less for public consumption than for the nationwide critics who Perry had so thoroughly discomfited at the New Music Seminar. While you were getting drunk and trying to get laid, it hissed, THIS is what you missed.

The Los Angeles press sided with Jane's Addiction. One writer compared *Jane's Addiction* to the Pretenders' debut album, "exhilarating" in the peaking levels of its own energy, "scary" in the possibilities that it laid bare. Others hammered the Led Zeppelin comparisons firmly into the ground, with *Buzz* magazine's Gina Arnold at the head of the pack. "Led Zeppelin was never this sarcastic," she vowed. "They were never angry. They were never, and here's the crux, brave. That's where Jane's Addiction has it over them 100 percent."

Barely (self-) produced, barely remixed, *Jane's Addiction* did more than simply re-create the awesome energy of the group in full flight; it actually improved upon it. Away from the mass of mosh-pit regulars who turned even the band's acoustic shows into the frenzied free-for-alls that Perry himself would eventually leap into, with the volume at least set at a comfortable level and the instruments finally distinguishable from the distortion of small-club acoustics, you really could, as writer Carlo Wolff cautioned, "hear how dangerous rock still can be."

The heavy-metal references of course came out in force, but they were tempered first, by the sheer impossibility of actually placing *Jane's Addiction* on the same turntable as Poison or Mötley Crüe. Later in the year, an enthusiastic notice from Robert Hilburn of the *L.A. Times* asserted that Jane's Addiction wove "the kind of seductive, almost unnerving musical spell that is at the heart of true heavy-metal music." True heavy metal, "*not* the tedious, cartoonish bombast of the many bands associated with the genre these days." This was an important distinction, in that it preserved intact the Led Zeppelin references that remained Jane's Addiction's most potent calling card. Perry made a mental note to thank Hilburn sometime. Sure.

Cashbox picked up on the album, marveling at the way in which its "raunchy metal and punk sonics swagger with lyrics from the littered streets." *Buzz* concocted an unholy alliance "between Led Zep, U2, and"—deferring to Perry's occasional taste in ladies clothing—"Culture Club—this band is meant to hit everybody right where it hurts." *The WARD Report* insisted that "the only problem with Jane is that those who hate her will never change the minds of those who love her . . . because the reasons for their passions are exactly the same."

Jane's Addiction broke its silence to tie in with the album's release. They were added to the bill of what ranked among their biggest shows yet, an all–Los Angeles celebration at the Irvine Meadows Amphitheatre, on August 15, 1987.

The very lineup was redolent with meaning and impact. Jane's Addiction appeared at the foot of a bill that even today would be regarded as sensational: punk icons Social Distortion, and the neo-legendary X. What Jane's Addiction needed to prove was that the pecking order was not immutable.

X were already on their way . . . if not down, then certainly out. One more live album, the following year's *Live at the Whiskey*, and that would be it for the group that literally redefined Californian rock.

As they played their respective sets, it was as if both X and Jane's Addiction comprehended the sheer gravity of the particular situation. Jane's Addiction would later repay X by including the band's "Nausea" in their staple in-concert tribute to the City of Angels, "L.A. Medley," along with the Doors' "L.A. Woman" and the Germs' "Lexicon Devil."

There was no room for sentiment tonight. The decade was getting old, and with it, the bands that forged it. That evening, the Irvine Meadows Amphitheatre witnessed more than a simple concert; it saw a changing of the guard.

The crowd was still filing into the auditorium when Jane's Addiction commenced their set, and Perry later admitted that the sight was off-putting.

He didn't show his bewilderment, though. Recalling the hours that he used to put in, leaping around his bedroom with the headphones on full blast, he explained that he had tricks that he had developed through many years of performing alone. "One of them is closing my eyes. That way you can give the exact same feeling as if there were a zillion people there."

Jane's Addiction played furiously, dropping any song that didn't conform to the 100 blitzkreig Perry knew would blow the audience away. "On every song, just pump it out. Then get off in half an hour."

That same month, August, Jane's Addiction made another of their periodic sorties into the world of Perry's British influences when they were invited to open for the Psychedelic Furs in Santa Barbara.

Truly adventurous, truly challenging, occasionally even punishing, the Psychedelic Furs were the decade-so-far's only true realization of Pop as Art. Their components were as offbeat as Richard Butler's "two-packs-a-day" vocals, a sax that roared like a vacuum cleaner, a guitar that could nail you to the wall, all falling into place within the band's almost secretively melodic barrage.

The venue would have been packed even without Jane's Addiction's traveling support; the Furs were enjoying a major hit album with *Midnight to Midnight*, and it would take a lot to even compete with the shouts of their own fiercely partisan fans. Even vocalist Richard Butler admits that Jane's Addiction, whom today he describes among his favorite bands of the 1980s, were in explosive form that night.

The Santa Barbara show was followed by a handful of low-key California club dates, and then it was back to the East Coast as the guests of yet another group of British tourists, yet another of Perry's own favorites as well, Love and Rockets. Jane's Addiction had been offered a number of different tours that fall, but there was something about Love and Rockets that appealed.

For a start, it was short. True to their word, Warner Brothers wasn't putting any financial backing into Jane's Addiction's road expenses, and Charley Brown acknowledged, "I don't want them to. The more we can do on our own between now and when the record comes out, the more credibility we'll have. When our record comes out, I want to have the ball rolling so much that Warners just has to kick in and give that extra push." The headliners' own schedule demanded that the tour break in mid-December and not resume until January at the earliest, by which time Jane's Addiction would be involved in recording their Warner Brothers debut.

Love and Rockets commanded precisely the kind of audience that Jane's Addiction knew they could share. The band had formed just two years earlier, from the two-year-old wreckage of gothic pioneers Bauhaus. Daniel Ash, David J, and Kevin Haskins were actually planning a full Bauhaus reunion when they first reconvened. Undaunted, the trio completed an album of its own, the monumental *Seventh Dream of Teenage Heaven*. Now, in late 1987, they were just releasing their third. *Earth Sun Moon* was already receiving widespread college radio acclaim; with the impetus of the tour behind it, it would eventually break the national Top 50.

The tour reached California in December, hitting the University of California–Irvine's Bren Events Center on December 5. Elsewhere around the country, Jane's Addiction had found themselves playing to Love and Rockets' own audience exclusively. Now it was time to show the headliners what home support really was.

Did Perry's pants rip? Or were they torn? According to the campus police, it was the former. Perry's gymnastics simply put too much strain on his already tightly stretched spandex trousers. The view from the audience was an eyeful of Perry's genitalia, flapping loose through a gap in the front of his pants. Robert Hilburn, writing in the following morning's *L.A. Times*, remarked that in the time it took before Perry finally covered up, pulling on a pair of briefs, "[his] manner was so nonchalant that many in the audience must have wondered if this brazen gesture was part of the act."

That nonchalance led Hilburn to just one final conclusion: Jane's Addiction were heading, inexorably, for "the big time."

It was reactions such as Hilburn's that convinced Jane's Addiction that they made the right choice in accepting the Love and Rockets tour; that, and the sheer compatibility of the two bands, both musically and personally.

There was a genuine sense of camaraderie on the tour bus, and one that Love and Rockets were to remember when they made their return to the U.S. five months later, in May 1988.

At their specific request, Jane's Addiction was invited to open the group's Los Angeles show, at the Wiltern Theater, on May 9. Stephen Perkins reciprocated by wearing a Love and Rockets T-shirt in Jane's Addiction's first video.

Cast Deep
Into Your
P o c k e t s
for Loot to
Buy This
Disc. . . .
If , You
Don't Have
Bread, See
That Blind
Man. . . .

e're a live band. We should tape the album live."

Perry had it all worked out. Jane's Addiction would commandeer an empty warehouse, ship all the luxuries of a studio into that wide, open space, and then let rip. Strategically placed microphones would not only catch the roar of the band, they would also pick up the sheer vastness of the room, the echoes resounding from the walls, the dust kicked up by the volume, the scurrying of the rats to get out of sonic harm's way, everything.

It was only when he sat down to price the project out that the shadows started to cross his face. Jane's Addiction had already won a major concession from Warner Brothers, the right to become the first unsung act since Prince to produce its own debut album. It was unlikely that the group would be granted another—the first unsung band since Prince to go so far overbudget on the first record that it ended up costing *double* the amount most groups spent on three.

"We'd end up in debt forever," he sighed, and when someone asked why they couldn't just make up the shortfall on some long-distant future project, was it just imagination, or did a peculiar shadow cross Perry's face?

Jane's Addiction ended up in the twenty-four-track Eldorado Studios in Los Angeles, and if making a noise was all they were concerned about, the complex swiftly proved itself to be up to par. Maybe they couldn't play until engineers Dave Jerden and Ronnie Champagne's needles rocketed into the red, Perry acknowledged, "but it still sounds pretty fucking loud."

They even managed to tape a handful of tracks live, slamming the whole song down in one take, although nobody could have confused the new versions of "Jane Says" or the CD bonus track, "Pigs in Zen," with those that had already appeared, over the past twelve months, on *Jane's Addiction* and *Scream: The Compilation*.

Jane's Addiction didn't want to be "slick and clean," Stephen insisted. Their first album "was grungy and live." That was the feeling they wanted to keep. "But still, we're a grungy street band."

"We are a very live band," Eric continued, "and I think that a lot of people would want to come home and listen to the Jane's Addiction they'd just heard [in concert], one that's raw and straightforward. I don't think they'd want to hear [it] polished."

When a band plays live, Perry explained, things go out of tune, "people make mistakes. We have mistakes on this record, too, but we kept the mistakes that worked."

Last time around, "if it happened, it happened, there was nothing [we] could do about it. This time, we could overdub. It's kinda like asking somebody to draw a picture and not stop, as opposed to somebody who has a chance to sit at home and erase. It's always gonna come out better."

Perry was swift to reassure the band's followers that "we didn't fuck with it too much. There's no synthesizers!" There were, however, horns, cluttered through "Idiots Rule," and they did take some getting used to, even though there was no questioning the credibility of the players: Flea, the trumpet-tooting bassist with the Red Hot Chili Peppers, and Fishbone's Christopher Dowd and Angelo Moore, all members of the mutual appreciation society around which the Los Angeles alternative scene still revolved. They were friends, they were passing, they played. It was as simple as that.

Other friends, however, would not be coming round very often anymore. As the band prepared to go into the studio, they finally parted company with Triple X.

Both parties have remained amicably tightlipped over the reasons for the split, and even the Los Angeles grapevine doesn't have any credible alternatives for the most common explanation; that while the band wanted their management to concentrate exclusively on their career, Heur, Brown, and Naleway were equally interested in pursuing the record label they formed around Jane's Addiction's debut album.

Triple X over the next few years expanded to become one of Los Angeles's most vital independents, loyal not only to the waves of new bands that were bursting out of clubland, but also to the old hands they had worked alongside in the past. Jeff Dahl and the Angry Samoans, Tender Prey and Human Drama from the Scream scene, and Christian Death's Rozz Williams—all became Triple X recording artists.

The legal separation, too, was conducted with dignity. Triple X retained the rights to the live album and, seven years later, would receive Perry's blessing (and participation) in the re-release of the Psi Com EP. When the label celebrated its fifth birthday, Perry brought the group along to play the party.

The group lost little time in recruiting a new manager; by the time Perry was ready to start lettering the album sleeve, Gary Kurfirst was already positioned at the top of the group's administration.

Dave Jerden was an inspired choice for the album's engineer. Today he ranks among the country's top producers, with credits that stretch from Alice in Chains to Love Spit Love. At the time of his recruitment by Jane's Addiction, however, Jerden was still an unknown quantity, albeit an unknown quantity with a career resumé that could disgrace more than a few of his peers.

Back in the early 1980s, Jerden was part of the studio team Brian Eno convened to produce Talking Heads' seminal *Remain in Light* album. That alone suggested a sonic sense that no number of big-shot studio superstars could ever re-create, and his contribution to Jane's Addiction's project was so great that Perry ended up promoting him to coproducer status.

The sessions passed off in comparative privacy. Although Warner Brothers was still a little worried about what their investments might be up to in there, the work-in-progress previews that would periodically land in the A&R department reassured them that yes, Perry was a perfectly competent producer; and no, there were no doubts whatsoever that this album would prove one of the biggest of the new year. Nobody involved in the sessions at Los Angeles's Eldorado Studios could think of anything to worry about, and neither, they hoped, would anybody else. In a perfect world, they wouldn't have.

As 1987 moved toward the new year, the world in general, and the music industry in particular, was far, far, from perfect. Before Jane's Addiction even delivered, there were forces abroad that not only endangered whatever they might come up with, but were working against a lot of the things that anyone might have been planning.

The music industry was now bound, according to a self-imposed code of voluntary ethics, to decorate new album releases with PARENTAL ADVISORY stickers, cautioning potential purchasers against any obscenities that might be contained within. The PMRC had set in motion a chain of events that not only exceeded that organization's own brief, they also ran contradictory to that most important amendment to the American Constitution, the right to free speech.

The forces of God and Goodness couldn't stop record companies from putting out distasteful records, but they could influence stores into not taking them, particularly the chain stores, which, throughout much of America, are the only places people can even buy records. With the chains out of the picture, the effect on a record's sales would be devastating.

Lyrics were no longer the only battlefield, either. Simultaneously, and quite coincidentally, late 1987 saw three otherwise wholly disconnected record *jackets* come under intense scrutiny, and this time it wasn't simply a matter of placing a warning sticker in one corner of the disc to hush the roars of approbation. This time, people really were running scared. Steve Baker, Warner Brothers' vice president of product management, put it best when he understated simply, "It's important for everyone to understand that record retailers are having problems all over the country right now."

The war of attrition, Jackets versus Justice, Designs versus Decency, began in the sixties, yet it remained remarkably arbitrary. While Jimi Hendrix liberally plastered his *Electric Ladyland* album with twenty pairs of naked breasts with no ill effects whatsoever, John and Yoko Ono Lennon's *Two Virgins* couldn't even show one breast (plus accompanying genitals) without being crammed into an all-concealing brown paper bag—and even that didn't stop police from confiscating thirty thousand copies from a Newark, New Jersey, warehouse. It was contradictions like these that derailed attempts to "regulate," or even offer guidelines to, the music industry's taste in record sleeves.

That is why there was so much dismay following the formation of the PMRC in the 1980s. Rock 'n' roll had faced some formidable foes in the past, but they were isolated.

The PMRC was the first organized resistance to rock 'n' roll to have direct access to both legal and institutional means of redress, and it grasped the opportunity. The PMRC's prime target was the Record Industry Association of America (RIAA), under whose umbrella the bulk of U.S. record labels fell.

With the advent of the PMRC and its potential censorlike control, there suddenly was a flood of jackets that might, in the post–Dead Kennedys/Guns/Prince climate of moral approbation, also deserve more than a passing glance of distaste. The Red Hot Chili Peppers' *Abbey Road* EP, the four Peppers naked but for one strategically placed sock apiece; Poison's sexually suggestive *Open Up and Say . . . Ahhh!* "Okay, what's going on around here, you ask?" demanded *Palm Beach Post* reporter Scott Benarde. "Is somebody trying to jog our jaded senses? Or infuriate the televangelists?"

Even before he revealed his contribution to the burgeoning controversy, Perry was equally questioning. "I've been waiting all my life to get some money to do art. It's the chance of a lifetime for an artist. You think I'm going to blow it now by considering [the reactions of] people who are unartistic? There's not a chance in hell."

When he unveiled precisely what he'd done with that chance of a lifetime, a sculpted image of Casey as a naked female Siamese twin, seated with both her heads aflame over the printed album title, *Nothing's Shocking*, he continued unabashed.

The image, he said, came to him in a dream. "[It] wasn't meant to be shocking. It was a separate idea to the [album] title. If I'd planned to make it shocking, it would probably have been a lot more pretentious. It was just a spontaneous idea that seems to have taken on a life of its own."

It did mesh with that title; meshed, too, with the sense that the only reason why nothing *was* shocking any longer was because society was now so desensitized to the notions of shock, horror, and disgust.

Everywhere you looked, from Hollywood fantasy to television news, from tabloid press to underground comics, it was not stories that sold, it was suffering, human suffering on a scale unprecedented since World War Two, and maybe even greater than that. Against that, a fantastical image of burning Siamese nudes was so harmless that it seemed all puerile to discuss it. Maybe the combination of deformity, nudity, and a fiery headdress was discomfiting, but individually, those ingredients were hardly new, in art or elsewhere.

The problem with *Nothing's Shocking*, then, was not its content, but the challenge that it threw down. At a time when the American people were suddenly becoming aware of just how far society's standards had slipped since their own childhood, there were an awful lot of things that were suddenly shocking . . . and being told that "nothing was" was one of them. AIDS, crack, the crime rate, the divorce rate—everywhere you turned, things were going down the tubes, and in a way, that was the point Perry himself was making.

What Perry wanted to do, he said, was emphasize what his generation has to face, "which is this media blitz to just kind of gross you out. Look at the talk-show people. They're trying to out-horrify each other [and] they can't do it. They're showing straight gore now on TV."

He admitted that there were occasions when he couldn't even bring himself to watch television anymore, because "I'd freak out. If I saw 'Oprah' or 'Sally Jesse' or the news . . . I'd go to the 7-Eleven and I'd go, 'Oh my God, this guy could be molesting his kid,' 'cause everyone on TV looks like everybody else at 7-Eleven."

Maybe Jane's Addiction were doing things that were censurable. The difference was, they were doing it with what Perry calls "enough premeditation and enough care and thought that it should be looked upon as something that's valid." Instead, they were condemned as ruthlessly as the very horrors Perry was commenting upon.

"Why is it," Perry mused, "that in a museum, painting and sculptures of nudes are considered fine art, while my sculpture . . my expression of art, is censored because it's on an album cover?"

If the burning twins were already standing in a gallery somewhere, there would have been no problem. The record jacket, though it could still be considered objectionable, would have simply been depicting an artifact that had already proven its artistic merit; but context is everything, and Perry's sculpture had not already been vindicated by the art world. Just as a museum gallery is entitled to pick and choose the exhibits it displays, so is a record store.

Nothing's Shocking's August 1988 release was still pending when the retail trade first made its feelings known about the artwork, with seven major chains of record stores announcing that they would not be carrying the album: Music-Land, Camelot, Hastings, Lieberman, Handleman, Target, and Sound Warehouse. Between them, they added up to a pretty hefty slice of the American market.

This was not a unique situation, either for the music industry or even Warner Brothers. Warner's, after all, marketed Prince's *LoveSexy*. This time around, the furor looked set to bite deeper.

"[*Nothing's Shocking* is] the second most repulsive cover I've ever seen!" Steve Marmaduke, VP of purchasing for the Texas-based rack-jobbers Western Marketers told *Billboard*, although he didn't elaborate on which was the first. "I don't like being put in the position of being a censor, but I know the sensibilities in the mass market are not in favor of that cover. This is not even questionable."

It was not necessarily even an issue of censorship. Marmaduke's opposite number at Handleman, Mario DeFilippo, argued that "we don't buy every record that is released, [and] nor does anyone else," neatly skipping over the debate altogether by hinting that Jane's Addiction's album would just go the way of the countless other no-name albums released every month.

The list of stores rejecting *Nothing Shocking* grew nevertheless. According to a report on Nashville's "Channel Two News at Six," Xanadu's, Sam Goody, Wal-Mart, and K-Mart had all waded into the fray. "For the K-Mart people, we want something that's not very offensive to them," the local K-Mart manager said. If Warner Brothers would consider an alternative sleeve, K-Mart would consider stocking the record. "We want the best for our customers."

Then the album's supposed allies came out against it. Steve Bennett, the president of one of the stores that *was* carrying the album, Record Bar, defended those other retailers by stating, "It's not that people don't support free speech; it's just that you have to make a conscious decision not to disrupt your business."

He admitted that even after his company opted to stock *Nothing Shocking*, he still nurtured some reservations. "We haven't received any negative comments [from customers, but] I wouldn't be surprised [if we do]."

Sensing a story that went considerably deeper than the issue of lyrical profanity and degradation, the Cable News Network tried to re-create the process by which an album jacket is arrived at, interviewing Jeff Gold, the VP of Creative Services at A&M Records.

"What usually happens is, we have a meeting with the artists, who nine times out of ten will come in with an idea, and my job is either to make that idea work and work well, or dissuade them from the idea they have got, and come up with something that works for them and works for us too."

The problem was that sometimes an artist couldn't be dissuaded. Jane's Addiction had stated their position long, long ago, even before they signed to Warner Brothers. Backstage at the last night of Scream's Embassy Hotel residency, some fifteen months before, Perry mused, "It's weird, because we do a lot of things that make a major [label] say, 'Please, fellas, don't do that!'" If he had shown anyone his idea for the album cover, that would have just been something else for the bigwigs to balk at. Please, fellas, don't do *that*!

Warners agreed to stick by Jane's Addiction, a decision that even the most cynical observer would admit was courageous. Public opinion hadn't yet scaled the powerful peaks it was to strike five years later, when the same label found itself embroiled in Ice-T's "Cop Killer" dispute. There were still shareholders to answer to, and the risk of the controversy spreading to other company interests.

The label remained adamant, however. "Nobody at [Warner] is going to force the band to change the cover based on people's tastes," Steve Baker insisted, while Perry himself recalled the moment he presented the cover design to the label heads.

"All the comments were really good. I never thought that there would be a problem like this." He acknowledged that once the complaints did start rolling in, Warner Brothers did ask if he'd be interested in designing an alternative sleeve, but his response was unequivocal. "If McDonald's doesn't want my artwork, who the fuck cares?"

That, Steve Baker continued, was that. One Los Angeles record dealer, Jeff Campagna, writing in *Album Network* magazine, agreed. "So what's the big deal about the . . . cover? We have a nice display on the wall and no one has objected yet (I think). Isn't it the music that counts anyway?"

Around the country even the most disinterested commentary on *Nothing's Shocking* made approving noises about the record, with several writers commenting that the controversy surrounding the cover actually outweighed the more sensitive issue of lyrical content. Did one reflect the other? Or were they separate entities altogether?

Richard Loerzel, discussing *Nothing's Shocking* in the University of Illinois's *Daily Illini*, agreed that the cover "does an excellent job of telling the potential record buyer, in some unexplainable way, how the music sounds . . . innovative, and unique." Was there another agenda at work here, one scarred by the creeping belief that the band "appear[s] to be trying too hard to make the world believe they are completely weird, dangerously insane and totally 'off the wall'?

"David Byrne, of Talking Heads, and Robyn Hitchcock both give the impression that they were born weird. With Farrell the weirdness comes across as nothing more than hype. He acts as if he took a class entitled 'How to act like an out-of-control serial killer and make a lot of money in the process.'"

It was a savage indictment of the performer (albeit one Loerzel did find forgivable purely on the strength of the music's "sincerity"), but it was also an understandable one.

Tracing back over the past year of Jane's Addiction's history, noting as Loerzel did that the album's cover was generating controversy before anybody even heard a note of the music within, it was becoming increasingly difficult to distinguish Jane's Addiction from any of the myriad other bands that erupt from nowhere and ride the back of headlines that have little to do with their songs, suddenly becoming the most talked-about thing since . . . The *Dallas Morning News* even called Jane's Addiction "first runners-up to Guns N' Roses as Los Angeles's most-hyped musical eminence."

With so many contradictions flying around, the resolution of the *Nothing Shocking* debate was almost disappointingly anticlimactic. Whether it was Perry's argument over artistic freedom that won the day, or simply the realization that, backed as it now was by several million dollars' worth of free publicity, *Nothing Shocking* was on course to become a major hit.

"The cover art, I love it . . . and I'm proud of it," Perry said. "But . . . if it wasn't for the music, it doesn't matter. I mean, the cover art's great, and I'm glad that the artwork is appreciated. But the music . . . I don't want it to be overshadowed." At the end of the day, and it had been a very long day, everything else was simply "gravy."

The *Boston Phoenix* pointed out that the music contained within *Nothing Shocking* was "not exactly above gimmickry." To the uninitiated, Perry's very voice was a novelty instrument, fed through the broadening battery of effects and echo boxes with which he was surrounding himself, and encompassing, in the words of the *Milwaukee Journal*, everything from "cryptic, hallucinatory lyrics to . . . jazzy, folkedelic hard rock."

It was a cunning blend, however, and one that swiftly began paying dividends. The Expand-O-Retail chart welcomed *Nothing's Shocking* at number 14, just two weeks after the album's release. Twenty college/alternative radio stations were already programming it, with half a dozen—three on the West Coast, three on the East—already registering it within their Top Tens. (Its showing on a national chart dominated by the likes of Van Halen, Pat Benatar, and Robert Palmer, a lowly number 103, may not have been too impressive.)

"The band's combination of power, artfulness, and incredible street buzz makes this a record people want to be part of," Warner Brothers' National Promotion Manager, Steve Tipp, explained. "Commercial programmers are playing 'Jane Says,' while hard rockers are leaning toward 'Ocean Size.' College response overall has been phenomenal. This," he gleefully prophesied, "is a record and a band that will go very far."

```
God  Knows
How   Many
P e o p l e
D  a  v  i, d
B o w i e ' s
S l a u g h-
t e r e d !
```

erry was frying on acid. A video flickered on his television screen, *Murder: No Apparent Motive*, and it fascinated him no end. Dancing through a series of dramatic interviews with some of America's most notorious murderers, a cast of Hollywood extras chopped, shot, bled, and bludgeoned their way through a never-ending parade of gruesome killings. That, thought Perry, was the attraction of the video, the fact that you were able to relive the "dastardly deed" through the dramatization.

Ted Bundy was one of the bludgeoners. Between January 1974 and February 1978, he murdered thirty women as far afield as Seattle, Washington, and Tallahassee, Florida. The song that Perry wrote while he was watching that video was called "Ted, Just Admit It," "because he's never admitted to his guilt."

The song itself, Perry explained, was not necessarily concerned with Bundy himself. "Within that song, there were a lot of ideas. It's about what the media does to the mind. The concept to that song, in my mind, sums up the spirit of the times." Jane's Addiction, he insisted, might write about killers and violence, but they also wrote about cats and bees. It was just that no one paid so much attention to the songs about cats and bees.

Despite the band's demands for a live sound throughout, *Nothing's Shocking* made liberal use of studio trickery, with "Ted, Just Admit It" a literal smorgasbord of brutal samples. Lifted from a variety of media broadcasts, they build into a cacophony of disorientation that rivaled the yowl of the band itself, a soundtrack for modern urban living.

A Syracuse journalist would later describe "Ted, Just Admit It" as "the 'Dazed and Confused' of the eighties": another, the *New Musical Express*'s Jack Barron, insisted the song "moves through more changes than a politician's mind, from ethereal whine zones via loping skunk, found voices, to all-out napalm attack."

Even if he wasn't the focus of the song itself, still Ted Bundy was to dominate it, both conceptually and later, when "Ted, Just Admit It" became one of the new album's most talked-about moments.

Bundy had already killed twenty-seven times when he was first arrested in June 1977 in Aspen, Colorado, yet he escaped through a second-story window of the Pitkin County courthouse and made his way to Florida. Arrested again, two years and three slayings later, he managed to escape a second time by starving himself to the point where he was able to simply slip through the bars on his cell.

Now, Perry joked, he was worried that Ted might make it out a third time and come looking for him; wondered aloud whether that's what Warner Brothers' legal department had in mind when they suggested Perry approach Bundy *before* adding his voice to the samples on "Ted, Just Admit It."

Perry ignored them. "We kept the voice in, because if anybody's gonna sue, it's gonna be Ted himself." As a lawyer, Bundy made a point of always conducting his own defense. Presumably, he would orchestrate his own attack as well. "Wouldn't that be wild? The guy is a mass murderer . . . and a lawyer. The way he was able to change characters was similar to David Bowie. God knows how many people David Bowie's slaughtered!"

Recaptured a second time, on July 31, 1979, Bundy was sentenced to die in the electric chair. Appended to his death sentence were two consecutive ninety-nine-year jail terms. Nine years later, Bundy was still protesting his innocence.

"There are bite marks on the bums of the women that he's bludgeoned to death," Perry complained. "They matched them up to his teeth. And he still says, 'I did not do it.'"

Bundy would not confess until the very eve of his execution, in January 1989. "I was kinda hoping he would escape again [before they killed him]," Perry joked later. "I was waiting for him to come and bludgeon me to death." And then say he didn't do *that*, either.

Mea culpa. You heard a lot of that as the Jane's Addiction campaign gathered pace, and the arrival of *Nothing's Shocking*, like Jane's Addiction themselves at the climax of a quite unprecedented media buildup, did little to diminish either the accusations of hype or the increasingly unconvincing excuses—"Not us!" Once again, the logical response to any trumpeting of either band or album was the most obvious one.

Reviews of the album mirrored the extremes to which Jane's Addiction was now so accustomed. In Winnipeg, the *Free Press* came down viciously on the side of the band's detractors: "Nothing's shocking—maybe so. But this . . . quartet almost gets a collective hernia trying to work up some shock value–as–titillation on its major-label debut." And, from the *San Pedro News Pilot*, "Contrary to its title, *Nothing's Shocking* is shocking. Shockingly dull and unappealing, that is."

Perry, in particular, was subjected to some quite astonishing savagery. Jane's Addiction, the *Orange County*

Register opined, "is undone by [him]. His scratchy, whining vocals don't match the strength of the music and his lyrics are often merely grandiose exercises in self-importance. When he starts chanting 'Sex is violent' in 'Ted, Just Admit It,' Farrell just comes off as an ill-tempered mock Jim Morrison." The most refreshing moment on the album, the review continued, was the lounge-club instrumental "Thank You Boys," "when Farrell shuts up for a while."

Even "Jane Says" was not above criticism. "This ballad tips you to what soundtrack these guys grew up on," penned writer Tom Carson. "Farrell's vocal sounds like a strung-out version of Rod Stewart's old fake-folkie empathy."

Misunderstanding or, at best, misinterpretation played a major part in further engorging the Jane's Addiction myth, a situation brilliantly parodied by Perry when he appeared at the Roxy, shortly before the album's release, on a performance-art billing pieced together by sixties acid guru Timothy Leary.

One of *Nothing's Shocking*'s key songs was "Had a Dad," a song widely accepted to be an autobiographical study of Perry's own relationship with his father. Perry himself denied it, argued that his relationship with his dad was never better, but that didn't stop the questions. Tonight, maybe he could.

Perry's performance opened with him sitting behind a desk, simply talking to the audience about the state of the world. Then the telephone beside him rang.

Perry listened intently for a moment and then told a "Record Producer" that he was not singing "God is dead" but "God is Dad."

He put the phone down and resumed his monologue, only for it to ring again.

"Oh, hello, Dad. . . ."

Perry himself wrote Jane's Addiction's first Warner Brothers press release, seven pages of scrawled handwriting which still remains a fascinating document, a manifesto both for the integrity and—because the band members themselves were both painfully aware of and hilariously impervious to it—the hype that surrounded Jane's Addiction.

"Jane's Addiction are the foremost experts on beauty," Perry penned. "They are the biggest braggarts, money-grabbers. Their mascot is a rooster. They can make a song out of anything. They say they can blow you away because they know they can." They weren't "macho monkeys," and neither were they "fags."

They weren't, according to Perry, a radio band either.

One of the conditions of Jane's Addiction's Warner Brothers contract, he told journalists, insisted that the band's records received no more than "medium rotation" on radio station playlists, further proof, Perry's growing band of admirers insisted, of their idol's firm conviction that Jane's Addiction claimed no place in the Top 40.

The desired effect of disdaining regular radio play was setting in stone Perry's age-old claim that he didn't "necessarily want to be popular."

Jane's Addiction was a band you were either madly in love with or hated with a vengeance. There was no middle ground, and everybody respected that. Already, Roberta Petersen of Warner's acknowledged, the group was reaching its "target audience," the heady brew of punks and metal heads who had so recently embraced the Cult—coincidentally, another Warner's (via the Sire subsidiary) act.

The Cult, too, made it on the strength of their street appeal; they were too weird and abrasive to have done it any other way. If that approach had worked once—twice, if you counted Guns N' Roses—then it could be made to work again for Jane's Addiction.

What it came down to was commitment, Perry agreed; commitment—to the audience, to the music, and most of all, to the band's own integrity.

"Think about what you're playing for, because the message is what's going to get you somewhere." Don't blend in . . . Be fearless . . . Be outrageous. The advice that Perry once so freely proffered to "new bands" was the advice he himself always followed, the advice that would, he vowed, sustain him throughout the next phase of his career . . . and there was that shadow again, passing over his face as he added, "However long it lasts."

In August 1988, just as *Nothing's Shocking* finally hit the stores, Jane's Addiction returned to Scream's new Park View Plaza basement to shoot the live portion of their first video, "Mountain Song."

Conceived by Perry and Casey as part of a longer, twenty-four-minute video called *Soul Kiss*, "Mountain Song" would nevertheless be many people's first exposure to the band. Album sales, although encouraging nationwide, remained highest in the Los Angeles area. Armed with a video, though, they thought might become a television band: a Music Television band.

David Bowie's twenty-two-minute "Jazzing for Blue Jean" enjoyed a profitable run in British cinemas (opening for Neil Jordan's *Company of Wolves*) before it even hit the video stores. A considerably shorter version, concentrating solely on the title song, was prepared for television.

This was the process that Perry, Casey, and Warner Brothers, who were financing Jane's Addiction's first video, envisioned. Or maybe it was only Warner Brothers who envisioned it. Before shooting even began, Perry was unequivocal over what he wanted from the video.

"I'm pushing for MTV to get off their ass. Let's upgrade this whole [video] thing. Videos have become formulated and I'm not one to conform because I really don't see that as an end, I see that as a beginning, because there's just so much more you can do."

The group, Perry said later, "had to fight fucking hard" to get Warner Brothers to agree that the one video for which they pledged backing would be this one. They were expecting moving pictures set to music. They received "a montage of images that lends itself to the song without being so fucking obvious." Before *Soul Kiss* was finished, it incorpo-

God Knows How Many People...

123

rated everything from sex and nudity to cruelty to animals (in one scene, Dave Navarro appears to slam his pet eel repeatedly onto the tabletop); from accidental arson, when Perry ignites a firework in his bedroom, to something approaching Armageddon as an invited audience erupts across the cameras on Scream's dance floor.

That performance of "Mountain Song" opens *Soul Kiss* in storming style; from there, the film lurches through a series of disconnected interview segments, followed by a lengthy sequence of increasingly surreal domestic scenarios.

Perry explained that there was no way he would make a storyline video. "I'm making video the way I want to," he said. He wanted to give people's eyes "something to dance to" while they listened to the music. Discussing the full-length *Soul Kiss*, however, he appeared proudest of the closing sequence, in which the band members kiss and embrace their friends and each other.

So did Eric, joking that he enjoyed this part the most "because I got to do it." But he was surely also relieved that it was not he who would have to sit down with Lenny Waronker, president of Warner Brothers, and try to get the video approved.

Waronker was no prude. Like his chairman (a position he would ascend to himself, following Ostin's retirement in late 1994), he believed wholeheartedly in the acts Warner Brothers signed. Just as he had done with Prince, it was Waronker who finally okayed Jane's Addiction's desire to produce their first album; Waronker who joined the front line of executives who stood firmly alongside the band during the battle over *Nothing's Shocking*'s jacket.

Perry was nevertheless not looking forward to the meeting. "I have to sit there with this guy," he mused on the morning of the appointment, "turn out the lights, get comfortable, and then here we go, there's my big ol' dick."

In the event, Perry's penis was not seen (or at least, noticeable) in the final cut of *Soul Kiss*. Indeed, most of the questionable material in the film was reserved for the nonmusical portions. "Mountain Song" ran into immediate approbation for the flashes of a bare-breasted Casey which littered it. Nobody was surprised when MTV declined outright to even air "Mountain Song" in its original form. Maybe, they asked, Perry would consent to prepare a suitably edited version instead?

Perry laughed at them. "Play it with the bits, or get out of my face!"

The nudity, he insisted, was included "because [it is] part of the expression. You might not like it, and it might not be worth a shit, but that's what I foresaw for the video." In the face of MTV's continued refusal to screen the unedited "Mountain Song," he simply shrugged. Either he would have to think of a way to create a new market for the video, he announced, "or it'll be seen in the clubs where the kids go." Either way, he wasn't going to sit around and think about what MTV likes. They simply weren't part of his life.

Soul Kiss went directly from the cutting room to the video stores. "Mountain Song" would never be screened on MTV in its entirety.

What did this latest controversy prove? Only that once again Jane's Addiction had made an awful lot of noise about a very little music. So what if *Rolling Stone* called the band "the brightest stars in the west"? Or if *Kerrang!* referred to them as "the second coming"? You read the same thing about other bands every day. The only difference was, "other bands" tended to play the media game according to its own rules.

Jane's Addiction, with two major censorship rows already under their belt, were taking the opposite approach. They weren't even attempting to redefine the rulebook. They simply contradicted it, and no matter how loudly Perry protested the integrity of his art, in the eyes of the world, the quality of the project took a very definite second place to the quality of the controversy. As 1988 rattled on, that fact was becoming increasingly obvious, and increasingly annoying.

For the outsider adding up Jane's Addiction's achievements, there was still very little that justified the claims being made on their behalf. Just one album, just one video, and most damaging of all, just one tour, the year-old memory of the Love and Rockets package.

To all other intents and purposes, Jane's Addiction was still little more than another name in the press, running through its screechy paces before the main attraction took the boards. Its very screechy paces. "Like the Doors' Jim Morrison at his sophomoric worst, Perry Farrell sings, howls and recites his bad poetry," complained an unimpressed *Washington Post*, and if Perry was bad, the band was even worse, as it accompanied him with "a pseudo-arty brand of heavy metal not unlike . . . the Cult or Billy Idol." As the reviews and notices continued rolling in, it was becoming exceedingly apparent that Jane's Addiction had exhausted its ration of controversy. It was time to put rumor to rest.

From the moment the possibility became actual fact, Perry knew that the next tour was going to be different. He didn't think Jane's Addiction had anything to prove to anyone, but maybe the knockers were right. Maybe it was time to prove they had nothing to prove. The day Perry heard that Jane's Addiction had been confirmed as the opening act on Iggy Pop's fall tour, he phoned all his friends with the news. Then he played Iggy's *Funhouse* full blast on his new stereo.

The Iggy Pop legend is enormous. Fronting the Stooges, a statement in musical nihilism long before that term took on the post-punk connotations that make it so fashionable today, Pop single-handedly hallmarked the notion of the *enfant terrible*.

From the first-generation British punk rockers, through to the latest crop of Los Angeles glam thunder lizards, Iggy's legacy was omnipresent. Even the band that would be backing up Pop around the United States this time around was drawn from the ragtag army of adolescent acolytes who literally grew up in awe of the legend: guitarist

Andy McCoy, whose molten riffing once underpinned Hanoi Rocks with such vitality, and now nailed Iggy's latest *Instinct* monolith into place; Paul Garisto, the Medusa-haired drummer who'd been powering the Psychedelic Furs when Jane's Addiction opened for them the previous year.

Perry, too, had been touched by the enormity of Iggy's achievements. *Funhouse*, the Stooges' second album, was one of his own all-time favorites, a record he would later claim literally changed his life. It was the first album he'd ever heard that didn't sound like it was made for commercial gain.

Perry himself had been compared to Pop, of course, a comparison that both pleased him and scared him, particularly as the opening night of the tour loomed closer. What if Iggy himself had read those reviews, and recruited Jane's Addiction so he could check out this latest in a long line of slavish Pop impostors? As Jane's Addiction awaited their cue to take Washington's Warner Theater stage on the first night of the tour, September 9, 1988, Perry just hoped that he'd be able to enjoy the show. If Iggy was out there he swore he'd keep his eyes closed all night.

For any band, opening for Iggy Pop was a tall order. For Jane's Addiction, opening for Iggy Pop was Herculean. The entire country appeared intent on proving that if life was easy for the group in Los Angeles, out in the real world, things were a little tougher.

There was something about Jane's Addiction, something about Perry himself, he said, that attracted random violence. He'd noticed it even back in the Psi Com days, the gunman at the Anti-Club, the knifeman in Victorville. "It's almost like bulls," Perry reflected. "They go toward the color red." And to psychos, Jane's Addiction was the color red.

The tour was into its third day, September 12, and Jane's Addiction had just finished their set at the Stone Balloon in Newark, Delaware. Changing into offstage regalia that was almost as captivating as its onstage equivalent, they headed for the nearest Denny's for an after-show meal. Nobody even looked up when Dave got up to visit the john.

The next time they saw him, they were rushing him to the hospital, his nose broken by the local redneck who took exception to the guitarist's appearance.

The redneck didn't like being answered back, either.

Jane's Addiction's first taste of the America on this tour left a sour and sweet taste in their mouths. The group set out to provoke a reaction, and almost every night, they earned one, but sometimes it was more extreme than they expected.

"We'll be in a place full of fucking cowboys going, 'What the hell, Jane's Addiction?'" Stephen mused, "and that night will turn into fucking craziness. We'll play the hardest, meanest songs we got . . . [And] the next two weeks you're going, 'Dude, that was the fucking greatest. We had the best time that night.'"

Asbury Park is Bruce Springsteen territoiy. He grew up just down the road, first playing the local bars and clubs, then immortalizing the place in his own musical mythology. Ever since then . . . you couldn't even say the place had a chip on its shoulder anymore. It was more like a ravine.

Nobody remembers the precise flashpoint, but somewhere around the midway point in Jane's Addiction's show at the famous local Stone Pony, Perry took a violent dislike to one particular guy standing right at the front of the stage.

The antipathy was mutual, and it just kept building. When the band kicked into "Had a Dad," Perry changed one line to "suck my dick," and sang it directly into his opponent's face.

The kid just laughed, so Perry gave him another line. Then another, and finally he'd had it. Swinging around, Perry picked up the bottle of red wine he'd been swigging from all evening, poured some on his own head, then emptied the bottle on his adversary's head.

That ended one confrontation, but Perry was still feeling antsy. When Iggy came out for his set, Perry threw himself into the crowd at the front, the only slam dancer in the whole room. New Jersey didn't know what had hit it—and neither did Perry, as the Stone Pony security leaped on him as one and threw him bodily out of the club. "My own gig and I'm not even allowed in there!" he whined in mock horror as he sat by the back door. "Maybe next time we play here, I'll throw all of them out."

No matter where Jane's Addiction went, nobody gave them an inch. "Iggy was great," Stephen enthused. "He had a good crowd for us. And Iggy's a cool guy." Nevertheless, the journalists who caught Jane's Addiction at the bottom of each evening's bill remained furiously unimpressed.

A month into the tour, on October 11, the entourage reached Houston. "Jane's Addiction undermines its daring—and occasionally on-target—sonic adventures with a pretentiousness that distances the audience," cautioned the *Houston Post*. "Farrell's pantomimes and the band's aloof attitude in general doesn't entice an audience into its circle."

The neighboring *Houston Chronicle* added, "Jane's Addiction showed its youth by doing little to draw the audience in with a show or a dialogue. Perhaps the aloof look is cool these days, but one doesn't have to be an animated phony, either." The group could, the general consensus constantly insisted, do a lot worse than take a few lessons from the headliner, and journalist Marty Racine sounded almost grateful, after Jane's Addiction's performance, to catch Dave and Stephen "still standing in the crowd . . . checking the old geezer out." Maybe there was hope for these young upstarts after all.

"I think it's great," Perry cackled. "If [people] hate us or they love us, that's great. I haven't found anybody that just thinks we're okay. It's either 'They can't play. They can't sing. They can't write.' Or they praise us for everything we do. And I just love it."

Peter B. King of the *Pittsburgh Press* must certainly have numbered among Perry's favorite critics, then. "You need to know three things about Jane's Addiction . . ." he wrote on the day of Jane's Addiction's September 21 visit to Pittsburgh.

"They can't sing . . . they can't write . . . they can't play. They really must be something live . . ."

Perry continued, "I'll talk to someone, and they'll be, 'I don't know if you really want to read this [review], they said you stink.' I think that's great. Of course I want to read that stuff. I don't want to hear that we're great all the time, and I don't want to hear that we're just okay and passive." When he read reviews by people who didn't like the band, he continued, "they go on for paragraphs and paragraphs [about] how much they don't like us—because we really got to them."

In mid-September, Jane's Addiction swung briefly away from the Iggy Pop tour to face the equally daunting challenge of opening a couple of shows for another American icon, the Ramones, in Providence and Pittsburgh.

Touring on the back of *Ramones Mania*, a compilation of "da bruddahs'" best moments from a decade of buzzsaw power pop, the Ramones surely boasted one of rock's most partisan audiences, there for just one thing, the moment when their vocalist barked out "one-two-three-four" and the band flew into yet another of their sonic speedball fantasies.

It certainly was a very different audience to anything Jane's Addiction had faced before, and one that was not easily won over by Perry's yelps and whining, and the band's full frontal metal-psych support.

"An ugly assembly of thrash chords, screams, flying hair and four-letter words . . . by the end [of the show]," *Pittsburgh Post-Gazette* writer Scott Mervis sighed, "there was a mutual distaste between Jane and the mob." Another report depicted members of the audience chanting "go back to L.A." throughout much of Jane's Addiction's set.

Jane's Addiction didn't care. They returned to the Iggy Pop tour to open the headliner's Detroit homecoming on September 22, then they took another short break while they headed over to Europe for their U.K. debut.

The British press had already embraced Jane's Addiction. In August, they took the cover of the weekly *Sounds* newspaper;

just months earlier, they had landed a full-page story in the same national publication, before most American magazines had even heard of them.

Melody Maker and the *New Musical Express* both turned over several columns apiece to reviews of *Nothing's Shocking*, and while the buildup maybe wasn't on a par with the Springsteen Is God campaign which highlighted Bruce's first British visit, thirteen years before, still it left a sense of rampant expectation. The band's name was even added to posters advertising a Living Colour show at the London Astoria on September 9, completely overlooking the fact that Jane's Addiction wouldn't even be in the country then!

Jane's Addiction had three major London shows to negotiate, beginning, with appropriate irony, halfway up the bill at the Brixton Academy's goth night, on September 24. Two headliners followed, at the Camden Palace on September 27, and a steambath at the Charing Cross Road Borderline on September 29. But it was the Academy that grabbed the attention.

If only on the hearsay evidence of the little-known but much discussed Psi Com EP, Jane's Addiction certainly shared roots with the evening's headliners, the Fields of Nephilim. Their reputation was as something garish, gorgeous, gregarious, qualities that had little to do with the self-conscious blackwrap of the gothic interns. When the concert reviews were published the following week, one of the loudest complaints was that "Perry Farrell isn't as elegant as I'd hoped . . . dripping with sweat, not jewelry."

No one left disappointed, though.

Instead, they raved about the kind of performance that, "in several years time, will have normally reliable types claiming that yes, they too were at Brixton Academy in '88"—particularly when they discovered that the overzealous fan who hauled Perry offstage early on in the show did more than breach the gap between performer and artist. Perry fell awkwardly and hard, returned to the stage and was immediately doubled up by a sharp, stabbing pain in his chest. After the show when he went to a hospital, he learned that he had cracked a rib.

When the reviews were published the following week, neither *Sounds* nor the *New Musical Express* even bothered to mention Fields of Nephilim.

Returning to the United States, Jane's Addiction rejoined the Iggy Pop tour in Houston, on October 10. Perry was still in pain from his cracked-rib souvenir, but aside from securely taping it up, there really wasn't much he could do about it. He wasn't going to get much chance to recuperate, either. Trouble was breaking out wherever they went.

Perry didn't see the gang of Cubans on the Fort Lauderdale street corner; might not have even known they were there if one of them hadn't suddenly clocked the gaily-clad figure who cavorted grinning and made-up alongside a group of ten or so friends, then yelled to his friends, "Look! It's Boy George!"

Perry wheeled furiously and shot back, "Suck my dick!" The whole street opened up like a gangland-style war. It just sprayed open with people chasing and running."

You couldn't tell who was who. People were getting whacked and whaled left and right, fists flew and feet, and someone "cracked my friend's fucking head on the sidewalk. It hit right on the curb. We thought he was dead. His wife was standing over him, going 'Oh my God!'"

The most chilling detail of the entire affair, however, was still to come. "I was dressed like a clown that night, for some reason," Perry remembers. "And when the cops showed up, I was standing over my friend in a clown suit going, 'Help him! Help him!' It was the worst!"

Jane's Addiction had barely been back with Iggy for a week when they stared to notice how things were turning around. The press was still apathetic at best, and usually downright hostile, but every night, the kids were wilder, the cheers were louder. "Keep on like this," promoter after promoter was telling them, "and next time you're here you'll be topping the bill." In a lot of those instances, they were back within a few months.

"Jane's Addiction, the latest band of world-beaters from L.A.'s ubiquitous rock underground, put on a show that was so full of bombast, innovation, and spirit that the group may well end up on the Food and Drug Administration's list of habit-forming substances." William R. Macklin, writing in the *Grand Rapids Press,* could barely control his enthusiasm, to the point of chastising Perry the next morning for swinging the mike cord round his neck midset. "That's an old and stupid stage trick . . really unworthy of the singer."

Squeezed into a Hertz Penske van so tiny that Perry reckoned he could identify his band members simply from the smell of their farts, Jane's Addiction crisscrossed America, through October until Christmas, and then on into the new year.

Chicago's Smart Bar, Boston's TT Bears, the Phoenix Underground, Houston's Numbers, Champaign's Mabel's, Minneapolis's 7th Street Entry, the Diamond in Toronto, New York City on Halloween night; the clubs were small, few boasted more than a thousand or so capacity, and some, like Grand Rapids's Club Eastbrook, let in as many guest-listed locals as ticket-buying customers. Almost every venue was filled to overflowing, and not only on the strength of overexcited word of mouth.

The new-year nominations for the thirty-first annual Grammy Awards contained the usual smattering of surprises, but none so much as those within a brand new category, for the Best Hard Rock/Metal Performance. The very existence of the category was regarded as a major leap forward. "When the traditionally conservative recording industry decides to bestow an award upon it, Heavy Metal has clearly arrived," *Billboard* remarked.

As a readily definable genre, metal had been around for almost two decades now, ever since Black Sabbath and Led Zeppelin first started playing the blues with their amplifiers turned to eleven. It had been in the last four or five years that the genre assumed its wildest popularity. One week in June 1987 alone, five of the top six albums on the *Billboard* chart were metal: Whitesnake, Bon Jovi, Poison, Mötley Crüe, and Ozzy Osbourne.

The Grammys were not so representative. Of the five nominees in the Hard Rock/Metal category, only two, AC/DC and Metallica, were truly genre-specific, and most observers felt that it was they who would be contesting the award. The remainder were simply along to make up the numbers: perennial English prog rockers Jethro Tull, Iggy Pop, and, howling totally unexpectedly out of the farthest left field, Jane's Addiction.

"It's flattering," Perry acknowledged, once the shock had worn off. "But I also have this fear of getting into large situations like that. There's something really great about finding things and discovering things, and being on the Grammy Awards takes away from that. It takes away from the esoteric fun if Granny can sit in her living room and watch us making fools of ourselves. It was nice, but we had a show to play. We couldn't be bothered."

While the rest of America tuned in to the Los Angeles Shrine Auditorium on February 22, 1989, Jane's Addiction was playing the last of two nights at Washington's 9.30 Club.

Jethro Tull, too, was missing from the awards ceremony, so when the band's *Crest of a Knave* album was announced as the winner, it was Metallica's James Hetfield who collected the award, scarcely disguising his own disdain as he did so. The entire auditorium erupted with boos and catcalls from the moment the victor was announced, and Hetfield himself, when asked how he felt about Jethro Tull winning, replied, "I'd have been happier if it had happened ten years ago."

First a controversial album cover; now a role in a controversial Grammy—*Nothing's Shocking* took its momentum from both of these things, but proving itself to have considerably more staying power than its detractors imagined, it continued selling fast. *Soul Kiss* was moving equally swiftly. And "Jane Says," pulled from the album as a considerably more media-friendly single than its predecessor, was already a college-radio staple, despite Jane's Addiction themselves frequently omitting it from their live show.

"To do 'Jane Says' every night . . . is tiring, but it also cheapens the whole thing," Perry declared. "The song means a lot. I like to pull it out at the end of the night, [but] you can't just do the same thing every night, you get too bored." Mouthing again the words that so many rock 'n' rollers have spouted in the past, Perry was not, he insisted, a puppet onstage to jerk off for the jerks who jerked his strings.

"Why should I compromise?" he demanded. "The Beatles went from thinking they had to compromise to realizing that they didn't. By the time they did the White Album [1968's *The Beatles*], they were doing what they wanted to do. I'm just starting out with our White Album. I've already clued the record company and everybody else about that. This is our music. We're not a PG [-rated], singles-type of band. Warner's is allowing us the time and freedom to develop naturally." Besides, "we're selling a lot of records for a band that gets no radio or MTV airplay."

But at what cost? Jane's Addiction had now been on the road so long, they were beginning to forget where their mouths even were. The group was selling a lot of records, but the schedule was simply too punishing. "I feel like I'm getting sucked dry, and it's too bad," Perry said. Suddenly he could understand "how someone can put out a shitty album. If you don't have enough time . . . it's like Tang. You know it's good stuff, but then someone adds too much water, and people who didn't know about it before never know why it was so good."

Jane's Addiction had vaulted from the intimacy of the tiny clubs and bars that were piled randomly on top of one another on the original date sheet, to a full-fledged headline tour. Supported first by the Slammin' Watusis—the immortally named Midwestern punk band with two major-label albums to their credit—then by the Buck Pets, a Dallas garage band that had recently been picked up for major-label support (by Island Records), Jane's Addiction found themselves checking in to seated theaters and old-time ballrooms.

Perry tried to make the most of it. "Anybody who's doing what I'm doing wants to be a success. We want people to hear our music and enjoy it, so we can continue playing it to them."

He privately wondered, Did it have to be this way? "We're experiencing so much now, soaking up so many cities, and the more you use your life, the less you have to draw from." What sort of life was he living now, this traveling, gigging, playing every night? What sort of experiences could he possibly collect? He'd entered rock 'n' roll because he wanted to change the way things were done. Instead, it now seemed it was he who was changing.

"We haven't even had a chance to rehearse our live show [as headliners], not once," Perry complained. When Jane's Addiction hit Seattle, early in 1989, they hadn't rehearsed for two weeks. Consumed not by the machine, but by the demands of the machine, they were suddenly in the position where it appeared as if "the last thing that counts is the music. It's gotten really pathetic.

"Isn't it weird? What we built our reputation on is the last thing that anybody considers." It was rush-rush-rush about everything else, delivering artwork, turning up for interviews, smiling for the camera, "all these other things. But when it comes down to the music, there's no time to rehearse. It's something that's really frustrating me right now."

There was no time to even write songs, and even if there had been, what was there for him to write about? "You're in a hotel room for a year. What are you going to write about? The Hilton Hotel? Kids can't relate to that unless they're on vacation in Miami Beach with their parents. You've got to write about things you understand, not traveling from city to city, gambling, taking Lear jets. I couldn't give a shit about that, and I don't think the people on the street really care about it."

All he could do, he sighed, was "see if I can pace myself and at least make a few great records."

To make amends for the unrehearsed Seattle show, Jane's Addiction returned to the Northwest in April 1989, headlining two nights at the city's Moore Theatre, right at the end of the tour. At first, it was just another few nights on the road, but just a few minutes into the first evening's set, it exploded into something else entirely.

The show was still young when Perry suddenly turned on the audience and demanded, "Who's gonna be the first to shoot President Bush?"

There was a lot of applause, but no apparent takers.

"I guess I'll have to do it, then."

It wasn't the first time Perry had made such remarks, and it wouldn't be the last. "You're such a bunch of cowards," he once chastised an audience. "There's one guy in the White House. There's a thousand of you. Jesus, what kind of odds do you want?"

This time not everybody who heard such talk was in approval. "How daring!" the *Seattle Times*'s music critic, Patrick MacDonald, remarked sarcastically the following day. "How shocking! Now that showed real intelligence and guts!"

In the midst of a review that had already established MacDonald, like so many other journalists, firmly in the anti-Farrell camp, his response was maybe only to be expected. And at least he recognized it as "[an] attempt to shock," no matter how "juvenile." It was obvious that it was not a serious threat. However, Perry claims that he later received a visit from "a guy who looked like a Ken doll" who asked him to come down to headquarters "to explain your sense of humor. Because we don't understand it."

"This should be printed," Perry told journalist Steve Martin, "because maybe it should be known in this country that if you do use your right to exercise the First Amendment, it's not as simple as you might think." He remains convinced that the CIA placed a tail on him for at least a month.

Outwardly Perry remained stoic about what was patently an absurd situation, but he could not help but admit it worried him, "because of what the British authorities did to Brian Jones, planting things on the guy." Throughout the late 1960s, Rolling Stones guitarist Jones was rarely out of the headlines thanks to a succession of highly publicized, and extremely dubious, drug busts.

"I don't need these guys to target me, to make my life hell just because I happen to speak up about something." Life was close enough to hell as it was.

No less than his fractious, fractured camaraderie with the rest of Jane's Addiction, relations between Perry and Gary Kurfirst, too, were falling apart. Privately, Perry was already telling friends that he intended dropping Gary as soon as he could; publicly, he appeared to be going out of his way to make Kurfirst look helpless at best, powerless at worst.

The end came as the tour finally closed. With *Nothing's Shocking* still moving in the stores, Warner Brothers announced that they wanted Jane's Addiction to begin work immediately on its successor. Perry refused, and when Gary Kurfirst added his weight to the demands, Perry refused even louder.

"When I got home, I was a nervous wreck . . ." and a physical disaster area. The rib he'd cracked in England back in October, and which had remained untreated ever since, had developed an infection. A torn cartilage in one ankle left him cast-bound and hobbling, and still played up when he put too much weight on it. He also contracted pneumonia.

He'd toured his ass off for 125 dates, and that still wasn't enough for the bastards. Finally, desperately, he did what any recalcitrant artist would do. "I got myself a drug addiction and booked myself into a hospital instead."

In late April, Perry checked himself quietly into a Beverly Hills rehabilitation center. It was time to rest.

The Ulti-
mate Cool
Mother-
fucker

9

Heroin, and the cultural accoutrements that accompany it, can be glamorous. The sunken eyes and wasted cheekbones, the soft slurred voice and the gangling frame, there's something about the look of death that translates perfectly to the roar of rock 'n' roll. Heroin is the rock 'n' roll drug, no question about it.

Other drugs have come and gone—marijuana and acid, amphetamines and coke—but they were fads, rooted to one time or mind-set. Heroin, however, had been there for Charlie Parker, blowing jazz through the forties, and it was there for Jimi Hendrix, jamming blues two decades later. It was there for Billie Holiday in 1959 and for Sid Vicious in 1979.

In 1985, First Lady Nancy Reagan took the initial steps toward undoing some of the drug myth when she launched her "Just Say No to Drugs" campaign, a media-friendly blitz aimed wholly, and solely, at "the MTV generation." MTV itself joined the fight the following year, with a series of public-service announcements under the banner title of Rock Against Drugs.

While Just Say No was targeted at schools and youth clubs, MTV's battle was fought almost exclusively along "role model" lines. Musicians ranging from Mötley Crüe's Vince Neil to ex-Pistol Steve Jones extolled the virtues of a drug-free life. "If I want to get high," Aerosmith's Steven Tyler told his audience, "I listen to music." (It was almost cripplingly ironic that at the top of his playlist he placed the Red Hot Chili Peppers' *Uplift Mofo Party Plan*.)

The Red Hot Chili Peppers' own battles with Anthony Kiedis's and Hillel Slovak's heroin abuse had scarcely been documented at this time; would not, in fact, become public knowledge until Hillel's death in June 1988. Even so, it was only within the band's own immediate circle that Slovak's passing caused more than a ripple of interest, and even there, did it make a difference?

"I did drugs after he died," bassist Flea confessed years later, totally confounding everybody who portrayed him, as Anthony once put it, as the "cleanster" of the group. "I thought, [Drugs] killed him, but they're not going to kill me.'"

Another of Hillel's friends, Thelonious Monster's Rob Graves, died from an overdose in 1990, a year after Thelonious Monster itself finally ground to a halt.

Within this whole druggy climate, riddled with secrecy and deception, word of the problems circulating within Jane's Addiction was both slow to emerge, and confused when it did so.

First was the escalating violence within the lineup. It was common knowledge that the band members were at odds with one another, but was that really news? Given the nature of Jane's Addiction's live performance, given the violence of their music and the savagery of their image, few people believed they could ever really have been friends to begin with. Their chemistry was that of the Who's, four people who came together in mutual antipathy, and the sound of their clashing was the music they made.

But so heavily did Perry's shadow hang over the group that any input Dave, Eric, and Stephen might have had was barely considered when the group's future was being debated and scarcely rejected. When the word crept out that Jane's Addiction was on the verge of splitting, worn down and worn out by a tour that might never have ended, it had to have been Perry's idea.

When a second rumor started creeping around, the whispered suggestion that someone in the band, as Guns N' Roses might have put it, was slamming with Mr. Brownstone, even before his visit to rehab became public knowledge, again that someone had to be Perry. Didn't it?

Perry initially laughed the stories off. There were so many rumors about him in L.A., and he was well aware that he himself had contributed to a great many of them. Let people talk. It kept Jane's Addiction's name in the news, kept their reputation afloat. They'd already proven that they could dish out the heat. Well, they could take it as well. Besides, how could anyone nurse a drug habit when they were being tailed by the CIA? When he went out, Perry spent more time looking behind him than he did watching where he was going.

When Jane's Addiction joined Fishbone, Thelonious Monster, and the Red Hot Chili Peppers at the Hollywood Palace on July 11, 1989, the concert was a wild celebration. The Red Hot Chili Peppers had finally completed work on their first album since Hillel's death, *Mother's Milk*, and already advance copies of its first single, "Knock Me Down," were creating waves. Fishbone and the Monster were close behind them, in terms of music, madness, and, after years on the road, mass acceptance. And *Nothing's Shocking* was now firmly on course for a quarter of a million sales.

The billing did not necessarily reflect the participants' stature, then. Fishbone headlined the concert, the Red Hot Chili Peppers languished in third place, and Jane's Addiction stormed the stage, sandwiched in between them, a blur of sound and vision that even left the bill-toppers feeling exhausted. Could this really be the same band that, a scant two months previous, looked so tired, sounded so slow? They were certainly firing on all cylinders now, and anyone who'd come along in search of clues about the smack stories would have left disappointed. After the show, as much as before it, rumor was all anyone had to go on. That was enough.

Perry was talking with Norwood Fisher, Fishbone's dynamic frontman, about the pair of them duetting together on a version of Sly Stone's "Don't Call Me Nigger, Whitey" for inclusion in what would become Perry's film, *Gift*. For all his own problems, Perry insisted, Stone ranked among the most important voices of his age, and he knew that Fisher felt the same way. What Perry wanted to do now was nail down a recording date.

Norwood turned him down. "Maybe Fishbone didn't think I was in my right mind anymore," Perry hypothesized, leaving *Melody Maker*'s Ted Mico to came right out and say it. "Fishbone refused to be in the film because of rumors of Farrell's drug addiction."

Fisher remembered Hillel, even if no one else seemed to. The two bands, Fishbone and the Red Hot Chili Peppers, had been touring together just weeks before the tragedy, and looking back, Norwood knew that the warning signs had already been flashing red. He hadn't been there for Hillel, because in the long run, nobody had been. If Perry really was going the same way as he did, Norwood didn't want to know.

Perry shrugged. This burgeoning new reputation suited him. He could have scotched the rumors right at the start, but he hadn't. He could have gone public about his rehab course, but so far, he hadn't done that, either. "Maybe," he reasoned, "I need to put myself in these stupid situations in order to fight my way out of them."

He was going to fight. The next thing anybody heard about the Sly Stone cover, Perry had already completed it, with rapper Ice-T filling in for Fishbone. Perry, Ice-T enthused, "is the ultimate cool motherfucker, deeper on more levels than you could possibly imagine."

The feeling was mutual. As the figurehead of the rap movement which began moving out of Los Angeles almost simultaneously with Jane's Addiction's first confident strides out of town, Ice-T had much in common with Perry. Like him, he was wildly outspoken; like him, he spoke for the street; and like him, he was contracted to Warner Brothers. The performance that the two turned in, trading Sly Stone's fiercely acerbic lyrics over a flaming Jane's Addiction–meets–Body Count accompaniment, was the ultimate consummation.

Perry and Casey started talking about what would become *Gift* even before *Soul Kiss* was completed. Like *Soul Kiss*, he described it as his attempt to wrest control of video back from the record companies, back from MTV, back from everybody.

So it was ironic that it was not until that early effort proved financially viable (*Soul Kiss* eventually went gold, racking up sales of 100,000) that Warner Brothers would even consider helping to finance Perry's latest dream child. They eventually came up with $300,000, and Perry remains convinced that the company would have been just as happy with a couple of short-form videos. They simply didn't share his vision. Share it? They didn't even understand it.

Gift was to be a quasi-documentary, dealing with the last year or so of Perry's life. He wove a fantasy sequence that begins with Casey's character (like Perry, playing herself) overdosing on drugs, and culminates with Perry being arrested on suspicion of her murder by two police officers.

Jane's Addiction remained on hiatus throughout the remainder of 1989. It was a necessary break; only by putting their careers on hold could the band members regain their equilibrium. *Gift* consumed Perry; he talked of nothing else. "It's not an exercise in mental masturbation. I was driven to make the film, and it has a strong story for me. The content of its scenes is a part of my life, and a part of many other people's lives. And given time, those images will be accepted."

Throughout the fall of 1989, through the spring and summer of 1990, visiting journalists, treated to advance screenings of the many hours of unedited footage, agreed. "The film could," *Melody Maker*'s Ted Mico hypothesized, "end up being a collection of bad home videos, or just another run-of-the-millstone junkie movie." But somehow Mico doubted it.

The cameras never slept; you never knew when something might happen that had to be filmed. One evening, driving home through Venice Beach, Perry spotted an enormous fiberglass clown, some two stories high, raised up over a newly opened cafe.

Immediately, he began plotting its destruction with the camera crew. Perry would scale its monstrous body, then spray-paint a message across the clown's chest—KILL ME—in massive, hate-filled letters. Then he'd douse its head in rubber cement, and set it ablaze. Only the technical problems of lighting, and the possibility that the clown's owner might happen across the carnage before the scene was completed, put the idea out of Perry's head.

The movie continued. One-off Jane's Addiction shows in Mexico City and Mount Baldie, California, were filmed in their entirety. Perry went surfing, and that was filmed, too. Harry Perry, a roller-skating guitarist Perry met on Venice Beach, appeared as himself, riding alongside Perry and performing one of his own songs on a scratchy electric guitar. A couple of scenes featured a snatch of buzzing electric anxiety contributed by John Frusciante, briefly the guitarist for the Red Hot Chili Peppers.

There would be plenty of weirdness: scenes shot inside Perry and Casey's own apartment in Venice, decorated with Perry's artwork; the posse of twelve security guards who accompanied Jane's Addiction wherever they went in Mexico

City. "I felt like Michael Jackson," Perry commented afterward. "They followed me around everywhere!"

So, he continued, did "Barton," Jane's Addiction's "one fanatical fan. Barton is everywhere—he always knows where I live. He's in the movie, right in the front row with a big grin." Perry joked about how he and Casey were planning to "do a freeze frame and put in a caption that says, 'Barton knows where I live.'"

The centerpiece of *Gift* was to be Perry and Casey's "marriage."

Both in reality and according to the plot of *Gift*, the couple had been together for close to six years. Now that Perry was finally off the road, it was time, he said, to "take her down to Mexico," and marry her in a quiet ceremony in a small village somewhere. Then they'd go surfing. The only question he avoided was, Who was really getting married? The real Perry and Casey? Or their eponymous counterparts in the movie? There were times when not even Perry himself claimed to know the answer to that one.

Discussing the ceremony, Perry explained only that it would not be conventional. "She is a woman that wants to be married," he would say, "and I'm a man who doesn't." The compromise, then, was to be united in a ceremony that was spiritually intact, but not legally binding. "I'll mime how much I love her," Perry said, "But I don't want a legal thing to be made about it. It should just be a symbol, a ritual. It's love mime. That's my show of love to her." Years later he said, "Would you call getting married in a film a legal marriage?"

The arrangements for the wedding were as convoluted as the reasoning behind it. According to *Spin* magazine, one plan, the most extravagant of them all, called for Jane's Addiction to travel into the Peruvian rain forest and combine the nuptials with a massive free concert for the local farmers and villagers at the headwaters of the Amazon River.

"Who gives a shit if nobody speaks Spanish decent enough to get the whole point of this ritual across to the locals?" asked journalist Dean Kuipers. "As the *pulque* [a

Mexican alcoholic drink] and the coke began to flow in abundance, the weirdness of this spectacle would be fodder enough for the cameras."

It was a great idea, but logistically, it wouldn't work. Back to the drawing board.

A year or so before, the English band Depeche Mode had arranged a radio-station competition whose winners would be heaped aboard a bus and driven from New York to Los Angeles, via the ghostly trail of the old Route 66. They would be filmed as they traveled, and at the end of the voyage, be admitted free into Depeche Mode's Rose Bowl concert, the last stop on their massive *101* tour.

Perry liked that idea; now, with the Amazon rain forest out of his system, he began working out his own variation on what had proven a remarkably successful venture.

"We'll have a radio contest. But they won't be stupid questions, like what color are Dave's socks, or what does Eric eat for breakfast," Perry cackled. "We'll get them on . . . oh, the history of American Pop Art, or postwar household appliances. Then we'll hire a bunch of buses, black out the windows, and ship the winners off into the desert." Jane's Addiction, and the wedding ceremony, would be waiting for them there.

That idea didn't work either, though, and in the end the cameras captured a simple, private, Santerian ceremony in the Mexican mountains. Under Perry's occasional narrative, "Classic Girl," the beautiful love song Perry wrote for Casey, played through the scene.

It would be another three years before *Gift* finally saw the light of cinematic day, but even in abeyance, Perry talked constantly of the project—often, some people felt, at the expense of Jane's Addiction themselves. The band's role in *Gift* was seemingly incidental.

The live performances aside, the group's only part in the plot would be a short studio scene. It was very easy to see Jane's Addiction's lack of involvement in *Gift* as another sign of Perry's waning interest in the group. What people still didn't realize was that Perry's retreat into *Gift* was less a cause of the still-burning strife within the lineup than it was a symptom.

Though it was still some time away from completion, *Gift* was already being discussed at Warner Brothers in terms of the "units it might shift," the "exposure it might bring." Perry himself was already suggesting that *Gift* was a companion to *Ritual de lo Habitual*, just as *Soul Kiss* was a companion to *Nothing's Shocking*; it was product, then, just as Jane's Addiction was product, and Perry Farrell himself was product. He loathed being in that position. "I've never hated as much as I do right now," he continued. "I've reached new thresholds of hatred for human beings. You know why? It's the result of people looking at me like product."

In January 1990, Jane's Addiction fired Gary Kurfirst as their manager. In April, Kurfirst announced that he was suing his former clients. Kurfirst's principle grievance was breach of contract, caused by drug problems that he alleged "clouded their judgment." Perry swung back wildly. When he decided to break up with Kurfirst, he was on the road and insists that he "wasn't that deeply involved in drugs. My judgment wasn't clouded at all." He was simply exercising his own, long-standing antipathy toward businessmen, he claimed. It infuriated him that the very nature of the music business required him to appoint anybody to a position of such power, particularly, he fumed, when "a management contract is the closest thing we have to slavery in this country. Management is one of the most ancient and conniving occupations there is, and the fact that people like [Kurfirst] earn money off what I do acts as a disincentive for me to do anything."

That was his defense against Kurfirst's allegations; that, and the fact that when the band needed him, Kurfirst simply wasn't around. "Hell, we're no angels," Perry admitted, "but when I was totally incapacitated . . . I had to get friends of mine to help me. Where was my manager?"

That incapacitation was what Kurfirst was relying on to win the case, and the fact that Dave Navarro was currently negotiating a methadone program. Like Perry and, as it transpired, like Eric as well, perhaps even for the same exhausted, frustrated, reasons as Perry and Eric, he, too, had fallen into drug addiction. The thing that the battery of lawyers who would be arguing Kurfirst's contentions didn't realize was, if it hadn't been for the drugs, Jane's Addiction might have shattered long before. All three of them had done what Danny Sugarman believes every drug addict in his heart wants to do: consolidated their problems into one.

It was Perry, Dave, and Eric's own decision to seek help for their problems. Jane's Addiction was already booked into the studio to begin work on their next album; tours would follow, interviews and countless other things besides. They needed to be clean. It was the cruelest irony, then, that Kurfirst's lawsuit should fall just as they set about completing the process. When the case came to court, the judge showed no hesitation about ruling in Kurfirst's favor, awarding him

what the *New Musical Express* described as "a healthy percentage of [Jane's Addiction's] future earnings."

The judgment devastated Jane's Addiction. Still arguing that Kurfirst had been on his way out of the picture long before drugs came into it, Perry simply couldn't understand how the guy could continue earning money from the band. Especially as the court's decision promptly set into motion another chain of events, which was also centered around money.

Perry had long since established his own publishing company, the amusingly named I'll Hit You Back Music, through which all of Jane's Addiction's own compositions were channeled.

The division of publishing royalties, too, worked in his favor. He was the band's sole lyricist, and in many cases, the sole tunesmith as well. The remainder of the band contributed to the songwriting process in the vision and arrangements they brought to the basic song, and the royalties reflected that—even when, as was increasingly the case on the latest recordings, Perry was fast becoming the sole contributor.

Now, with their share in the band's earnings eroded by Kurfirst's award, the rest of the group was eyeing Perry's lion's share of the publishing. "They wanted to split the publishing evenly, which is fine if the songwriting is even, but it was my work. Songwriting isn't something to carve up democratically. There's an art to it, and it takes a lot of time, even when it looks simpler." The "bad standoff" that Perry says then ensued would ultimately "be the death of the group."

For the time being, Perry amused himself by changing his name to Don Perry Farrell Niccoli. That, with its champagne connotations, cheered him up a little. But it was Iggy Pop who offered the best advice. "[He] told me I'd forget about it in two or three weeks. It was the funniest fucking thing anyone's ever said to me."

Over the next few months, Jane's Addiction did the rounds of Los Angeles management companies. None of them impressed them, particularly as it quickly became apparent that word of their drug use had got around before them, and wought considerable damage while it waited. According to one source, one company even insisted that the group submit to a dope test, to prove that their minds were no longer "clouded by drugs." Another wanted to set up a 1–900 telephone line, so that fans could listen to the band members' voices. Jane's Addiction walked out on them all.

"Managers are like politicians," Perry spat. "We pay them money, they fuck up, and we wind up cleaning up the mess and doing it ourselves. Well, fuck them. I'm not going to pay some asshole to take my money and have them kick back and enjoy it while he's making things worse." Jane's Addiction would continue to handle their own affairs. "I have no responsibility to anyone but myself," Perry asserted. The eventual recruitment of a management team he could trust, the American Tom Attencio, "who does the major music-industry schmooze," and who also managed the British band New Order, and Australian Ted Gardner, ensured that would remain the case.

Gardner first arrived in America in 1982, with the Australian band Men at Work, touring in the wake of a massive and wholly unexpected hit single, "Down Under." His job now was to remain "right by our sides at all times. If you want to have a really well-functioning musical unit," Perry swears, "you gotta have a guy there daily, because shit happens daily." Gardner was there, all the time, band manager, road manager, wet nurse, and security chief. "He's well-built for this work," mused *Creem*.

Not all of it, however, was very easily handled.

Kurfirst's action made a sizable dent in Jane's Addiction's finances. More than that, though, it undermined the sense of suspense in which the group delighted in keeping its audience.

Jane's Addiction, both musicically and conceptually until this point, had remained purposefully vague. The ambiguity of Perry's dress, and his remarks regarding his own sexuality, his attitude toward authority and the established order—Jane's Addiction, as journalist Gina Arnold wrote, captured the wailing of "crazed children howling over . . . car alarms and police sirens and the deadening strains of classic-rock radio." That was probably why so many people loved them and just as many despised them. Jane's Addiction contradicted everything, then turned around and contradicted themselves.

The revelation that the group had had, in the eyes of the law, "its judgment clouded by drug addiction" betrayed that love (and hate); betrayed that ambiguity, too. The group was no longer dancing on the edge of taboo. With the admission that they really had used all the drugs they might only have hinted at in the past, they overstepped one crucial boundary; how many more might they break in the future?

For Perry, the only answer to that question was even more ambiguity. Thirty years ago, science fiction author Robert Heinlein, in his novel *Stranger in a Strange Land*, created the Fair Witness, a person who would speak only what they knew to be incontrovertible fact: "What color is my dress?" "I don't know, I can only see one side of it."

It was with this same flair for literal observation that Perry now handled questions about his drug use. Even with the judicial ruling standing against him, he refused to be drawn in on the subject of his, or anybody else's, drug use. Instead, he cloaked everything behind coy innuendo. Maybe I did, maybe I didn't.

What, journalist Roy Trakin asked, was Farrell's own experience with heroin?

"That it's great," Perry responded. Was it his experiences he was discussing? Or the experiences of those people around him? He wasn't saying.

"I don't think it's anybody's business if I want to sit there and bang myself on the head with a board. Maybe I'm just too damn smart and I'm doing it for a reason." He never actually explained precisely what the antecedent for "it" was: The drug? Or the business with the board? "Maybe I just need to chill out a bit. If you don't get anything extra for being healthy, why should you be penalized for being sick?

"If anybody thinks they want to live like me," he continued in measured tones, "they're completely moronic." Whatever he did, Perry was adamant that he did it simply "to amuse myself on this boring planet." Did that give people a right to judge him?

When Roy Trakin described an advance tape of the forthcoming third Jane's Addiction album as "all in all . . . the druggiest, most fucked-up album since the daze of [the Rolling Stones'] *Exile on Main Street* and [Neil Young's] *Tonight's the Night*," Perry finally snapped.

"I'm simply writing like Bob Dylan when he said he married Isis, man." [In the song "Isis," on Dylan's 1975 *Desire* album.] He was, he said, "just dreaming it all up. I mean, did [Dylan] *really* go riding in on a horse on the twelfth day of May in the drizzle and rain?" Could you believe everything your idols told you?

The title of the new Jane's Addiction album, *Ritual de lo Habitual,* echoed this same lack of concern.

"What I'm trying to say is that everybody has a habit, and some of them are good, and some of them are not so good, some of them are stupid and make no sense at all, and some of them are healthy and they make you so healthy that they make you stupid. But everybody's got to have it."

It was the ritual behind the habit that created the habit, he explained, and if people wanted to emulate his habits, they needed to emulate his rituals, too. The only alternative was to absolve him of all responsibility.

Despite his constant dancing on the edge, Perry had steered remarkably clear of the traditional tenets of rock mythology, "the Keith Richards kinda thing," as *Metal Hammer*'s Mark Day put it.

When Lou Reed learned that an impromptu gathering of rock critics had voted him second to Keith Richards in the "Rock Star Most Likely to Die Next" poll during the mid-1970s, he was not only flattered. "Oh, that's really fabulous. It's a real honor to be voted after Keith."

Perry denied that he possessed any such motivation. "I get off on [the mythology]," he admitted, "but I'm not trying to be like it. I enjoy it as a story. It's an exciting story. Elvis was the greatest, really cool. But I don't want to be Elvis. You can't be Elvis . . . unless you're Billy Idol."

"The people who do drugs—I can see it in their eyes—they want me to hail them. . . . What can I say?" Perry asked helplessly. "Life is short, get carried away. Be smart so you live to see another day. The whole point about drugs is to wake up and tell the story to your brothers . . ." Heroin was dangerous, but so were the freeways, and so was the ocean. Perry Farrell was still driving and surfing, though.

T   h   e
Breasts
Are Okay,
But   the
Penis Has
to   Go

itual de lo Habitual never threatened to be an "ordinary" album. Neither, though its birth pains felt remarkably familiar, did it threaten to be anything like Jane's Addiction's first album.

The cover design was bright and colorful, cluttered and busy. On a bed surrounded with both religious and quasi-religious (a tiny bottle of methadone) paraphernalia, lay a sculpture of three bodies embracing—Perry, Casey, and Xiola Blue. When Perry unveiled the design to Warner Brothers, the only problem anyone could foresee was . . . "Well, it's only a little thing," the joke went round, "but there's the chance it might get bigger." The red sheet with which Perry draped his family grouping had slipped, just enough to show his flaccid penis.

(The same sculpture dominated one wall of Perry's living room; would, in fact, play a big part in getting him evicted from his Hollywood apartment. It disturbed his landlady. She'd put up with a lot, having him as a tenant. Maybe he simply forgot that the world is full of landladies.)

"When Warner Brothers first saw the cover, they kind of smirked and said, 'Oh no. Here we go again,'" Perry laughed.

When he was called in to meet with the label chairman Mo Ostin and president Lenny Waronker, they were unequivocal in their feelings on the subject. The topless women were fine, and the bushes of pubic hair. The penis, however, would have to go.

Perry sat, unflinching, while they talked. The art department had already been to work with its airbrushes, preparing a transparency that was now ready to go. Perry took one look at the safely doctored photo, then pushed it back across the table. No way. Afterward, he proudly related, "I refused to compromise."

It wasn't that he didn't understand people's concerns. "I can see why an image that represents three-way love would threaten some people, for the same reason I can see why the very first people got married. They were probably pissed off and jealous about their lover leaving, so they made a law." What alarmed him was that it wasn't the ménage à trois that alarmed people, it was the penis. "It's a sick cultural attitude, that it's okay to show a woman's breast and [genitals]," he complained, "but it's not okay to show a man's [genitals]. It's a real double standard."

The Warner Brothers executives relented. They may even have agreed with him. The company had weathered one storm over Jane's Addiction's artwork, it could easily withstand another.

This time, however, it wasn't just a storm that was brewing. It was a fully formed hurricane.

Ritual de lo Habitual was scheduled for release in early September 1990. The first promotional posters were delivered to record stores across the country a few weeks before that. The authorities swooped in within days.

On August 21, Rick Berry, the owner of Off the Record, a music store in Royal Oak, Michigan, was ticketed on the misdemeanor charge that he "displayed [an] obscene poster in the south window along Main Street." The officer's ticket continued, "Jane's Addiction poster displays women's privates." Not, interestingly, men's.

If found guilty, Berry was informed, he could be sentenced to anything up to ninety days in prison, and a hundred-dollar fine, and as Berry wondered what to do next, he could not help but ponder the most ironical aspect of the saga. At the same time the city was planning to raise a statue of two naked people outside City Hall.

Warner Brothers immediately agreed to fight alongside the store owner, even to the extent of covering his court costs. The American Civil Liberties Union made a similar pledge. The incident in Michigan was followed by others, and then the Warner Brothers sales teams were reporting on their own difficulties, trying to persuade nervous store owners to stock an album whose cover had already landed others in court. "If we don't get this sorted out soon," Lenny Waronker is reputed to have complained, "we'll be lucky if we sell one thousand copies."

Perry began reconsidering his position. It was the double standard that still savaged him. He knew that bowing down to Warner Brothers' initial suggestion of airbrushing out his own genitals would have been to acknowledge, perhaps even condone, that double standard. Plus, it wouldn't solve the Michigan affair. What Perry wanted to do was nail it once and for all.

Having won Warner Brothers' promise that they would continue to print the original jacket in whatever quantities the market demanded, Perry set to work on an alternative sleeve for *Ritual de lo Habitual*: a plain white wrapper decorated with the First Amendment and the inevitable PARENTAL ADVISORY—EXPLICIT LYRICS label. In its own way, this simple juxtaposition was more effective than any more overt stand Perry, or anybody, could have taken on the same issue.

"I just wanted to make the point that if you start restricting the media and the arts, it leaves you defenseless from the people who want to use propaganda to destroy our culture," Perry explained. "Censorship can only lead to our worst nightmares. I don't want to be a political spokesman, but it's not funny anymore. I think it's time to speak up before it's too late."

And do that he did, on the album's inner sleeve, in a paragraph he addressed "to the mosquitoes," to all the parasites who sucked on his artistic lifeblood. "For some reason, I want to talk to these people, these jackasses," he swore. "I want them to understand where I'm coming from, what my intents really are. I didn't want to come off too hostile, too malcontent. I wanted to simply talk—and ask them, what do you call obscenity when you live in a toilet anyway?"

"Hitler's syphilis-ridden dreams almost came true," the first lines of Perry's warning insisted. If people didn't protect their First Amendment rights, Perry wrote, such nightmares would become the law of the land.

Perry preferred to be making music and not concern himself with censorship. "It's really a shame . . . that we actually have to worry about protecting such a basic freedom."

The First Amendment, he continued, was so straightforward. That was why designing an alternative cover was so difficult.

The whole issue also allowed Perry to maneuver his way through the thornier issue of accepting Warner Brothers' suggestion in the first place. As Perry had said in the latest Jane's Addiction press release, "He who wants only to get his art out uncensored will work deals to do that." It was up to the public whether or not that art was acceptable.

Apparently, it was. Two years earlier, around the same time, coincidentally, as *Nothing's Shocking* hit the streets, the heavy-metal band Lightning released their debut album, *Lightning Strike*, with two different jackets, one innocuous mug shot and one bedecked in the band's grisly logo, a skull and crossbones emblazoned with the word *mother-fucker*. The photo cover was outsold by its counterpart approximately five to one.

Now, according to Perry, the same thing was happening to *Ritual de lo Habitual*. Within weeks of the album's appearance, he was boasting, "people are buying the art cover almost five to one over the plain cover with the First Amendment. [Warner's themselves claimed a more conservative three to one.] The cover that they thought was going to be the one they could sell has become a collectors' item!"

It turned out that many shops were actually carrying both covers, not so that they could give frail listeners a choice but because "people are buying the second cover as a collectors' item, and the first one is what everyone assumes is the real record!" The only retailers who regularly stock the First Amendment jacket today are the mail-order record clubs.

The sense of absurdity with which Warner Brothers' internal qualms were solved was only heightened by the fate of the various prosecutions.

Shortly after Rick Berry was ticketed, the city of Royal Oak was notified by Oakland County that it did not have the proper authority to charge citizens with obscenity. It was ordered to apologize formally to Rick Berry. Only the State of Michigan could press such charges. The State of Michigan wasn't interested. When Royal Oak promptly turned the evidence, a copy of the offending poster, over to the county prosecutor, Richard Thompson, he decided that the poster wasn't even obscene enough to have warranted legal action!

There was a darker side to what was fast becoming a very laughable affair. The fact that the complaints were made in the first place proved that the moral climate in America was still shifting to the right, had drifted even farther in the two years since *Nothing's Shocking*.

Jane's Addiction, having weathered this latest censorship row, crossed off Florida from the itinerary for their upcoming American tour, punningly dubbed "The Tour of the Old and New Worlds." Partly they were showing solidarity with their own First Amendment convictions, but they may have been saving their own skins as well. It was Florida which recently had been the scene of obscenity trials involving 2 Live Crew's album (2 Live Crew was acquitted of the charges brought against them).

"While we're just here to do our music," Perry explained, "we've learned over the years that there's a lot more to deal with than just that. We deal with a lot of problems, [and] we stand up for ourselves. [We] don't let anyone pull any shit with us. My main goal is just to get the art out, that's the most important thing to us."

As with their first record, the album's production was handled by Dave Jerden and Perry, the pair of them conspiring in a sonic barrage which even the sensitive ears at *Stereo Magazine* conceded was "performed 'like nothing else'" and "recorded 'in your face.' Listening to *Ritual de lo Habitual* is not a passive experience!"

Much of the credit for the album's sound goes to Dave Jerden. "He makes guitars sound fucking great," another of Jerden's clients, Love Spit Love (and former Psychedelic Furs) vocalist Richard Butler, enthuses; indeed, Butler admits that it was Jerden's association with Jane's Addiction that prompted him to recruit the producer for Love Spit Love's eponymous debut album in 1994. "I love the way he made Jane's Addiction records sound."

There were so many key moments: "Classic Girl," the opening "Stop," and, of course, the song that was to become as integral to *Ritual de lo Habitual* as "Jane Says" was to *Nothing's Shocking*: "Been Caught Stealing." Over a naggingly insistent acoustic guitar sequence, its intro swamped in the warning barks of a guard dog (actually, Perry's pet, Annie), its close an increasingly frenetic explosion of guitar, bass, and percussion, "Been Caught Stealing" was Jane's Addiction at their peak.

It was only appropriate, then, that later in the year, when MTV began airing the corresponding video, questions should immediately be raised over the very morality of the song. It did, after all, side with the shoplifter. Perry snorted in the face of approbation. "I enjoy stealing. It's fun. That's all there is to it."

"I let out a lot, that's for sure," Perry admitted when discussing the album. "I questioned whether I should even sing [some of] it, but then I thought about when I [die], it'll be beautiful for someone then, it'll become anonymous and people can hold on to it and feel safe with it." Every artist dreams of immortality. Perry now talked of it as well.

"It's kinda hard living amongst your art. I make it for when I'm dead. I write for a person that lives a thousand years in the future, because I think if he or she can still relate to it, then it's timeless." In a similar vein, he continued, "I don't write about current affairs or current events. I talk about things that have been going on since the beginning of time." He aspired, he said, to the fame of the ancient Greek writer Aristotle, "the way you'd pick up something [he] wrote and say, 'I know what he's talking about.'"

It was not, he insisted, "like I'm trying to write a novel or precalculated long-term story or anything." *Ritual de lo Habitual*, he asserted, was never intended as a concept album, and he repeated that Jane's Addiction was not part of an ongoing plot. "It's a vibe. It's just stuff that I'm into at the moment, a mixture of it all."

Paramount in this new mix was Perry's latest religious experiment.

The late 1980s saw the American media turn its attention, briefly but brightly, toward what for many people was simply another cult flourishing in the land of McCults: Santeria. Adherents of the belief were locked into what they viewed as a life-and-death struggle with local authorities, regarding their right to perform animal sacrifices during their ceremonies, a right that other, more established religions have never questioned.

Santeria was not a new fad; was, in fact, a remnant of a faith that was at least as old as the United States itself. It developed from the religious traditions of the African Yoruba people, snatched from their homelands in modern Nigeria and Benin to work as slaves in the plantations and mines of the New World. There, their beliefs were cross-fertilized with the Catholicism of their Spanish and Portuguese captors; in Brazil, their faith became the Macumba; on Haiti, Voodoo; and in Cuba, even today, it is said that if you scratch a local Catholic you will find a Santeria believer.

The Santerias, Perry explained, "basically mind-fucked the Christians and convinced them they were worshipping saints, when they were really worshipping their own gods. They posed as Christians, but in actuality they were praying to pagan demi-gods." To a Santeria believer, the Yoruba warrior goddess Chango became the Catholic Saint Barbara; the patron of miners and workers, Oggubn, became Saint Peter. "They used Christian symbols to goof on their captors because they didn't want to get flagellated." It was a deception, of course, with which he could identify.

"The Santerias built their faith with sticks and stones, small pieces of ceramic, bits of metal, hoping that it would be okay for them," Perry expounded. "And I can appreciate a person who can put faith into sticks and stones and a piece of cloth. The family, the child, the mother, the Holy Spirit, everything is so basic."

In Los Angeles, Perry could only scrape the surface of the faith by dropping in the small stores, or botanicas, where he could buy "potions, incense, [and] fetishes." His interest in Santeria was not the dilettante flirtation with "a higher power," which has, over the years, embroiled so many other rock musicians. "I was just drawn to the colors and sly joke of it all," he admitted. "I also responded to the pageantry."

He did not follow the religion. It was the art and the form of it, the little icons with which he decorated *Ritual de lo Habitual*'s album jacket, that he loved. He found folk art "touching." It wanted more from life than what it possessed, and to Perry, "all inspiration comes from wanting." That is what he took from Santeria.

"To me, the whole of life is about a rush. Santeria gives me a rush, it gives other people a rush, and anytime there's a rush to be had, the source should be looked upon as something worth saving." Jane's Addiction was one such source—for other people, anyway. For Perry, even as he reveled in the reviews that poured enthusiastically into the Warner Brothers press office, the sooner he got away from it, the better.

The *New Musical Express* probably summed *Ritual de lo Habitual* up best, with a nine, out of a possible ten rating, and Mary Ann Hobbs's impassioned (if ultimately erroneous) belief that "Los Angeles has produced only two truly great rock bands since the mid-1980s," one of which, Guns N' Roses, "will never make another album." So that left Jane's Addiction, who have "written the New (rock) Testament . . . *Ritual de lo Habitual* is a work of genius."

Thrust agreed. "Chaos and beauty metamorphose in *Ritual de lo Habitual,* creating an album that will speak for the nineties as [the Beatles'] *Sgt. Pepper* did for the sixties." The *Cleveland Patrol* was so intrigued by the album that it published four different (and wildly differing) reviews of the record in one issue; and *Spin's* Dean Kuipers concluded, "Building on 1988's *Nothing's Shocking,* [it] hits like the nighttime shrieking of a boy who suddenly knows the savage power of his own desire and his own poetry." It was only in Los Angeles, Stephen puzzled, that reviews were less than enthusiastic; were, in fact, "mediocre. They say side one is great and that side two is a bore. [But] I don't care."

Those criticisms drew their sustenance from what was, indeed, the most challenging thing on the album—the epic, ten-minute spread of "Three Days," which opened side two, and which Phoenix's *New Times* described as alternative radio's answer to "Stairway to Heaven." It was surprising, then, that when it came to choosing the first single from the album, Perry and Warner Brothers alike agreed that this behemoth should be the one.

Perry argued that they should release the track in its uncut ten-minute glory; Warner's held out for a more conservative, and certainly more radio-friendly, three minutes. The dispute could have run and run, but this time, Warner Brothers was in no mood to play. Time is of the essence in the music business; a new album demands a new single, even if it's only for the radio stations, so not only, accuses Perry, did they go ahead and chop the song down without even consulting him on the edit, they also commissioned a remix of the track for Perry's approval. Perry felt it was horrible.

"The drums were gone," revealed an incredulous Perry. "It was a drum machine! They took away all my vocal effects, which is one of the few things that is progressive in the band. They took that away. I'm left with a dance song, and it was like holding an eggshell where someone had put a little pin in the top of it and sucked the yolk out! I told them . . . they couldn't put it out. It was embarrassing!"

The remix remained in the can, but the edit made it out regardless. Reluctantly Perry set about selecting sufficient footage to compile a video for the edited "Three Days," then cackled with glee when MTV promptly censored it after they spotted what Perry called "five seconds of nudity—me and Casey lying together on our deathbed."

The pure intensity of the full-length "Three Days" might have been whittled away to insignificance on the single, but still the song retained its power, the perfect introduction to an album that, as much as its predecessor, grabbed the listener not through the force of melody, but from the sheer weight and strength of everything that was going on within, musically and lyrically.

Perry had undergone a massive transformation since he last spoke to the music press. Before, he was a rebel with an artistic bent, denying that he was a simple performer at a time when all he could do was perform. Now, he insisted, he worked only to prove that it was possible to make a living as a successful artist, be it a musician, a movie maker, whatever, and retain both your own dignity and that of the people around you. There was no way he was going to allow "the assholes that keep trying to drain me like vampires" to reduce him to their level. Not again.

"I need to be able to stretch out and let my thoughts and ideas grow naturally. You can't force the soil," and you couldn't force him to bang out another quickie for the kids, a hit single or a top album.

What he could do, he insisted, was make the album that had been in his head "for a long time. It's a blend I've been waiting to achieve for five years, and now, here it is. It's the end of a five-year project, and everything's peaking." Back at Warner Brothers, a few people checked the Jane's Addiction press file. A five-year project . . . they'd read that before, somewhere. Ah, the hypester at work again.

The album's songs catapulted back and forth through Perry's life. "Ain't No Right" was one of Jane's Addiction's earliest compositions, dating back to the time of the Radio Tokyo demos; the inspiration behind "Of Course" stretched back even further, to a time when Perry's older brother would pin the younger boy's arms back and make him slap his own face, then jerked forward to discuss heroin addiction; and "Been Caught Stealing" time-slipped back to when a five-year-old Perry stole something from a store, only for his father to make him take it back, red-faced and apologetic.

Amidst so much talk of the past, was there nothing Perry had to offer the future? Apparently not. Instead, Perry ruminated on the latest set of rumors to be sweeping the record industry, that their next outing would be "the last Jane's Addiction tour for a while." Then he dropped his bombshell. "I'm not even sure I'll come back to that name. It's nice, but it's a shell. I want to step into something different. This is probably gonna be my last album with these guys. I'm trying not to outgrow Jane's Addiction, but at the same time, I am. And I feel it."

Publicly, the band regarded Perry's remarks with equanimity, nodding in silent agreement with his words and individually agreeing with his motives. Eric revealed that he, Dave, and Stephen would probably stay together as a unit, regardless of what Perry did. Privately, they were not so willing to let Jane's Addiction slip away from their grasp.

Perry remained adamant, though. Since the group first came together, he insisted, "I've told them . . . that I look on this as a cycle. We could go on and turn into some 'Doing it for the bucks, no time to clear your head, be happy and have a big house' kind of band. Or we could continue to be stimulated." The only way Perry felt he could retain that stimulation was to move on.

"Think about it, bands are not a very old concept. Bands are pretty new. We haven't got everything right with bands. There's problems—you put out your life in your first two records," and what are you going to do after that? "The kiss of death—starting to write in the studio, where the band doesn't get the chance to get stimulation. Rock stars don't see how far back they've slid from being human beings."

Ritual de lo Habitual, then, was Jane's Addiction caught before they started to slide. Had they really reached their peak? Or just the end of their contractual obligation? In private, the band members batted the possibilities around—and there were so many of them. Jane's Addiction was arguably on the verge of something enormous; in fact, scratch "arguably," they *were* on the edge of something enormous. Calling it quits now wouldn't only be madness, it was commercial suicide.

Perry wouldn't budge. He'd had enough.

"Look at us! Even when we agree with each other, we fight. Yes, Jane's Addiction could be huge, we could be the next Beatles, we could be New Kids on the Block. But I'm tired of the fighting. I'm tired of the routine. I'm tired of playing rock 'n' roll."

The squabbling continued at Warner Brothers. Someone put forth the notion of the band going on an extended hiatus, with a reunion scheduled for one, two, even three years away, and a live album to break the silence midway through. Perry simply snorted. "I'm done. I'm through. Next subject."

As he broke away from the band (whenever he could), Perry also found himself breaking away from Casey as well. Six years: It had been a long time. Maybe too long. Sometimes it

The Breasts Are Okay, But . . .

165

was as though they could barely stand the sight of each other, until it was hard to believe that barely one year before, they'd been on a mountain in Mexico, marrying each other.

Except they hadn't really, had they? Perry had been miming his love, and since then, he'd been miming the role of a husband as well. Just like he mimed everything else in his life: a pop star, an artist, a gaily painted iconoclast.

He needed to escape. He needed to surf. When the surfboard manufacturers Bronze Age offered him a free promotional trip to the Playa Zikatela in Puerto Escondido, Mexico, he grabbed it with both hands. That was exactly what he needed to be doing, hanging out on two miles of unbroken, blinding-white sand while some of the best surfing waves in the world crashed around him. He'd spend time with other surfers, and maybe forget who he was, what he'd become.

Peter DiStefano was six years younger than Perry, but had been on the road forever. "My dad played guitar in the Tennessee Williams play *The Rose Tattoo*. He brought the whole family along with him on the road. I had so much fun, I decided that music would always be my life."

Right then he was playing in a surf band called K38. They'd been at it for eight years now, but they were a dying breed. The western seaboard had been full of groups like this once, traveling the beaches and playing on the sand, running through their time-honored repertoires of old Ventures and Surfaris songs, "all positive and fun and full of love." Now the surfers brought their own entertainment, radios and Walkmans and portable CDs.

Perry liked K38, though, and the Sicilian-American DiStefano, as it transpired, idolized him. "Jane's was my favorite band in the world," DiStefano enthused. Long into the night they would talk. "I kept telling Perry, 'It's a bummer you guys gotta break up.' Perry was really unhappy, he needed to change."

At the end of the trip, back in Los Angeles, the two continued hanging out together, enjoying free-form jams in Perry's rehearsal space, and just letting rip in each other's presence. "He's the best musician I've ever met," DiStefano marveled. "He's very fanatical and very precise. He doesn't settle. If you are weak in any way, he'll let you know."

With Perry's boiling enthusiasm to push him along, DiStefano knew he could try anything. The first time he and Perry ever played together, the guitarist turned up with a boxful of effects and a violin bow. "I've wanted to do this every since I saw Jimmy Page do it in 'The Song Remains the Same,'" he laughed, then paused. Perry had probably seen enough Led Zeppelin–isms to last him a lifetime.

Perry looked curious, though. "Go on, then." As soon as Peter started playing, Perry was adlibbing alongside him, a half-joking song about a girl he knew who'd never experienced an orgasm, but thought he was the one who could change that. It wasn't the best lyric Perry had ever come up with, but he was impressed with it anyway. "If that's what we come up with the first time we play, who knows what'll happen in the future?" It was a future, he was adamant, that couldn't arrive soon enough.

Perry was now verbalizing his frustration at every available opportunity. "I'm as pissed off as I can be," he growled to *L.A. Music Scene*. For all his hard work distancing Jane's Addiction from the rock 'n' roll marketplace, success had arrived regardless, and with it, all the attendant bullshit. Though he'd also worked hard at conceiving the image of rock 'n' roll's number-one prankster, this time people knew that the joking had stopped. Suddenly, they were no longer measuring Jane's Addiction's life span in terms of tours. They worked in terms of individual shows, and any particular one, they knew, might be the last.

On August 19, Jane's Addiction prepared to break their year-long live sabbatical, boarding a plane to London, en route for an appearance at the annual Reading Festival. Given their reputation, and the burgeoning strength of their European reputation, Jane's Addiction's inclusion on that year's three-day festival billing was guaranteed from the moment it became apparent that the band would be back in operation in time. It was also one more piece of evidence for the growing belief that, in terms of what market forces now defined as "alternative music," the United States had finally came into its own.

"[There's] bands playing that I had never even heard of, that were like three spots above us," Perry marveled. "And I kinda felt that we got gypped. Maybe that's bold, but I really felt I wanted to go on when everybody was ready. Nick Cave and the Cramps are the greatest, but the other bands . . ." He paused to consider for a moment, than admitted, "Maybe they're great, and I'm real slow." Somehow you got the impression that he doubted it, and *Melody Maker* journalist Ted Mico noted how he "innocently muses how much stage will be left intact when Jane's Addiction finish their epic bombardment."

Jane's Addiction arrived in London a week before Reading. *Ritual de lo Habitual* was a week old; the band should have been on top of the world. Instead, they privately were at one another's throats. There was the money, there was the future, and most of all, there was a workload that threatened to become at least as punishing as that which had almost brought them to their knees eighteen months previous. This time, though, there would be no chemical safety net for the band members to fall back upon.

Dave and Eric had completed their drug programs and, as Ted Gardner put it, "they were clean and sober. Their attitude was, 'This is the way I want to live.'" Even before the first shows of the new tour, they had announced that when the gig was over, they'd be out of the door, back to their hotel rooms, for some clean peace and quiet. "If you guys want to party, fine," they informed Perry and Stephen. "But don't try and party with us."

The line was drawn, and even Perry didn't feel like crossing it. Not too often, anyway. Instead, he acknowledged their feelings and concentrated on maintaining as unified a face as the band could muster. Maybe some journalists noticed that when Perry did bring another band member along to interviews, it was usually Stephen, but they didn't think anything of it. All that really mattered was that the band was back together.

On August 21, Jane's Addiction appeared as special guests of the Ten-Legged Groove Machine at London's Brixton Academy. The following evening, they headlined their own show at Subterrania, in the old hippie stomping grounds of Ladbroke Grove.

The show sold out weeks before, but that didn't discourage hundreds of ticketless fans from descending upon the dingy venue in the hope of—what? Gaining entrance regardless? Or Simply seeing Jane's Addiction arrive?

Either way, the seething mob that greeted the group when they reached the venue was something Jane's Addiction had never experienced before. Back home, no matter how high their stock rose, their audiences simply came, saw, and passed judgment later. At Subterrania, there was an almost intuitive embracing of the group, as people and as icons; a suggestion in the borderline hysteria of the fans that for all his talk of touching people a thousand years from now, Perry had already made a profound impact, and it was not years, but miles, that he bridged.

Midway through that night's concert, when Perry went stage-diving into the audience, his crucifix slipped from around his neck. He realized the loss almost instantly.

"Wait! Wait a second here! Has anyone seen my cross? I was wearing a cross, is it somewhere down there?"

The band stood patiently, silently, and watched in utter disbelief as the crowd before them parted, shuffled, crouched, searching for the missing jewelry. Moments later, a hand reached from the throng to hand it back to Perry.

"Thank you," he replied, his face split in a grin of total gratitude. "Good things will come to you." At the end of the show, he announced, "We've realized you guys realize who we are. So we're gonna play here tomorrow night, too."

It took ages to come down from that show; ages, too, for Perry and Stephen to emerge from their dressing room, back into the throng. They were all apologies. "I was in the back there," Perry explained, "just pouring water over myself to try and clam myself down for over an hour. Steam was coming off me like I was a cigarette. I was up to like a hundred and thirteen degrees in the head . . ." Then he reconsidered. "One-thirteen? No, I'd be dead. Let's say one-oh-four. No . . . I'd be one-thirteen. Sure!"

Tickets for the following night's show went on sale immediately, and sold out within minutes.

The show didn't happen. Awakening that morning, Perry discovered that his voice had disappeared. At first he thought it was just strained, from the unaccustomed exertions of the previous evening. It had been a long time since he last played live, even longer since he'd played that hard. The problem only worsened as the day progressed, and when medical assistance was finally sought, the diagnosis was the worst that any singer can hear. He had contracted some kind of virus, which had gone straight into his larynx. There would be no singing tonight, none for another week or so. Stephen, Eric, and Dave headed down to Subterrania alone, hoping to see that night's show through with a handful of instrumentals, but their halfhearted doodlings were no substitute for the real thing. They left the stage in mute disarray.

A couple of days later, Stephen ventured down to Reading. He was accompanied by Marc Geiger, head of the American booking agency Triad, which Jane's Addiction shared with the Pixies. After all the trumpeting and boasting, after all the major spreads throughout the British music media, Jane's Addiction had been forced to cancel their performance.

It was Stephen and Geiger, then, who would experience the magic of Reading firsthand; Stephen and Geiger alone who would pack its details in their hand luggage when they left the country the following morning—Perkins to return to the United States with the band, Geiger to the next leg of the Pixies' European tour.

While Jane's Addiction left its British audience with the promise that the group would be back in October for a full tour, and a return bout at Subterrania as well, Perry took with him a blueprint for the future.

Rooting
Around in
H   i   s
Trousers
for   His
W i l l y

ane's Addiction was offered the opening slot on Guns N'
Roses' latest tour, but Triad turned it down. Instead, they
announced, the group would be headlining its own thirty-
two-date concert tour, and the wisdom of that decision
was revealed within hours. Every venue reported an insane
ticket demand. As Guns N' Roses watched their own tickets barely trickle out of the box offices, they must have
cursed Triad's choice every day.

　　"The crowds have grown double or triple since last
time," Perry proudly related. "The promoters were telling us
to take it to an arena, but that's not where we're coming from.
We want our fans to have the intimate theater experience, and
we work hard to set a certain vibe that will probably not work
past a certain-size venue."

Precious few of the venues on "the Tour of the Old and New Worlds" would exceed a 2,500 capacity. But still there was no doubting that in a season already awash with high-profile tours, Jane's Addiction's was one of the highest, because Jane's Addiction made a crossover that none of the other groups on the road during the fall of 1990 ever would.

"I don't look at it like it's alternative or metal," Perry reasoned when asked. "I just see ourselves as a group of musicians working on songs." Jane's Addiction soared up both the alternative and metal charts, but according to Perry, that said more about the state of metal than it did about the nature of Jane's Addiction.

"Metal kids might just be a little bit bored with traditional metal. We're not angling toward metal at all. I've been open with the fact that I think metal is pretty dated, [but] I think guts, volume, and power are always gonna be in. So if you can present that, fresh and exciting, with energy, people will get off on it and want to hear it.

"I'm more proud of 'alternative,' and I hope the alternative people are always surprised when they hear my music. These people have their ear to the street, and they're always waiting for something else. Metal people are willing to hear something else, but there's a format there. The fact that metal people like [*Ritual de lo Habitual*] is more a reflection on the state of metal than it is from us angling the product. It's a good sign, though, and about fucking time."

For everyone who turned up in denim and scruff, wanting only to head-bang themselves to oblivion with a clutch of smuggled six-packs, there were others, like *BAM*'s Bill Holdship, who admitted that "Jane's Addiction almost made me wish I was still stupid (and young) enough to consume mass quantities of acid." The news that the band had recently recorded Grateful Dead's "Ripples" for the forthcoming Dead tribute album *Deadicated* didn't change his mind.

"We're going to add a real strange presence to the theaters we play," Perry predicted. "We're going to get back to something we should never have left behind."

During Jane's Addiction's earliest self-promoted days years before, Perry and Casey had engineered some of the most startling visual displays witnessed onstage. As Jane's Addiction progressed up the concert ladder, the pair dreamed of being able to do that once again.

"What happened was, we actually de-evolutionized," Perry complained years later. "We actually went backwards as far as putting together all these great things." The simple economics of touring with a troupe of freaks and friends was beyond the band—"the idea of having them out for a song or two, [we] couldn't pull [it] off." It would be another couple of years before Perry could truly resurrect his multimedia dreams, but at least now he had the means to make a start.

Every stage, he promised, would be festooned in Christmas lighting, then flanked by sculptures and scenery. In an age when so many bands were going onstage with nothing more showy than jeans and white T-shirts, Jane's Addiction was erecting seeming cathedrals. Before they'd even played a note onstage, Perry would brag, "We're better than we've ever been before."

Jane's Addiction returned to Europe in September 1990; and it was worth the wait. Before they arrived, the *New Musical Express*'s Mary Ann Hobbs counseled her readers to "get on your knees for a ticket if you have to," and apparently they took her advice.

"We did about five weeks," Stephen enthused. "That was unbelievable, all sold out. The shows were pretty incredible, it was a lot of fun."

Perry, too, was excited about the outing. "I'm excited about the mixture of the new record with the old material." He admitted that although he once pledged that there was no way he would still be singing "Pigs in Zen" at forty, for as long as he was still performing with Jane's Addiction, "I could never abandon any of the old material. I hear [the songs] in the set, and I always want to keep it in balance. Besides, leaving those old songs out would be an emotional letdown for the audience, and I couldn't have that."

He knew from his own past experiences what it was like to go see a band and be bombarded with new songs all evening long, "then maybe if you're lucky, they'll do a couple of hits for the encore." Jane's Addiction didn't always do an encore, so they did their oldies beforehand.

The European shows did not pass off without incident, of course. In Amsterdam Perry was joyously flaunting his love of hash in front of journalists, as though daring them to comment on his lifestyle, and though few of them would, still he was making a point. As he himself allegedly told people, in increasingly unsubtle stage whispers, if people didn't like the way he conducted himself, they could just find someone else to hang out with. "I think I've proven what I am," he wrote in the booklet that accompanied *Ritual de lo Habitual*, "and I'm really comfortable with myself."

There were whispers, though, that maybe he was taking his indulgence too far, whispers that reached a deafening pitch when Jane's Addiction arrived in Amsterdam, and promptly canceled that night's concert. The official explanation was that he'd gone down with the flu, but Amsterdam is the drug capital of the world. If you can't find a cure for what ails you on the streets of that city, then it can't be ailing you too badly.

The canceled show was hastily rescheduled for the following week. Up onstage a week later, Perry was his normal, attention-seeking self. "I am a Jew by birth," he shouted. "So thanks for hiding my ancestors during the war."

No one could tell what sort of response he expected—the audience included. Perry's remarks were greeted with silence. Undaunted, he continued. "No, really, if it weren't for you people, I wouldn't be here right now. The folks back home asked me to say thanks."

The silence was stretching into infinity.

Indicating his stagewear, a pair of baggy trousers held up with suspenders, and an athletic T-shirt, Perry rambled on. "This is not a Nazi look. This is how we looked in the concentration camps." Now he was beginning to appear uncomfortable. "That's a joke."

No one laughed. Finally, he shrugged. "I guess you don't understand my sense of humor."

"Oh, we understand it allright," a Dutch girl at the back of the hall whispered to her companion. "We just don't think it's very funny."

Afterward in the dressing room, the group remained silent about their leader's outburst. It was left to Stephen to find anything to say about . . . anything. "Holland is beautiful," he remarked. "And the girls there are—There's just so many! Ninety-five percent of them are the most gorgeous ladies I've ever known!"

Every city turned out to greet Jane's Addiction. In London, the Subterrania audience included Depeche Mode's Dave Gahan and his girlfriend Teresa Conway—who had once worked Jane's Addiction's PR. Gahan loved Jane's Addiction, raved about them whenever he could.

The three-man band Love and Rockets were there as well, and that was more to his taste. "Shit, I love it!" Stephen raved. Jane's Addiction had just added an old Bauhaus song to their live repertoire, "Burning from the Inside," "but we do it with Bob Dylan lyrics," Stephen continued. "It's called 'Bobhaus.' It's only about three minutes of the song, but it's pretty cool, and then we go right into "Pigs in Zen.'"

The British press went crazy. Every writer who was assigned to cover Jane's Addiction came back with just one objective, to outdo whatever had been written before. *Raw* even described Perry as a "sex symbol," albeit an "unlikely" one. Because not only were "girls screaming like stuck pigs" every time he shook his butt, it was also "fascinating without being particularly entertaining . . . watching [Perry] root around in his trousers for his willy."

The group returned home in mid-October, running straight into the second, American, leg of their "Tour of the Old and New Worlds."

Things had skyrocketed during Jane's Addiction's absence. Five weeks after its release, sales of *Ritual de lo Habitual* approached half a million copies in the United States alone, pushing the album itself to number 25 on the *Billboard* chart. Five weeks after that, with MTV beginning to commit "Been Caught Stealing" to heavy rotation (it would eventually win an MTV video award), *Ritual de lo Habitual* joined the Black Crowes, N.W.A., Gregg Allman, Bette Midler, and Randy Travis among November's certified gold discs. It eventually peaked at number 19 on the *Billboard* chart, eighty-four places higher than its predecessor.

The American leg of the tour was scheduled to kick off in La Jolla, near San Diego, on November 2, 1990. Two days before that, however, the band announced a surprise warmup show at the Henry Fonda Theater on Hollywood Boulevard on Halloween night. Tickets, placed on sale just hours before the theater doors opened, sold out in near-record time. "Isn't it great to have the best band in the world come from your hometown?" Perry asked the crowd that evening, and at that moment, the only possible response was a rousing roar of approval.

Even amid so much excitement, the band's internal mechanism was creaking badly. Crossing the country by bus, their entourage—Dave's wife, Tanya, included—was simply packed in all together, living, breathing, eating up one another's twenty-four-hour presence.

It was too much. As they did in Europe, Dave and Eric's fellow travelers agreed to maintain a drug-free zone around them, but visitors and guests—and there were so many of them—were another matter entirely. By common consensus, the pair was granted exclusive use of the bus's rear lounge, whenever they needed to escape from whatever might be going on up front.

"They pass no judgment," *Spin*'s Dean Kuipers reported after he spent some time on the road with the group. "They have simply learned that they cannot use drugs of any kind without becoming slaves to them, and that slavery is death."

Kuipers, however, was seeing everyone on their best behavior. Behind the closed doors of the bus, the band members erected even more closed doors of their own.

Perry tried to reason his way out of his bandmates' condemnation. "If I need drugs to do everything," he admitted, "then I suck, really. I go back and forth. I don't want to be asshole stupid idiot to the real world," he objected. But neither did he "want to be a traitor to the drug world." Instead, he'd remain in the middle, and if certain people didn't like that, it was tough on them.

Tough on Jane's Addiction as well. "We weren't getting along to the point that nobody was listening to musical ideas," Perry sighed. "If I said, 'Hey man, let's try being adventurous here and putting, say, a flange on this instrument,' if you're not friends, you don't listen to me. You tend to block out any suggestions. Suggestions grounded in love are always accepted." When they're not . . . "I don't hang around where I'm not wanted," and it was becoming apparent that he wasn't wanted here.

Entire legs of the trip were undertaken in comparative silence. When journalists asked them about the group's future plans, Eric and Dave just looked blank. They'd even stopped trying to persuade Perry to keep the band going. There was no future.

The tour was three nights old when Jane's Addiction played Phoenix, and from the start, the Celebrity Theatre security guards regarded the growing tide of female stage invaders with leniency, even humor.

Things were cool, and they remained cool when the band kicked into "Stop," and one more stage invader materialized. "I like people onstage," Perry mused later. "I appreciate a kid with guts to get up there."

This night, though, it was more than simply a kid. With one young woman having made it onto the stage, wrote the local *Republic*'s Salvatore Caputo, another quickly followed . . . "then another. Then another. Then a young man made it to the stage, and he, too, was cool, dancing with the band and the women without getting in the way of the show." Then all hell broke loose; hundreds of fans swamped the stage, overwhelming the security, drowning the vinyl pants and plastic skirt–clad Perry.

Jane's Addiction continued playing, but it was getting tight up there. The security team marshaled their defenses and rose up as one, clearing the stage and then preventing a recurrence by linking arms at the edge of the stage. Nothing was going to get past them again, nothing except a sly nod of approval from the band, who rewarded the audience for its enthusiasm with a gentle "Jane Says." The crowd responded as one. Jane's Addiction still seldom played their signature song; when they did, it meant they were especially pleased with the way things had gone. "If I felt people were really giving from the audience, then I would give back," Perry explained.

The enthusiasm that greeted the Phoenix show, every show, didn't surprise Perry. "We haven't played in about eighteen months," he said, "and if I was a kid, I'd dig this. It's got energy and melody. It's got slow, fast, beautiful, ugly." And it was about to get even uglier.

Through New Orleans, Birmingham, and Atlanta, on to Virginia, where the support band, 24-7 Spyz, joined Jane's Addiction onstage for a funked-up encore of "Mountain Song"; onward two nights at a converted New York City church, the Limelight—when Jane's Addiction hit Philadelphia on November 19, 1990, they looked and sounded ready for anything. Anything except for what they actually got. . . .

The group had been onstage for about fifty minutes . . . eight songs . . . little more than half the length of the average Jane's Addiction concert . . . when suddenly the band downed tools and left the stage. Even worse, the crowd had heard more insults than music.

Perry, flailing the stage in a floral print dress, appeared bummed out from the beginning. The first song was barely over and he was complaining, "This is bullshit." The audience needed enemas, he sniped. "You're all white . . . you can't dance." They were nothing but a bunch of "young, disaffected, suburban kids," and Perry spat the words like a curse. "I bet you think this is loud!"

Not until he walked off, with the rest of the band behind him, and the onstage silence stretched from moments to minutes, was the full import of his tantrum revealed. Ten minutes passed, three thousand fans illuminated by the house lights, and the catcalls and obscenities grew louder by the second. One segment of the crowd found ironic use for the band's name, amputating the final syllable, then roaring the remainder at the stage: "Jane's a dick . . . Jane's a dick . . ."

Around ten-thirty, the crowd erupted, pouring out of the Tower Theater like lava, onto 69th and Ludlow, battling among its own number, pushing aside anything that got in its way. The police waded into the hail of beer bottles—riot-helmeted officers being called in from as far afield as Chester and Philadelphia, forty departments in all. The warring continued unabated.

The mob spotted Jane's Addiction's tour bus, parked behind the theater. The band members themselves were still inside the building, but that didn't matter. One section of the crowd put its full weight against one side of the vehicle and began pushing. Another hammered against the backstage door, a third battalion continued its rampage, "smashing," said one press report, "everything in sight." By the end of the evening, twenty-three people would be arrested on charges of disorderly conduct; many others, including a police sergeant, would be treated for injuries.

"It was a total mob scene," a fan told the *Philadelphia Inquirer*. People "were trying to . . . tip the bus. There were sirens, police were pushing the kids, the kids were fighting back. It would have made a great scene from a Stanley Kubrick movie."

It would have made another great scene for *Gift* as well, but Perry wasn't watching. Backstage, he was locked into a furious debate with the show's promoters, Electric Factory

Concerts. Under the terms of the band's contract, they were to play a minimum of eleven songs, three more than they had performed, but Perry was adamant. The show was over, come what may.

"That old adage 'the show must go on' might be fine for Basil Rathbone or Sarah Bernhardt," he said with a sneer. "But you've got to remember entertainers were slaves back then. Who am I trying to please, anyway? I think I did the right thing."

Later, he compared performing that show with "having an epileptic seizure in a subway," and when Electric Factory raised the matter of payment and the fact that the band wouldn't be getting any, Perry's response was unequivocal. "Shove the money up your ass!" Electric Factory later offered a five-dollar rebate to any ticket holder who mailed in one of the $15.50 concert ticket stubs.

"The band was at fault for what happened. . . ." Electric Factory project coordinator Adam Spivak later said. "They didn't realize how serious it was, or how serious it could have been." He said that the dispute had been patched up, and for a time, there was even talk of scheduling another Jane's Addiction show at the same venue, with reduced ticket prices for anybody who had attended the ill-fated November 19 bash. "[The band has] been apologizing to us and to the press, and want to do something to make amends," Spivak continued. It didn't happen, though. Jane's Addiction was nearing the end of its tether once again. There would be no extensions.

Plus, did they really need to make amends? After all, not everybody who attended the concert was disaffected. One fan told the *Philadelphia Daily News,* "We can blame Led Zeppelin and Bruce Springsteen and the Grateful Dead for conditioning people to expect marathon shows. One of the best bands I've ever seen only played for twenty-nine minutes—the Beatles. Another was Jane's Addiction. There were moments Monday when they were on fire."

Perry, too, remained unrepentant, if apologetic. "I regret anyone getting arrested or hurt in Philadelphia," he

mourned in a swiftly penned press statement released two
days later by Jane's Addiction's public-relations firm, Levine
Schneider. "I know people may have felt they did not get their
money's worth out of us. It's unfortunate that I'm not a
wind-up toy that can perform anywhere, anytime, under any
conditions."

He described the venue as "restrictive," and complained, "I felt nothing, and so rather than fake an orgasm, I
decided to get dressed and leave."

What he might also have done was point com-
plainants in the direction of an interview he gave to the
Philadelphia Inquirer, which was published on the morning of
the Tower show. "Whatever I do, I try to make it feel like it's
the first time I've ever done it," he told journalist Tom Moon.
"I imagine that nobody knows me, so I do what I like."

It was, he said, "a very different philosophy from
the stardom thing, where once you start getting known, you
somehow have this moral and social obligation to act a certain
way. With me, it's always been little Perry. Nobody's gonna
cast a social obligation on me!"

What was most interesting about the whole situation, however, was the fact that Jane's Addiction had played
similarly brief sets in the past and encountered similarly out-
raged (if considerably less violent) responses as well. "Many
in the Tucson Garden audience . . waited more than two hours
to hear Jane's Addiction play for fifty-five minutes," wrote the
local *Citizen's* Chuck Graham on January 9, 1989, a full
twenty months before the Philadelphia outburst. "Was this an
economical investment of time?"

The Tucson audience thought not; seemed, in fact,
"a bit stunned by the whole incident. One minute the Los Angeles quartet was thrashing through a more or less typical
L.A. club-band performance, then suddenly all the musicians
ran offstage."

Again, the immediate response was that the band
would be back in a moment, to simply pick up where they left
off. Only slowly did the realization dawn on the crowd that the

show was over, and that was when the booing started. "Finally," Graham reported, Jane's Addiction "did return to rip off three brief encores," and there was little doubt that the term "rip off" was very deliberately chosen. "Maybe if another modest hit or two crops up, the band will work up an additional thirty minutes of material," he concluded. Or maybe not.

24-7 Spyz left the Tour of the Old and New Worlds following the Virginia Beach show, to be replaced by Buck Pets, who in turn gave way to former Black Flag vocalist Henry Rollins's own eponymous band, a steamroller of noise that at least rivaled Jane's Addiction's own. Then came the awesome West Coast tour with Primus, the Pixies, and Jane's Addiction.

That particular stretch of the Tour of the Old and New Worlds opened on December 9 in Seattle, Jane's Addiction's first stop there since the George Bush quips that had set the CIA on Perry's ass eighteen months previous.

Seattle Times critic Patrick MacDonald was still around, though, lying in wait with a concert preview that referred readers back to the last shows, then sniffed, "That's just the kind of juvenile stuff Farrell is always doing." But, he was forced to admit, "it pays off. The *Ritual . . .* album is a chart success . . . the next one probably will be a smash." Had Perry not spent much of the past six months denying that there would be a "next one," it would have been hard to disagree.

Jane's Addiction returned home to Los Angeles on December 18, 1990, to find scalpers already collecting up to $125 a ticket for the first of the band's three Palladium shows. Box-office tickets sold out in just thirty minutes, and that statistic raised more than a few wry smiles. Why, it was only a few minutes less than Jane's Addiction played that evening, after a sandal sailed out of the crowd and clobbered Perry on the head—his "overfull head," as *Village View*'s reviewer rather unkindly put it afterward.

From the start, the Palladium audience was a mixed bag, half of them there to cheer on the local heroes, the other half intent on cutting them back down to size. The attendant critics felt the same way as well; afterward, they all happily agreed that Jane's Addiction was the best band Los Angeles had going for it right there and then. The question was, did that mean Jane's Addiction was great? Or that Los Angeles was in serious trouble?

"Each time Farrell opened his mouth to speak, he came off as such a pretentious, profane, ill-informed Valley [snob] that it nearly spoiled any illusion about this being a significant band with useful ideas to impart," complained the *L.A. Times'* Chris Willman. "His bandmates ought to slap a gag order on him."

The sandal, one of a host of missiles that were raining down all evening and had already chased the Pixies off the stage early, effectively did the job for them, although not before Perry, as the increasingly uncharitable Willman wrote, "complained at even greater length, unappreciative of the irony that he who lives by the missile dies by the missile." But Willman saved his best barb till last:

"It's this kind of loutish thinking out loud—with a muddle-headed mix of hippie-ism, hedonism, and insults—that makes Axl Rose sound like a politically informed intellectual by comparison."

Perry retaliated by taking the stage the following evening high on acid, or so he insinuated. "So, this is L.A. on LSD?" he asked from the stage, and journalist Sean O'Neill, distinctly underwhelmed by a band he believed to be suffering "the proverbial sophomore slump," could only respond, "Maybe Farrell was tripping, for the entire set felt tentative."

A fog machine made a poor substitute for the stage paraphernalia that had so delighted earlier audiences, and "the entire evening," O'Neill condemned, "had a tossed-off feel, as if the band was going through the motions."

The answer to that question lay deep within Perry's heart. It suddenly seemed very possible that he, at least, was indeed simply doing what he had to, until he could stop. "Touring in itself is a great thing," Perry had mused in 1989.

"You're going to faraway places to play music for strangers that have heard about you. It's a heavy kinetic connection."

It *was* tiring, it *was* boring, and ultimately, it *was* self-destructive. Perry wanted to experience life, then write about it. That is what he'd always said—that, to judge from Jane's Addiction's back catalog at least, is what he did.

It was not touring itself that was wrong, though, it was the system. Though the idea was still only half-formed in his head, he knew that things would be different in the future. "I'm going to change it. I know how I want it handled."

The girl on the other end of the line sounded sincere, and very, very worried. The Los Angeles Health Department was accustomed to calls like this, of course, but this one was different. The girl had only recently been diagnosed HIV-positive, and she'd been able to contact just about all of her past sexual partners to advise them to get tested. There was one left, a public figure . . . Was there any way the Health Department could get through to him, tell him what had happened?

"And who is it?" the concerned voice on the other end of the phone asked.

"The singer with Jane's Addiction. Perry Farrell."

The warning hit Perry like a thunderbolt. "I was literally sick from worrying about it." Awakening in the morning, he would simply lie lethargically in bed thinking, "Look how skinny I am. My face is changing. I'm dying." The Health Department told him to get tested as quickly as possible, but really, what was the point? "Today let us eat and drink," he would tell himself, "for tomorrow . . ." He'd have the test tomorrow. It was always tomorrow.

When Perry said "Name something degrading, I've done it," he knew it would shock people. Now it shocked him. Something degrading, *anything* degrading. The needles he might have used, the people he may have slept with, at the time it was just another high. He hadn't thought, he didn't know. When he finally made the appointment for his AIDS test, his voice rose several octaves, and wavered like a seismograph reading.

The whole incident turned his life upside down. He still slept around, but that's all he did, sleep. In the days before he was tested, he ended up in bed with three or four different people, but he didn't even try to have sex with them. "I just couldn't say to them, 'I don't want to give you AIDS.' That's fucking unsexy."

When the results came back in and he was certified HIV-negative, then it was all a big joke. The rumormongers, as usual, were still several steps behind reality, so while Perry was celebrating his reprieve from the illness, a lot of other people were only just finding out that he might have the disease. Perry, proud that he was only the second person in Los Angeles history who'd had the Health Department hunt them down over AIDS ("like I was running around like vermin or something"), simply smiled, laughed, and let people get on with the legends. Now that he knew he wasn't going to die, it didn't matter if everybody thought that he was.

The rumor spread, across town, across country. Two decades before, there'd been a big scare about Paul McCartney, about how he'd been killed in a car crash and replaced with a double, and it had all been hushed up by their record company. The rest of the Beatles couldn't keep quiet, though, so they strewed little clues in their songs and on their record sleeves, and let the pop culture detective sort out the tangle.

People were studying Perry's jackets now, looking for clues about his life as well. As innocently as the Beatles, who hadn't even noticed the license plate on the Volkswagon parked on the *Abbey Road* jacket, let alone figured out that Paul, like that number, would have been 28 IF . . . Perry hadn't even known it at the time, but there was one helluva big clue on *Ritual de lo Habitual*, halfway down the front, on the left-hand side.

A wedding album lay open to two scenes from *Gift*, taken during the Santerian ceremony in the Mexican mountains. Tucked into the page was a certificate, and if you looked at it hard enough, got a magnifying glass out and squinted . . . *Spin* broke the news, describing "a mysterious clinic report [which] implies that Perry has tested positive for the HIV virus." The certificate even had his name on it.

Perry roared when he read that one. Yes, he did have a clinic report, but whether it had come back positive or negative, it wouldn't have had his name on it. Not even his real name. AIDS is still a sensitive issue, so sensitive that its victims don't even have names anymore. They are given case numbers.

It wasn't a clinic report on the cover, Perry claimed, it was a homemade pregnancy certificate, another piece of red-herring debris from the marriage that never was. Perry had intended fooling people into thinking he'd created life.

Instead he had them believing that he was on the edge of death, and once that story—which he had to admit was a far juicier tale—appeared in print, "I couldn't get laid for six months. Every town I go to, every old friend I've ever had comes running up to me asking how long I have to live." After a time, it wasn't even funny anymore. As much as he hated to do it, he took to carrying around a small plastic card that certified that he was HIV-negative.

Still, rumor, innuendo . . . "Jane's Addiction is all about reaction," noted one Midwestern journalist as he contemplated the outrageous assault of the band's live performance, and Perry was swift to support that diagnosis.

"I want to be interviewed by people who can't stand me," he told writer Steve Martin, "instead of people that like me." Martin was a friend, an ally. "So if I told you that somebody else thought up all the songs for me, you probably wouldn't believe me, right? If you hated my guts, you might think, 'Oh, wow, this is hot gossip. The guy didn't even write his own songs.'

"I can't do that to you, 'cause we're friends, but I'm gonna start throwing interviews, because you read other people's interviews and they have these opinions about *shit*, like they don't wanna be political, they wanna be a *band*; they don't wanna be rock stars, they wanna be a *band*; it's all so obvious, and it's all so full of shit."

Jane's Addiction took Christmas and the early new year off, but was back on the road throughout the spring of 1991. Triad booked them into larger venues that the previous tour's ticket demand, at least, suggested they should have been playing six months before.

This was no ordinary large-capacity tour, neatly programmed sets being kicked out for a sedately seated audience. Horrified at the sheer size of the halls—the six thousand–capacity ASU Activity Center in Tucson, the Universal Amphitheatre in California, the Municipal Auditorium in New Orleans, the twice-that-size expanse of Madison Square Garden—Perry demanded that every venue, including the Garden, secure a small-capacity general-admission area in front of the rows of reserved seats.

"It's nice to do [the larger venues]," Perry said, but "all of a sudden you feel lonely, like you're not making contact with anybody." The standing-room-only crush immediately in front of the stage, was reassuring, then; it restored Perry's "balance," and let him know, too, "that we can always go back to a small-club situation in my head, when I get disoriented."

It was also interesting as this second tour got under way in Arizona in mid-January that, at last, Florida figured in Jane's Addiction's itinerary. Perry had previously omitted it as a protest against, if not a reaction to, the near-draconian treatment the state almost traditionally reserved for rock 'n' roll.

The concern that Perry's closest friends and associates felt about the inclusion of five shows, in Pensacola, St. Petersburg, Miami, and two in Orlando, was nothing to do with the things that he might do wrong. Far more disturbing was the possibility that he might start doing things right.

The end of Jane's Addiction, the split he'd been dreaming of for almost a year, was still nowhere in sight. "This will be our last tour," he'd insisted, but nowhere had he said how long this last tour was going to be. Triad set the dates, Perry rolled out to play them. He did it so dutifully, there was only one conclusion left to draw. The system had finally got him, and Perry had given up fighting. If it wasn't for the fact that Jane's Addiction was scheduled to play in Miami that evening, he might even turn up at the Grammys!

It was inevitable, when the Grammy nominations were announced, that Jane's Addiction would be back in contention. They were among the real favorites as well.

In the Hard Rock category, with no Jethro Tull to queer the pitch, and the Metal bands all shunted off to their own private party, the competition was stern: Faith No More, Mötley Crüe, AC/DC, and the eventual winners, Living Colour. In the Best Jacket Design section, though, there was no question about it. *Ritual de lo Habitual* was a clear victor. The penis that scared America half to death had finally won the approval of its peers.

This Is It, Home- b o y s , Y o u t h R e v o- lution!

J ane's Addiction was still touring in the spring of 1991, and there was no end in sight. This tour was already scheduled to bleed into the early summer, three months of touring crammed into a single five-month window, and Perry's frustration was obvious, in the way he talked, in the way he danced, in the way he simply did whatever Triad asked him to. Everywhere, the word was out. Maybe this was Jane's Addiction's final tour, but Triad wanted more, Warner Brothers wanted more, the kids wanted more, and Jane's Addiction was giving it to them. Maybe, the thinking seemed to be, it was time to give something back to Perry.

When Triad first approached him about continuing the tour into the late summer, Perry responded exactly as everyone expected him to. With a frown, a whine, and an expression of absolute horror.

"Then they told me that I could do whatever I wanted," Perry recalls. "[They said], 'We're giving you the license to do with your tour whatever you want.'"

Perry just looked at them curiously and said, "*Whatever?*"

Suddenly there was so much raw material to play with, so many dreams and schemes flooding his mind, and slowly they coalesced. He dreamed of organizing a touring schedule. It would be a multimedia event, "using music, art, and military discoveries and weaponry as forms of entertainment."

Like a Gathering of the Tribes? he was asked, a reference to the festivals staged by The Cult's Ian Astbury a few months earlier.

No, like a Lollapalooza, he retorted. He, too, had brought together a cross section of both musical and political groups, and with considerable success. "It means someone or something special, excellent, or exceptional," Perry explained. "It also can mean a giant lollipop." He'd stumbled upon the word channel-surfing one night, and getting sucked into an old episode of the Three Stooges. Having appropriated it, Perry guarded it with jealous passion. When the Ford Motor Company attempted to run a television commercial using the word around the time of the 1994 tour, Perry slapped an immediate injunction on them. Lollapalooza, he informed Ford, was above such base commercialism. The settlement the Lollapalooza organization received from the case, he added, should be donated to a rain-forest charity.

That sense of altruism permeated Lollapalooza's birth. Reactions from Marc Geiger's peers, when he first floated the untried idea of a traveling festival, were generally incredulous. "[They] ranged from 'You've got to be crazy,' which we were, to 'It won't work, it's never been done before,'" Geiger swears, still overlooking the example of the Gathering of the Tribes just months earlier. "Some promoters were really behind this, others said they wouldn't touch it with a ten-foot pole, and others had to have it forced down their throats."

Don Muller, one of Geiger's colleagues at Triad, could not help but be enthused over the project. "I thought it was a great idea. At the time, Jane's Addiction was consistently selling out five thousand– to seven thousand–seat venues across the country, even places like Indianapolis. I thought, boy, if we can do that kind of business, with other bands on the bill, maybe we wouldn't be able to sell out everywhere, but we'd be able to do ten thousand to fifteen thousand people a night."

Everybody involved dismissed out-of-hand Ian Astbury's belief that Lollapalooza was modeled squarely on his own Gathering of the Tribes; and, in fact, carefully avoided any mention whatsoever of the festival in their own acknowledgment of Lollapalooza's predecessors. According to Geiger, "Basically, we stole the idea from festivals in Europe, except that ours is on the road and theirs is not."

The Reading Festival was an influence, of course, but more important, so were events like the remote desert festival Psi Com played some six years before. Perry continues, "The spirit of Lollapalooza came from those days way back when—when the Minutemen and the Meat Puppets played on some ship that cruised in San Pedro Harbor. Those shows, that's where I cut my teeth." The excitement of those shows was what he now missed. "When I got into this business on a major level, I thought it'd be exciting." Instead, he was bored. Lollapalooza reawakened his mind.

Every stop on the tour was an excuse for Perry to telephone in to Triad to check on the festival's progress, and to throw some new dream into the melting pot. "We want the army there!" he roared one evening. The numbskulls he'd met at Camp Pendleton all those years ago still bothered him. "I want the army there to tell me why they're so fucking keen about killing folk."

Another time, he was demanding the National Rifle Association be there, at the festival. He wanted

Greenpeace, the Sierra Club, Refuse and Resist, an attempt to see what would happen with what he called a "major exchange of information." Perry disliked the idea of the world being controlled by the news media. He thought ideas needed to be exchanged in another forum.

The biggest factor in this sense of awareness among people was the Gulf War, the United States–led squabble that was organized the previous summer to blitzkrieg Iraqi forces out of the Kuwaiti territory they had invaded in August 1990.

Perry himself opposed the Allied coalition, although he was not above incorporating jokey references to how the dispute should be resolved into his live repartee. "What do we have all those missiles for?" he asked one audience. "Why send anybody over there to fight? They could all stay at home and have fun, and let the missiles do the job for them."

In truth, however, "I don't like what my country is doing. I don't agree with it. But as we know, most political leaders are scumbags and I've got to wonder about the other guy [Iraqi leader Saddam Hussein] as well. I don't agree with what's being done, [but] as far as who's wrong, I don't know if either one is right."

He blamed his indecision squarely on the role of the media in reporting what was going on, both before and during the January 1991 war. "Most of the opinions that have been coming out have been prowar because the news closely covers what the government does. It doesn't mean it's right. It just means it's well-publicized, and what is publicized usually becomes public opinion."

What people didn't understand, however, was that if they equated that same principle to something else, to music, for instance, "most music that's popular sucks, right?" Vanilla Ice sold a lot more than Jane's Addiction, he said, "but that doesn't mean it's good music. It just means it's more popular, and the same thing with war. It looks as if most people are in favor of the war, but that's not true. You're getting opinions from people who stand to earn a profit from it.

"At this point it seems more people are for the war because of the fact there are more stupid people."

And "stupid people" were one of Lollapalooza's primary targets. Stupid people, and the thought processes (or lack thereof) that fed their stupidity. In the back of his mind, Perry pondered, "Maybe I'm wrong, maybe it's war that we need. A lot of people really believe that was what was necessary." He paused and smiled. "I guess the war's been bugging me a lot."

While Ted Gardner was able to run down an extensive list of the organizations that had agreed to set up booths at Lollapalooza, most of the right-wing organizations that Perry invited turned him down. "I've tried to get the military involved," he said later, "I've tried to get the NRA to come down and say their piece, and they don't want to."

"Perry, he's a thinker," Marc Geiger said as the Lollapalooza project gathered weight. "He wants to enlighten people. He wants to make a difference in the world, and I've no doubt that slowly but surely he will in some way."

He already had. The all-out musical firestorm that Jane's Addiction had patented was spreading. In Europe, Urban Dance Squad and EMF had both embraced the sound, and the look, which so set Jane's Addiction apart from their peers; EMF vocalist Derry even shared Perry's predilection for dreadlocks.

Perry acknowledged those bands' debt to Jane's Addiction, but it was not something he was concerned about. "The thing about being from America is that instead of being haunted by history, you can deal with the present and invent the new. Our music deals with things they just don't have in Europe, gangs and the ocean and a funky beat."

It was true. When EMF tried covering Iggy and the Stooges' "Search and Destroy," there was simply no way you could visualize them running around with hearts full of napalm. But the Red Hot Chili Peppers pulled the same song off, and Jane's, if they'd wanted it, could have done much the same.

Such comparisons could, in any case, be deferred as the final lineup for Lollapalooza began taking shape. Even though at least three of Perry's original choices, Living Colour, the Red Hot Chili Peppers, and Nick Cave, all turned him down, still it represented a blistering cocktail of eclecticism that not only defied conventional concert-bill logic, it defied audience toleration levels as well.

"[We] looked to try to get younger bands, newer acts," Ted Gardner explained, blending them with some of Perry's own favorites. Siouxsie and the Banshees, the wildly experimental British band that had exploded out of punk, single-handedly pioneered goth, and was now being blamed for the late-eighties psychedelic revival, was one of the first confirmed performers; Ice-T, described by Gardner as "the definitive rap artist who's also gone heavy metal," was next.

The industrial cult band Nine Inch Nails, riding the release of their *Pretty Hate Machine* debut album; the Butthole Surfers, screaming Texas hardcore funk defiance; Henry Rollins's Rollins Band, with whom Jane's Addiction had so successfully toured the previous spring ("We asked him if he'd be interested," Gardner continued, "and he said yes") . . .

"This is a pioneering tour," Ice-T confirmed. "All the groups in their own way have pioneered a certain form of music. None of us get played on the radio; to be able to pack arena shows, that people want to hear [what we are saying]. It's also a very educational experience. Everybody's taking a pill they're not used to." They were enjoying it as well. "In twenty-one cities, 430,000 predominantly white kids waved their fists in the air and screamed 'Cop Killer' along with us."

"There was a lot of thought about mixing and making [the bands into] a multifaceted bill," Perry explained. "I wanted to integrate—racially integrate, musically integrate—and I think it's a good start." He talked of trying to maintain Lollapalooza, and its crosscultural billing, as an annual event. The success of his vision can be gauged from the fact that it would be another five years before any artist— namely, Hole's Courtney Love—raised any objection. In early

1995, before that year's Lollapalooza line-up was even confirmed, Love complained to a New York audience about being invited to appear on a bill with rappers Cypress Hill and Snoop Doggy Dogg, "presumably," *Rolling Stone* ruminated, "because of their lyrical associations with misogyny." Perry was furious. "As far as I'm concerned," he told that same magazine, Hole was now out of the running.

As the July 18, 1991, launch date for Lollapalooza grew closer, there was one question that industry observers could not help but ask. Was this the right time to be launching such an ambitious project?

The recession that had been cutting swathes through America since the mid-1980s, gnawing at the music industry's profit margins, finally hit rock 'n' roll hard in 1991. Record sales plunged more than 10 percent on the previous year's already disappointing figures, while touring revenues fell by an even more terrifying 25 percent, and that was the conservative estimate. Some reports put the shortfall as high as 35 percent.

Guns N' Roses and George Michael were among the headline acts left counting empty seats when they toured that summer, empty seats that simply could not justify the million dollars–plus the latter tours, at least, cost to mount. David Lee Roth and Whitney Houston joined the growing ranks of artists who canceled projected tours altogether once they got a look at the sales figures.

In Florida, the influential Cellar Door Concerts promoters stripped their larger presentations down to the bone. In 1990 they staged sixteen stadium concerts. The following year they didn't put on any.

Neither was the multi-act nature of Lollapalooza a contributing factor in the venture's ultimate success. Several other, similarly esoteric, packages also set out during the 1990–91 concert season, at least one of which, featuring the Sisters of Mercy and rappers Public Enemy, scarcely even made it across the Rocky Mountains before calling it a day.

The metal-oriented Operation Rock 'n' Roll, combining Judas Priest, Alice Cooper, Motorhead, Dangerous Toys, and Metal Church, also fared poorly.

Lollapalooza succeeded because it was envisioned, marketed, and sold as an event. The new audiences were wary of being marketed to. Talking to *Music Express* magazine, one promoter, Louis Messina of the Texas-based Pace Concerts, admitted as much when he said, "We need to make the concert the experience it once was. For many years, the music business has been on automatic pilot, and we're shoving crap down the fans' throats. Until people like myself start making the fans the priority, and really knowing what they want and seeing the different changes, and being price-sensitive and artist-sensitive, and until we get the feel, the spirit of the music back into the business—not the business into the music—it's going to be an awakening for a few more people."

Perry agreed. "There are a lot of people that want to make a dollar and are willing to work very hard for it. If you just keep giving the kids the same thing they have, and keep working on the same old formulas, it's going to get boring." He personally didn't even go out to gigs very often anymore. "You go to a concert and it's the same fucking thing all the time. There are no surprises. What are you giving people? You are trying to entertain them, but are you giving them anything any different?"

Lollapalooza was launched with all those factors in mind, and as journalist Tina Clarke stated, "It was one of the most successful tours of the year." Perry himself bellowed at the end of one performance, looking out over the audience that undulated in frenzied waves toward the stage, "This is it, homeboys, youth revolution!"

"[Lollapalooza] got a better reaction than we anticipated," Don Muller continues. "Chicago sold thirty-two thousand tickets; we sold out in Detroit in a matter of minutes."

In fact, with a gross of close to $8.5 million, it came in as the twenty-fifth most profitable outing of the year,

a statistic that left nobody in any doubt that if the venues were larger, the billing could have filled them. Even though the Lollapalooza organization had already anticipated the public demand for tickets, insisting that no venue hold less than ten thousand people, while some were as large as thirty thousand, the response when tickets went on sale was overwhelming.

Of the eighteen shows, only eight failed to sell out completely, a success rate that could scarcely be bettered even by the giants of the concert circuit.

As Lollapalooza gathered headlines, however, the biggest story switched from the ever-profitable weight of talent and diversity that Perry attracted to the bill to a whole newly disclosed "purpose" to the tour. At long last, after over a year of increasingly unsubtle hints and threats, Perry had finally resolved one of the longest-running cliffhangers in American rock. Lollapalooza would become Jane's Addiction's gravestone.

"I was miserable," Perry remarked later. "We didn't get along. It had run its course. I heard laziness." The band had fulfilled its side of their Warner Brothers contract, delivered two albums, and as for the option—well, it was only optional, wasn't it?

"Just playing with Jane's forever would be like listening to the same radio station for t`e rest of my life," Perry commented. "My intention was never for us to just keep getting bigger and bigger, anyway. What people have to expect from me is not to expect anything." He applied that same logic to Lollapalooza, he said, and to life itself.

Lollapalooza, and with it, Jane's Addiction's fiery career, officially ended on August 28, 1991, amidst a blistering mind-fuck performance that blasted from the King County fairgrounds in Enumclaw, Washington, straight into the heart of nearby Seattle. Exactly four weeks later, an unknown local cult band named Nirvana would release its own second album, *Nevermind*. A record-company spokesman proudly predicted that if the group worked hard, they might sell as many as 250,000 copies.

* * *

From the stalls, it really did look as though he was masturbating. Perry had stripped his clothes off a song or so before, and if his mere nakedness did not catch the imagination, the dancing that accompanied it did. But it was the moment when he took himself in hand, so to speak, that broke the camel's back.

"He only touched himself for a second. . . ." "He did dance naked, but he did not masturbate. . . ." "He wasn't masturbating. . . ." Even with Perry's onstage activities now spattered over the following morning's local press, there yawned a very genuine divide between what the audience saw and what certain members of the audience *thought* they saw.

The ROCKER'S NUDE PRANCE–type headlines that engulfed the Honolulu press for days after the event were to be expected. The evening in question had already gotten off to a surreal-enough start. How fitting that it, and indeed, the band that made it possible, should end in a similarly bizarre fashion.

The queues outside Honolulu's Aloha Towers were excited, but skeptical. Jane's Addiction had been booked to play here before, back in the early summer. They pulled out, the ubiquitous official spokesman said, through "sheer fatigue," and then, observed the local *Star Bulletin*'s John Berger, "took off on . . . Lollapalooza."

Since then, the story only grew stranger. The group had broken up, that was certain. Of course there had still not been any official announcement to that effect, but that, Perry himself admitted, was only because he'd not officially told anyone yet—anyone, that is, aside from the constant stream of journalists who actually bothered to ask him if it was true.

So the rescheduled Hawaiian shows were just that, rescheduled contractual obligations that didn't affect the band's status one way or another. Another forty-eight hours and—who knows? The shroud of secretive exaggeration that was Jane's Addiction's stock in trade pretty much since its inception descended once more, but this time it slammed into place with a vengeance.

Perry's future was always up in the air, changing with the weather, or at least with the temperament. He talked of abandoning music once and for all, throwing himself into movies or travel. There was a whole world out there that he had only seen through the glass of a tour-bus window. He wanted to travel, he wanted to paint, he wanted to do a thousand and one things, and most people believed that he would.

On the other side of Los Angeles, musically if not literally, Guns N' Roses was on the edge of destruction. Alcohol and drugs, the very same elements that so cemented their place in the mythos of eighties rock 'n' roll, now appeared to be the ones that would send them reeling to oblivion.

Who was keeping score anymore, anyway? Guns N' Roses was huge, bigger than Jane's Addiction, bigger than the Cult, almost as big as the Stones, for chrissakes. If they couldn't look after themselves, who could?

For the members of Guns N' Roses, every night was a party, like being a kid in a candy store.

One kid, though, was fed up with the candy. "After this tour's over . . ." Guitarist Izzy Stradlin spoke quietly, almost meditatively. "I'd like to go hang out in Europe, preferably somewhere near the ocean, and keep writing songs." Two months later, he quit the group.

The grapevine was buzzing with possible replacements: someone the rest of the band knew . . . someone who could play with the same brain-crushing power . . . a proven musician . . .

The guys in Guns N' Roses, though, they did consider their options, and when they realized just how limited those options were, when everyone else realized the same thing as well . . . well, it *had* to be Dave Navarro, didn't it?

Dave kept his head down and his mouth shut. Even when Axl Rose acknowledged that Dave was at the top of Guns N' Roses' shopping list, Dave preferred to keep his own counsel. But tonight in Hawaii, even rumor could swiftly be expounded into fact, and for everyone on line who hoped that it would never happen, there were two others who were not only convinced that it would, and were busy passing on the latest bit of street gossip—that Navarro had already joined Guns N' Roses, and would be bringing his new friends out for the encore tonight.

Assuming anybody actually got into the show, that is. Trusting Jane's Addiction's original pledge that the canceled shows would be rescheduled, a lot of people simply hung on to their unused tickets and presented them on the door. That, after all, was what they'd been instructed to do.

The earlier tickets were only valid for one of the two shows—tomorrow's. And you didn't find that out till you'd stood in line for forty-five minutes or longer.

Security was tight. The promoters, Goldenvoice, had foregone the usual route of hiring private security teams in favor of recruiting off-duty members of the local police department. The first anyone knew of that, of course, was when they entered the theater and received an even more rigorous than usual pat-down. Empty your pockets, take off your hat, the works. Which was bad enough in itself, but it didn't get any better inside, as journalist Chris Alpern reported, because that was when the cops started getting restless.

"One drunk guy made the mistake of accidentally bumping into one of the bored cops. The cop chased and tackled him, eventually pushing his face into the parking lot." Another reason, Alpern remarked, why promoters should hire from the private sector. "That way, at least we can sue them after they beat people for no reason."

Those were the abiding memories of the first show. As for the second, that headline from the *Advertiser* probably summed it up best: "Rocker's nude prance gets mixed reaction."

Interestingly, the story was not generated locally. Rather, the claim that Perry "'masturbated and pranced' in the raw midway through the show" was pulled off the Associated Press wire service. But immediately the *Advertiser*'s telephones were ringing red-hot as "angry parents" called to demand how the state officials who operated the Aloha Tower could ever have permitted that to happen. What about the police on duty that night?

The concern promoters, Matthew and Michael Grim, immediately leaped to the defensive. Acknowledging that the majority of the police were stationed around the bar area, and would not, therefore, have been in a position to witness the actual performance, Matthew Grim did admit that he was surprised to see Perry remove his clothes. "I did see him nude onstage," he told the *Advertiser*, "and that was somewhat shocking. It actually didn't seem lewd, it almost fit the show. He wasn't doing it in terms of being naked and talking sexually—this was the band's last show ever, and it was more like he was giving everything he had. Even his clothes."

As for the possibility that the Grims were aware beforehand that Perry was planning something of this nature, Matthew was adamant, as he told the *Advertiser*, that nothing could have been further from his mind. His own mother was at the show—she came along to see him play in his own band, booked to open for Jane's Addiction at that night's performance.

"And what's the name of your band?" the *Advertiser* asked.

Grim must have wished the earth could have swallowed him up as he answered that question. "Naked Angel."

Yet somehow there could have been no more appropriate an epithet for Jane's Addiction. Perry himself certainly couldn't think of one. He admitted as much as Jane's Addiction launched into the last encore of their last-ever show. "Well, this is the end. We don't have a statement or anything. Just keep rocking."

A few days later, Heidi Robinson, Jane's Addiction's publicist, confirmed that the group was taking an indefinite sabbatical, a break "that could last three months, six months, a year or forever."

Interviewing Perry some eighteen months later, *Rolling Stone* made one final, valiant stab at unearthing the reasons for the breakup. "Can I ask," ventured journalist Kim Neely, "how much of the problem was due to . . ."

"Drugs?" Perry asked.

"Yeah."

"Sure you can ask," he replied. "But I'm not gonna tell ya."

Woodstock Isn't a Bad Word

Perry had seemingly left the headlines, but the headlines wouldn't leave him. Less than three weeks after the Honolulu show, he was arrested at the Holiday Inn in Santa Monica by police officers responding to a call from the hotel staff.

According to the local press, "Hotel officials refused to divulge the circumstances which led to the arrest on investigation of misdemeanor charges." But Sergeant Robert Oliver confirmed that Perry had been arrested on suspicion of being under the influence of drugs and granted one thousand dollars' bail.

Perry remained silent, but he was reeling inside. The drug bust was beneath contempt; in fact, no charges were ever brought.

"It was time to dump the money-making machine," he told people. He found that the more successful he became, the less opportunity there was to experiment with what he called "the darker side of life . . . Let Madonna *really* play with her pussy onstage." And that, he insisted, was *it*. "Case closed."

The case wasn't closed, and Perry, no matter how much he might have wanted it, would never be able to simply drop out of sight and paint, or travel, or indulge in any of the idle daydreams he once spoke of.

Lollapalooza did more than rejuvenate the concert circuit, earned more than what Perry himself confessed were "incredibly nice" comparisons with Woodstock. It also thrust Perry into a whole new limelight, characterized, at year's end, by both *Spin* and *Rolling Stone* acclaiming him as the Artist of the Year for 1991. More accolades flooded in for *Ritual de lo Habitual,* and there was another invitation from the Grammy committee, who nominated "Been Caught Stealing" in the Best Rock Song category. The competition included Sting, Bryan Adams, and Metallica. Perry turned them all down.

Rolling Stone asked him to appear on their cover. Perry refused. "I know the only reason they put people on their covers is to sell magazines. It's not because they value people's work. I mean, they put stupid "Beverly Hills 90210" people on their covers. Why would I want to be seen in that context?" Warner Brothers came to him with their plan to release a live Jane's Addiction album. Perry slammed the door in their faces. "I don't want to hear about it."

When he and Casey broke up, there were no outpourings of grief. Their relationship had run its course, now the courts could sort through the debris. Like Perry himself admitted, he and Casey would simply be "happy to God to never see each other again as long as we lived." Perry would end up paying out $75,000 in palimony, but at least, he smiled wanly, he wouldn't have to hear her describing him as her husband anymore.

He had a new girlfriend, a beautiful Asian named Kim Leung; a new family as well, as he moved into the Venice home he'd only just had built with Kim and her two-year-old son, Donovan. The fans who tracked him down there and knocked on the door told their friends that she was lovely. "But we didn't catch a glimpse of Perry."

Very few people did as the fall of 1991 rolled into the new year of '92. Trading in his old pickup truck for a dark green Lexus, "very sexy and great for long freeway driving," Perry would sometimes show up on the beach, sometimes turn up at a club. But most of all, it seemed, he stayed at home, the head of a unit that *Spin* quickly christened "the image of a sweet hipster family, postmodern 20th-century fairy-tale groove kids."

The handful of visitors he did entertain were musicians. Peter DiStefano dropped by a lot, and Stephen Perkins, the only member of Jane's Addiction the press didn't portray Perry as being at constant, bitter loggerheads with. They jammed together, messed around with new songs, and talked.

Perkins had only just got back from a side show of his own, touring with Mike Muir of Suicidal Tendencies in a new band, Infectious Grooves. In a way, it was an exorcism for him, a chance to simply kick back with some white-hot metal, and let other bands bathe in the pressure. Infectious Grooves only did one tour, opening for arch "bat-biter" Ozzy Osbourne on what was widely billed as the headliner's last tour. A lot of people probably didn't even notice the opening act.

The three-piece unit of Perry, Perkins, and DiStefano maintained an air of obscurity. Away from the prying eyes that they knew would automatically be focused upon whatever Perry did next, they had gelled instantaneously. Christmas out of the way, they were already talking about forming a band, and thinking they'd already got one. All they needed now was a bass player.

Surreptitiously, the word went around, but the handful of mock auditions the trio staged turned up little of any real interest and nothing whatsoever of use. Finally, Di-Stefano suggested that maybe he ought to call up one of his own friends. The others agreed. There was nothing to lose except the plane fare. The friend was over in Holland.

DiStefano had met Dutch-born Martyn Le Noble in a Los Angeles club. Le Noble was playing with Thelonious Monster at the time, and when he walked in "with a gorgeous girl" on his arm, DiStefano hurried over to introduce himself.

"I asked him who she was—'my wife,' he said. 'That sucks,' I said. Then I asked him what he did. All I knew was that I wanted whatever he had." When Le Noble smiled, you saw that one of his front teeth was missing, and DiStefano almost knocked his own teeth out that evening, "because Martyn looked so cool."

DiStefano called Le Noble in Holland, and they fine-tuned his return arrangements as best as they could. His passage into the new band was not going to be easy.

The morning of his audition, Le Noble was evicted from the apartment he'd only just moved into. When he left for the rehearsal his car broke down. Grabbing his instrument and completing the journey on foot, Le Noble wondered why he was even bothering. He'd barely finished his first cup of coffee of the day and already his world was falling apart. Maybe he should just turn around and leave. He simply didn't need any more headaches.

"But when we started playing, I knew."

So did Ted Gardner when he first heard the band. "You're going to know it's Perry Farrell because of the voice and the lyrics," he acknowledged. "But musically, it's totally different."

Perry recruited a local Venice Beach hip hop performer and turntable artist, Skatemaster Tate, to add to the proceedings. He began talking about a stage show that would make the wildest multimedia fantasy appear tame by comparison. Musically, if you could imagine a combination of Astrud Gilberto, Bad Brains, Duke Ellington, and Adrian Sherwood, then you might come up with what he envisioned it sounding like, a stew that *Rolling Stone* eventually christened a "new modal grunge–Middle Eastern hybrid."

Porno for Pyros had been born.

When he read that, Perry shrugged. They could call it whatever they wanted. "Porno sounds a little like Jane's, but I think we've stepped it up." Even if they hadn't, he didn't, he laughed, "give a hoot." All that mattered was that the group wasn't targeted "at some schmuck who's walking Melrose on Saturday."

The band's sound would incorporate everything. There would be samples, Gardner continued, "though not to the point of noticing it's been ripped off," scratching ("It's very rhythmical, very melodic.), maybe a female singer, and it was very strong music to fuck to. That was what everyone who heard the stuff said, whether it was leeching through the walls of the band's rehearsal space on Venice Beach, or on the three-song demo that Porno for Pyros hammered out one afternoon. It was a sound, Gardner continued, that was "very much in Perry's heart going way back. It was just a matter of putting the musicians together."

It was an explosive combination, and of course Perry came up with a name to match. While the group's members were flicking through a pornographic magazine one afternoon, a flyer flapped out from the pages. It advertised fireworks, and for a moment he was baffled. Fireworks for flagellation fanatics? Pornography for pyromaniacs? He called his bandmates that evening. "We don't need worry about a band name anymore." By the end of March 1992, everything was in place.

Porno for Pyros would be making their debut on April 4 at a Hollywood Palladium benefit for the Earvin "Magic" Johnson AIDS foundation.

Since his own brush with AIDS, Perry admitted that his own sexual habits had been reined in considerably. He admitted he was like a hyperactive high school student in terms of promiscuity, but that now he always carried a condom.

The bill for the Magic Johnson benefit was incredible, as impressive as any Lollapalooza. Fishbone, the Rollins Band, Primus, and the Beastie Boys were all scheduled to play, together with the Red Hot Chili Peppers—raving Johnson acolytes who had even titled a song after the athlete on their breakthrough *Mother's Milk* album.

But all eyes tonight were on Perry Farrell, even the Red Hot Chili Peppers. "Porno for Pyros was beautiful, man," Flea enthused afterward. "It was a great night of music."

Porno for Pyros themselves were less happy with their debut. "The expectations of the world, yeah, I feel it in my stomach," mused DiStefano. "People have high expectations. Our first show, it's like everybody's already there checking us out. We wanted to feel what it was like to party and have a good time and be a little loose." Instead, they were reviewed by *Rolling Stone*.

"*Rolling Stone* shouldn't have been there," Perry agreed. So far as he and the rest of the group were concerned, they did "pretty good for being together for two months." The party was over now, the cat was out of the bag. He knew that Porno for Pyros was not going to be allowed any period of natural growth. In their own minds, they were a new band. To the media, however, if not Jane's Addiction Revisited, Porno for Pyros at least was Jane's Addiction II, a sequel to a blockbuster, and people couldn't wait for it.

"It's really hard to come back and do it again," Perry mused. "People tend to judge you against your past. . . . Are the players better? Is the music better? If the public turned around and said, 'Eh?' Warner Brothers would bail on us like that!"

As it was, the label had no hesitation about re-signing Perry with or without Jane's Addiction. They didn't even know what he was planning when they did so, but "Hey, it's Perry Farrell! How bad can it be?"

Porno for Pyros' live set was short. Insistent that he would not be raking over the coals of past glories, Perry refused to include any Jane's Addiction material in his new band's live repertoire, not even as audience-pleasing encores at the conclusion of a very well-received performance.

"I don't want to be like Chuck Berry," Perry averred, "doing the duckwalk across the stage singing 'Maybelline,' just because some fucking eighteen-year-old jerk never got to see him do it. To me it's like, 'Well, you never got to see me do it? Too bad, look at a film. Let me get on to something else. I'm bored.'"

New material, too, was still hard to come by. "Orgasm," the first song he and Peter ever wrote together, was there, and enough other tracks to at least fill out a forty-minute set. If Perry was suffering from a dearth of new material, that situation would swiftly change.

It has since become part of the Porno for Pyros mythology—how the group's name was unveiled just days before Los Angeles erupted in flames, following the April 29, 1992, acquittal of the four white police officers who were videotaped savagely beating a black motorist, Rodney King. In actual fact, close to a month elapsed between the two events, but still there was a serendipity about even this weak coincidence and one that, even as the neighborhoods burned, Perry was not going to pass over.

Porno for Pyros was in Crystal Studios when the fighting broke out. Perry had recruited Matt Hyde, who had already overseen the soundtrack recordings on *Gift*, to produce the group's debut album, but all talk of the project trailed off as word spread about the eruption on the streets outside.

The situation only worsened as the afternoon turned into night and the violence started spilling all across the city—all across the United States, in fact. For a while there, even Perry admitted, "It got kinda scary." The police were nowhere in sight; only the media remained on the streets, and the scenes they witnessed, but never even tried to prevent, underlined their impotence. Perry remembers, "We were like, 'Man, I kinda like wanna go back out on the street without thinking someone's gonna shoot me. I wanna go to a club, y'know?' We were a little tired of this."

The self-imposed imprisonment was unbearable. The television was on, but someone had turned the volume down long ago. You could hear, and smell, the destruction easily enough already. Finally, Perry had had enough. "Well, I'm going out there. It might even be fun."

"It was not a fearful riot," he said later. The first night of unchanneled violence was over, and with it the horrific images of random beatings and assaults that were fed out of a transfixed nation's television sets. Now Los Angeles was a looter's paradise, as crowds simply assembled and dispersed at will, converging upon the defenseless stores in which they had shopped all their lives, simply taking the goods they once would have bought. "Pregnant mothers were stealing diapers," Perry marveled, "their three-year-olds walking beside them with a six-pack for Dad. It was real basic, very humble. Adorable."

But it was also opportunistic. Joining in with one of the looting mobs, Perry bragged that he himself got a set of huge bronze peacocks. Other people, just as well off as he was, made away with hi-fi equipment, televisions, anything that they could possibly carry. The law simply stood by and watched, powerless to intervene as entire neighborhoods were systematically denuded. The National Guard, armed but without ammunition, joined them on the sidelines. It would be three days, and three nights as bright as day, before Los Angeles Police Department chief Daryl Gates could confidently predict that his men were regaining control of the streets, many months more before the besieged city returned to normal.

Throughout the fighting, Perry wrote constantly; wrote, and the song "Porno for Pyros" describes masturbating in the "fire and smoke." The riots, he laughed now, "They were damn sexy, weren't they? The excitement—I mean, let's face it, you can get a boner if someone slaps you in the face. Nine times out of ten."

The song "Black Girlfriend," too, took its inspiration from the carnage as Perry intoned, too solemnly for many people, that "ever since the riots," all he'd "ever wanted was a black girl." And you could make of that what you would.

The final details of the second Lollapalooza tour were unveiled around the same time as Porno for Pyros emerged, in late March 1992. Once again, Perry insisted, "I wanted to try to find diversity in the lineup, as far as what each band was best at and what they represent in the musical field. You can't always get your exact dreams, but there are always a few that are the top of what they're doing, and these bands represent that."

Don Muller expounded on his thinking. Planning for the tour actually commenced as early as October 1991, the moment Perry returned from Hawaii, and quickly the organizers drew up a not particularly short list of seventy bands that might work the main stage, everyone from R.E.M. and Neil Young on down. It was then simply a matter of whittling it down to seven.

214

The first bands to be confirmed were two with whom Perry had already established personal relations. Lush was a British group that had opened a handful of shows on Jane's Addiction's 1991 U.S. tour. "Music to soothe the savage beast" was how Perry described their soft, guitar-led meanderings.

The Red Hot Chili Peppers, of course, were old friends. Perry had invited the Red Hot Chili Peppers to perform on the original Lollapalooza; they turned him down because, with their own new album, *Bloodsugarsexmagik*, imminent, they wanted to preserve their energies for their own headlining tour. Still, they had watched Lollapalooza's progress with interest, with vocalist Anthony Kiedis now admitting, "If I didn't get off on it so heavily last year, I wouldn't have been so inclined to be part of it this year." If his band hadn't been signed with the Triad agency, they may not have been given the opportunity.

Accusations that Triad jealously dominated its stake in Lollapalooza were not new. Perry himself invited the Rollins Band onto the 1991 tour, but according to Rollins himself, their inclusion was not confirmed until the group itself signed with Triad.

This year, Perry wanted to include the Ramones, the hard-hitting New York punk quartet that was now, unbelievably, racing toward its twentieth birthday. According to singer Joey Ramone, though, Triad nixed their inclusion, too. The Ramones, after all, weren't one of their acts, and weren't about to become one, either. "A lot of what Lollapalooza is," Joey complained, "is a real political situation."

This impression was hammered home ever further later in the year, when Anthony Kiedis added his voice to the media chorus that insisted that Lollapalooza was "way too male," and "way too guitar-oriented." Kiedis's own attempts to at least partially redress the balance by having the all-girl band L7 inserted into the lineup came to naught, however, when he contacted Triad and was brushed away brusquely.

"L7? They don't mean anything."

"What do you mean?" Kiedis shot back incredulously. "They rock, and they're girls."

Frustrated, Kiedis tried to contact Perry directly, "and they wouldn't even give me his phone number." Instead, Kiedis was told to fax Farrell in care of Triad. "It was kind of upsetting to me," he murmured. Like the Ramones, L7, it might be noted, were not represented by Triad.

Marc Geiger tried to defuse the controversy. "We knew that Anthony wanted L7," he acknowledged, "but Perry wanted Lush. So what do you do?"

It remained a tense situation. How, people argued, could Lollapalooza begin to claim that it was opening the music industry up from the inside, when it was still controlled from such a narrow angle?

It didn't even seem important that this particular argument overlooked perhaps the one essential determining factor in Lollapalooza's success. The fewer conflicting interests that are involved, the easier it is to hold the whole thing together, and that was as true for booking agencies as it was for record companies, and even musical genres. The basic categories into which the 1991 and 1992 Lollapalooza performers fell—industrial, rap, punk, post-goth, and straightforward, guitar-based "alternative"—have remained constant ever since. So has the dominance of one booking agency's clients. In 1992, four of the final seven bands—Lush, the Red Hot Chili Peppers, and the Seattle pairing of Pearl Jam and Soundgarden—were represented by Triad.

After the pioneering hyperbole of the original Lollapalooza, the organizers admit that there was considerable pressure on them this time around to maintain the same standards, both of musical variety and commercial feasibility.

"We kind of watched records and knew when records were coming out," Don Muller says. "We knew Ministry had a new record coming out [*Psalm 69: The Way to Succeed and the Way to Suck Eggs*], we knew the Chili Peppers were the obvious choice to headline, and I had kind of a hunch that Pearl Jam might come on." The Seattle hard-rock band was, in fact, readying itself for a tour with the Red Hot Chili Peppers when the invitation arrived on manager Kelly Curtis's desk.

Muller continues, "Soundgarden is a very important band for the genre of music they play; they kind of cross the alternative, harder edge. We thought Ice Cube, with the riots and prior to that, was an important figure who needed to be seen. A lot of white kids don't go to his shows, they're afraid. So we thought it was important to get him out and let him be seen by the people who are probably buying his albums.

"The hard thing was trying to see the future and see if those bands would be happening by the time this thing hit the road."

In almost every case, the intuition was correct. By the time the tour kicked off, Pearl Jam's *Ten*, the Red Hot Chili Peppers' *Bloodsugarsexmagik*, and Soundgarden's *Badmotorfinger* had each certified gold, while Ice Cube's latest had gone platinum. And while it was true that the lineup this time around was nowhere near as esoteric as the first year's, was certainly geared more toward the "successful" side of the alternative marketplace, still it was a powerful alliance. It was also an uneasy one, particularly where the two top-billed bands, Ministry and the Red Hot Chili Peppers, were concerned.

"I didn't want to be part of this whole picnic-circus," growled Ministry frontman Al Jourgensen. "But this band really is a democracy, despite what people may think, [and] basically I was outvoted within the band, within management, within everyone else." Howie Klein, of Ministry's label, Sire, agreed. "It took me weeks to convince [him] that it was the right thing to do."

The problems with the Red Hot Chili Peppers went somewhat deeper than reluctance. In May, midway through a packed-out tour of Japan, the band was shaken when, completely out of the blue, guitarist John Frusciante quit. He'd endured enough of the madness, he said, the madness that was inevitable when you are suddenly catapulted out of total obscurity and into one of the wildest bands of the era.

For a moment, the Red Hot Chili Peppers were stymied. Their initial dream of replacing the errant Frusciante with Thelonious Monster's Zander Schloss fell apart before the group even reached Los Angeles again. Once there, however, the solution was simple: Dave Navarro.

Having turned down Guns N' Roses, Navarro had been hanging quietly since the demise of Jane's Addiction, working with Eric Avery on their own Deconstruction project. From the outside, there really didn't seem to be much happening. But when Kiedis called, Navarro turned him down flat, and not, speculated *Melody Maker*, for musical reasons.

Relations, the paper continued, were "reportedly . . . frosty" between Navarro and Perry. With the Peppers' Lollapalooza engagement less than a month away, Navarro was wary of accepting any job that might bring him into the orbit of his old vocalist.

Perry's involvement with Lollapalooza II was peripheral, to say the least. Hopes that he might debut Porno for Pyros to the rest of America via the traveling festival were dashed when Ted Gardner announced that this time the singer would be expending most of his energies on the nonmusical aspects of the tour.

"Sting will look after the rainforests," Gardner quipped, "U2 will look after Greenpeace. Our [concern] is to look after local issues, specifically runaway kids and the homeless, as well as things like handgun control and the beauties of body-piercing."

They certainly gathered the right people around them for that. Among the headlined offstage attractions was the Jim Rose Circus Sideshow, a Seattle-based aggregation of aggressive carnival-freak turns whose self-torturing specialties ranged from swallowing swords to suspending heavy weights off their own nipples.

Perry said he got off on stuff like that, admitting that he boasted "several" piercings of his own, far beyond the nose ring he still sported offstage, if not on. He said he had to stop wearing it because kids at concerts kept trying to pull it out. "I guess they thought, 'Hey, it might hurt him a little, but I would have it forever.'" Now he was talking of having his penis pierced, and smiled when it was pointed out that that would really give the kids something to tug on. Either that, or he would think twice before ever repeating his Hawaiian disrobing.

Concerns that Lollapalooza was becoming too big for its own boots, then, left Perry cold. How big—read, commercial—could you be when you had something like Jim Rose on the bill?

"The Lollapalooza tour was an experiment last year," wrote the New Jersey *Star Ledger*'s Jay Lustig. "It has already become an institution." That much was true. But Perry and Ted Gardner still worked hard to maintain Lollapalooza's independence from any commercial interests.

Despite a few telltale suggestions that maybe they hadn't remained totally true to their word—the giant Bacardi bottle that turned up outside the Cleveland show, the Domino's pizza trucks that were spotted at various southern venues—

Lollapalooza certainly resisted several offers of sponsorship, including a union with the monthly magazine *Alternative Press*, the only mainstream publication in the country that not only understood, but also gave prime column inches to, the kind of music Lollapalooza was trying to popularize.

The idea was for the magazine to produce a tour program, which would be distributed free of charge to concertgoers. The stumbling block was the corporate advertising that would help fill the pages, and was the only way to guarantee that the venture broke even. *AP* demanded it, Perry resisted it, and when the deadlock couldn't be broken, the whole thing was forgotten.

"I've heard that Lollapalooza is supposedly crossing over," Perry mused when these issues were raised. "But I'm not *interested* in the mainstream. They've got Madonna, they've got Michael Jackson. I'm bored shitless with all that. I want something weird to happen!"

Appointing a Director of Oddities and Curiosities, Peter Barsotti, was one way of ensuring that; the recruitment of the Jim Rose Circus was another. So were the other sideshows that were arranged for the outing: displays of street rods and landscape art, a charity gambling tent, a cyberpunk computer technology exhibit, and a film show.

"I'm working very hard to complement the music," Perry explained, adding that there was no single element to the festival he considered more important than any other. "The politics of it all, the kick-back atmosphere, the learning aspects of it all—all of that to me is as important as the music." Responding, once again, to the comparisons between Lollapalooza and the two-decade-old spirit of Woodstock, Perry reiterated, "I don't think Woodstock is a bad word. But time marches on and things are a little different. At Woodstock, people painted each other. Now they pierce each other."

The Castaic Lake Amphitheatre held four thousand people, and as Porno for Pyros prepared for their official concert debut, on July 11, 1992, all four thousand places were taken.

It was the first rock show ever to be staged at this unique and beautiful counterpoint to the sweaty clubs of the conventional Los Angeles circuit. Five miles out from Magic Mountain, the entire scene was bathed in the kind of beautiful balmy sunshine Southern California specializes in. As Rage Against the Machine ran through their raucous opening set, the omens looked bad for the rest of the show.

Backstage, Perry was admitting once again, "We don't have many songs," almost as if he expected the brevity of Porno for Pyros' scheduled performance, a mere forty-five minutes, to unleash another of those firestorms he'd suffered in the past.

What he didn't add, the watching critics later commented, was that he didn't have many ideas, either. Replacing the flash pyrotechnics of Jane's Addiction's live performance were a couple of scantily clad females. It was no competition. Perry appeared to know it as well. Looking, said reviewer Steve Hochman, "a lot like the *Rock 'n' Roll Animal*–era Lou Reed," in his shiny black leather suit and golden hair, the singer spent much of the show wandering "lost or, worse, empty."

The reviews were merciless. According to *Rolling Stone*, both Perry and his music were "quite devoid of purpose or impact," with the only stand-out track in a setful of new material the languid semi-epic "Pets"; the only memorable quip, Perry's reminder that "this year's an election year. Don't forget to vote—but more importantly, keep on fucking."

Lollapalooza II kicked off seven days later, at the Shoreline Amphitheatre, on July 18. All Perry's newfound detractors could do was hope that the fare there would be a little more inspired.

It was. Taking the second stage very early in the afternoon, on the podium otherwise reserved exclusively for local bands who would play for no pay, Porno for Pyros ran out in front of an audience that had been expecting nothing more than Cypress Hill and Boo-Yaa Tribe.

"Before hordes of worshipful fans yelling 'Perry!',"
reported *Entertainment Weekly*, Porno for Pyros ran through
a set of "what could only be described as vaguely Middle
Eastern–influenced art rock—imagine mantras sung on a
roller coaster, with Farrell's taunting whine rubbing against
the whole shebang." Perhaps it was the nature of the performance, unexpected and thus unhindered by expectation, that
did it, but this time, Porno for Pyros pulled out all the stops,
and never put them back in again. Then, to prove that it
wasn't a fluke, they turned up again at a few other shows.
Porno for Pyros was now ready for action.

The action still wasn't ready for them. The group
completed its first album in just three weeks, so quickly,
laughed DiStefano, that "Warner Brothers didn't even know
we were recording. We handed them a record and they were
like, 'Wow . . .'" So "wow" that there wasn't even time to
schedule the album into the pre-Christmas release sheets.

It would be the following spring before *Porno for
Pyros* would see the light of day; in the meantime, the band
whiled away its time with a string of unannounced shows in
Tijuana, Hawaii, and Las Vegas, allowing themselves the
luxury of further refining their live show, and giving their fans
a chance to learn the songs from the unofficial live tapes that
suddenly lay as thick on the ground as Jane's Addiction
bootlegs were during that band's infancy.

It was during this interim that the magic began to
wear off.

Porno for Pyros was released in April 1993 and
crashed straight onto the *Billboard* charts at Number 3. The
following week, it began crashing out again. That in itself was
not unusual; it was, in fact, the way in which the charts oper-
ate in the 1990s. Just five years before, in June 1987, Mötley
Crüe created a sensation when they had an album debut at
Number 5 on the chart, the highest new entry, *Billboard* reported jubilantly, since Stevie Wonder came in at Number 4 in
1980. Since then, a combination of higher expectations and
considerably lower sales had seen this feat repeated over

and over, until even the appearance of Depeche Mode at Number 1, in their first week on the chart, was no longer worth raising eyebrows about.

Porno for Pyros itself wasted little time—just three months—in going gold; it was nevertheless debatable whether Porno for Pyros had attained that plateau. For all the acclaim that attached itself to Perry the showman, Perry the performer, and most recently, Perry the entrepreneur, he remained a marginal figure, unknown outside of the cozy confines of the "alternative" scene. He was as ripe for a whipping as anyone.

Gone was the truculent upstart who had swaggered into Warner Brothers and announced that he was going to do what he wanted. He had been replaced in the public eye by the considerably more insouciant Nirvana frontman, Kurt Cobain. Perry refused to appear on a *Rolling Stone* magazine cover, and that was a remarkable decision. But Cobain agreed, then turned up for the session in a T-shirt that insisted, CORPORATE MAGAZINES STILL SUCK, and that was not only remarkable, it also impacted upon far more people than Perry's nonappearance ever could. The most daring thing Perry had done lately was to flash a magazine photographer.

Nirvana's third album, *In Utero*, arrived bedecked in a collage of fetuses, a vision that sent their label, Geffen, scurrying toward the revised-art department even faster than the chain stores could cancel their orders. All Perry offered by way of competition was a devil in a rocket ship, blasting toward the stars, and blasting another gaping hole through his once impregnable mystique.

Perry often argued that he didn't need gimmicks, and certainly didn't need to shock people. Yet what other reason could there have been behind the announcement, several months in advance of *Porno for Pyros* itself, that one of the key elements in the album jacket's design would be a Yantra, an ancient Indian symbol that innocently combines the Jewish Star of David with a swastika? When it didn't appear, where was Perry's explanation? In the absence of both, it was only inevitable that people would draw their own conclusions.

There is no denying that the appearance of the Yantra on the sleeve of what would certainly be a high-profile album release would set a whole new cauldron of controversy bubbling, and the fact that both Perry and Warner's chairman Mo Ostin were Jewish would not quell the protests of an American Jewish lobby that was at least as powerful, and certainly as influential, as the police.

Even before the controversy was given the chance to get under way, the former *Melody Maker* journalist Ted Mico, now working as Perry's publicist, was angling to limit its potential damage. . . . What damage? The Yantra was already gone. It wasn't meant to be a Star of David with a swastika, but it could have been perceived that way. So when "various people saw it and said 'Oh!'" Perry "changed his mind."

"Oh!"? Perry had stood his ground against tougher condemnations than that in the past.

His sensitivity over the issue nevertheless won him some friends. The associate dean at the Simon Wiesenthal Center for Holocaust Studies, Rabbi Abraham Cooper, spoke for many people when he told the *L.A. Times*, "He's right to do this [change the artwork], if for no other reason than to spare Holocaust survivors some pain. In the music industry, you don't want young neo-Nazis picking up the album and looking at that symbol. . . ."

But what replaced the Yantra? Only the most harmless sleeve that could be imagined. Even the grinning devil who rode the spaceship into the skies, and whose image was adopted as Porno for Pyros' own icon, looked somehow playful, impish in the most childlike fashion.

Even more critical, it was legend alone that insisted that when Perry finally finished the sculpture, after two months of work, his attempts to launch the little rocket into space ended with him setting his house on fire, with just three photographs to show for his efforts. That scene, too, had already been played out, in the *Soul Kiss* video six years before, when Perry let off fireworks in his and Casey's bedroom.

As the album's reviews rolled in, so had the critics' patience. "There isn't a single reason this album deserves any press," *Alternative Press* condemned, "except for Farrell's celebrity status. If this is the extent of his invention and effort, then a lot of people have been duped." Even more condemnatory, however, was the observation that "if it seems more than ever that the art follows the money, you are beginning to see the visions of St. Perry."

On April 23, 1993, Porno for Pyros previewed its forthcoming first full American tour by headlining the first night of Phoenix radio station KUKQ's birthday bash at the local Compton Terrace.

It was a tentative evening. On a bill that almost out-Lollapalooza'ed Lollapalooza in terms of diversity—Porno for Pyros sharing a stage with Robyn Hitchcock, the Tragically Hip, and Rage Against the Machine—the local *Tribune* could complain only that "the band we were most anxious to see, Porno for Pyros, suffered from dull, uninspired material" and, although their performance was "tight and lively," uninspired hijinks as well.

When Porno for Pyros took the stage, both Best Kissers in the World and the Phunk Junkeez had displayed their bare behinds to the audience. "The very drunk Farrell . . . only showed us part of his." The rest of the stage was taken up with the clowns and jugglers whom Perry had recruited to the live show.

Perry continued to attract tired glances when *Gift* was finally released to home video in August 1993. The film was two years in the making, and people had long grown accustomed to its release being "imminent."

Perry had talked not only of full-scale theater releases, but also of select festival screenings and so on; as it was, *Gift* hit video a full month before its theater debut (at the annual CMJ conference in New York in September).

Previews of an album that, at the time of the filming, was still to be released; the study of a relationship that, again at the time, appeared to have an eternity ahead of it—

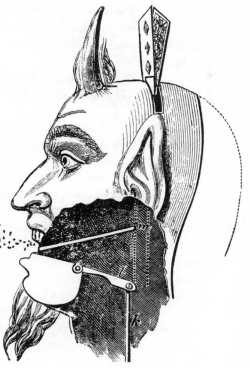

stirrup leotard
leggings scoop-neck
bodysuit unitard
muscle tights
half-zip ribbed

they would have been wonderful in 1991. By 1993, unfortunately, *Gift*'s intended symbolism was so warped by time that even its most twisted ironies were somehow shallow, even irrelevant.

The *L.A. Times* was especially flippant: "Drugs, sadomasochism, pizza delivery, necrophilia, drug rehab, old ladies from Bakersfield . . . welcome to the world of Jane's Addiction."

Balanced against such caustic irreverence, the best responses to *Gift* appeared in the mainstream press, beginning with the *L.A. Daily News*'s cute, if misleading, description of the video as "a shoot 'em up in the *Sid and Nancy* vein," and on to the *New York Post*'s insistence that "it's *Hard Day's Night* on smack."

Gift was neither, although read in the light of another of the *Post*'s comments, that "parents should not let their kids see this film, because . . . it glorifies narcotics," both assumptions are at least understandable, because those movies, too, were perceived (if not promoted) as portraying real life. People once truly believed that the Beatles lived in one long four-doored house! They also believed that the moon was made of cream cheese.

Very little about *Gift*'s depiction of a junkie's life can be considered glamorous or glorious, least of all Casey's mock death, or, before that, the livid bruises that can be glimpsed on her arms and legs, the scars of her needle chasing the last uncollapsed veins. Yet Perry's popularity, and the fact that he, too, is depicted using drugs, weighed heavily against that condemnation.

It was the same old dilemma, the notion that what a pop star does, a pop star *is*, a conundrum that was only emphasized by the public confusion Perry sowed regarding the status of his "marriage," the apparent documentary stance adopted elsewhere in the film, and, of course, the use of his, Casey's and the band's real names.

They Never
Ask How
Big My
Dick Is

T he Porno for Pyros tour opened on May 28, 1993, on a deeply tragic note. Stephen Perkins's brother had died just days before, and many people expected a whole string of shows to be called off. Instead, Perkins bravely agreed to play on. Porno for Pyros' second night at San Francisco's Warfield Theatre was canceled so that he could attend the funeral, but the first went ahead as scheduled.

It was not a good show. Even allowing for Perkins's emotions, much of what Jane's Addiction once stood for seemed to have escaped through the window, visually if not musically. The strengths of *Porno for Pyros*, the sheer inventiveness of its finest moments, were simply swamped onstage, lost amidst the gyrating dancers who had joined

Porno for Pyros onstage at previous shows, but were back in far greater quantities. "J.A. liked to fool around with dancers and props," condemned the Hayward *Sunday Review*'s Dave Becker after the San Francisco show, but their presentations were nothing whatsoever like "the overblown presentation Farrell choked the stage with."

Within the warm intimacy of one of America's most accommodating old-style theaters, ballerinas bounced and go-go dancers writhed. "Janet Louise," introduced by a carnival barker–style Perry as "the only six-foot-two hermaphrodite with a twelve-inch penis," sprayed the audience with a giant dildo during "Cursed Male," and two girls tried to out-Madonna Madonna with a simulated lesbian sex scene while the band rocketed through "Cursed Female."

A fire eater then emerged for "Porno for Pyros," a gymnast cavorted through "Meija," there was an outbreak of body-piercing through "Blood Rag," and to round off an evening of exhilarating visual carnage, a clown emerged to attempt what Becker could only describe as "some kind of symbolism during 'Packin' .25.' There was even a high-wire act to complete the circus-like atmosphere."

But this wasn't a circus. Such visual hooks may have been effective for a song or two, but their use throughout the performance simply added up to overkill and accusations. Add to that Perry's own refusal to speak to the crowd, his silent disdain for the cries for Jane's Addiction material, and that constant bane of his career, complaints over yet another short show, and Dave Becker readily concluded, "In the end, Farrell may have pulled off more of a performance-art routine than even he intended—ritual commercial suicide before a large crowd."

The singer still had to make a silent, beaming curtain call before the audience would finally vacate the theater, so chalk up one for Porno for Pyros regardless. The audience loved them even if the journalists didn't.

Becker's words, and so many subsequent journalists' criticism of the clown, hit Perry hard. "The whole image

of clowns really appeals to me," Perry defended; he had, in
any case, a long history with the imagery. Wasn't it a clown
he'd wanted to torch in the movie? Wasn't he wearing a clown
suit that evening in Fort Lauderdale when the Cuban gang
members attacked him? Maybe that memory was still with
him when he continued, "The obvious thing to do when using
a clown is either have him exceedingly funny, or exceedingly
sad, and it's been done both ways a lot. I would like to use
clowns for something . . . to think of a clever way to use the
image of a clown."

He openly discussed the clown's role in society; in
modern society, in which the notion of the "killer clown" had
already sustained tales as diverse as Stephen King's *It* and
Marvel Comics' *Obnoxio*.

"I've seen so many stories where the clown is the
. . . killer. If you already go, 'Oh, it's gotta be the clown,' then
the clown thing has been done too much. But . . ." And now
his mind was racing forward toward the already germinating
dream of a successor to *Gift*. "I can't figure out whether to
make him something of a clown gone mad, which has been
done before, [or] a clown being the happy clown, [which],
being an adult, doesn't work either. It only works for children,
[and] maybe that's it. In real life, those people are . . . if you're
a real happy clown, you're weird. I almost wouldn't buy it.
That could be odd."

The Porno for Pyros tour moved on, a string of
concerts that ran throughout the spring and summer of 1993.
The majority sold out easily, although it was surely coincidence alone that dictated that the best-attended shows should
be those that occurred in the areas Perry once called home—
in California, in Miami, where they packed the Bayfront Park;
and right at the end of the outing, in mid-June, when they sold
out two nights at New York's cavernous Roseland Ballroom.
If Nirvana hadn't chosen the same venue for their surprise
New Music Seminar comeback just one month later, it is unlikely that anyone could have topped Porno for Pyros' reception that evening.

"Their set looked like the inside of a big top," wrote the *Island Ear*'s Dave Gil de Rubio. "PFP's music coupled with the love concept of a kind of performance art/sexual sideshow in a circus setting is far beyond anything P.T. Barnum could ever have imagined."

If the American press in general regarded Porno for Pyros as something less than spectacular, the band's arrival in Britain in July, to appear at the annual Glastonbury Festival on July 25, was greeted with rabid enthusiasm. *Porno for Pyros* was still hanging around the upper echelons of the chart, but more than that, it was as if the entire country felt as though it had a personal stake in Lollapalooza—"because it was our festival which gave you the idea"—and wanted to share in its success. Perry was greeted with open arms, full-page magazine spreads, and a roar that was still echoing around the festival grounds long after the band's performance was over.

The band returned to the United States for a string of open-air shows, then it was back to England for the Reading Festival on August Bank Holiday weekend. At last, Perry could meet his baby's spiritual father.

That baby, meanwhile, was going from strength to strength. Lollapalooza 1992 had doubled its pioneering predecessors' income, both financially and in terms of bums on seats. Even before the lineup was announced, Lollapalooza III looked set to improve on that.

There was increasing opposition to its continued growth. Shortly after the last night of Lollapalooza '92, the Triad agency was bought out by the enormous William Morris Agency, which not only inherited most of the smaller company's acts, Porno for Pyros included, but it also got its hands on Lollapalooza. Triad had not, by any means, been a small company—it employed over three hundred people at the time of its purchase—but suddenly, Lollapalooza was out of the alternative marketplace. Now it was in the bullring with the big boys, and that made a big difference.

It was not only the music press that sensed the change. Triad's own employees could see which way the wind was blowing. "It became too corporate, too bottom-line oriented," Triad's John Rubeli complained. "[It] was not about music anymore." He quit the company shortly after the buyout.

Marc Geiger, more than anyone at the company the traveling festival's godfather, followed.

Shorn of one of its principle organizers, and with Perry, too, feeling the strain of trying to make his voice heard within the hard-nosed atmosphere of the new-look organization, Lollapalooza '93 didn't stand a chance.

Perry himself was disgusted by the whole affair. His own ideas, he complained, were "kind of brushed aside. . . . People just went, 'Ah, another of Perry's ideas, maybe if we appease him he'll go away.' Who the fuck knows what's going on over at William Morris?"

Angrily, he tried to wash his hands of the tour. "I don't have time to baby-sit them, and my name's attached to all of it. I just have to grit my teeth and pray that I don't get embarrassed too many times.

"People got carried away with themselves, and forgot how things got where they were. People just stopped thinking it really was more than just a rock 'n' roll concert. To me, it's more about youth culture, and music is an important part of youth culture. But they just thought, okay, now that we've got it established, let's just fill in seven bands"—including, for the 1993 festival lineup, five from the William Morris Agency's own roster.

These accusations look set to continue for as long as Lollapalooza itself continues. Before the 1995 schedule was even confirmed, Stone Roses manager Doug Goldstein complained to the *Los Angeles Times* that the British band had been knocked off the festival shortlist because they signed with the International Talent Agency, rather than William Morris. Don Muller subsequently denied this.

Talking to *Rolling Stone*, Perry went even further, finally lending his voice to those that had been raised in opposition the year before. The music, he asserted, was the worst part of the whole thing. "It becomes very political as far as who gets on the stage. Man, when the money starts rolling in . . . it's *your* fucking project, and all of a sudden you're hearing secondhand who's gonna be on. It scares me!"

Perry owned the actual name Lollapalooza, a hefty commercial property even without the corporate sponsorship that queued, patiently but increasingly despondently, at its door, and for a while, he was seriously contemplating selling it off.

"I did put the word out to see whether it was a good idea to sell it, to bury it," he admitted, and according to Ted Gardner, he was very serious about it. "I don't know if I want to be a part of it anymore," the singer pondered at the time. "I give ideas and stuff [but] Ted Gardner knows more about it than I do."

Perry changed his mind about selling when he remembered the ethics that had spawned Lollapalooza in the first place. He'd conceived it as an alternative to what was already out there. If it was slipping away from that ideal, it was his job, his *duty*, to bring it back.

Gardner convinced him of this when he admitted of the 1993 Lollapalooza, "We lacked that certain amount of imagination that Perry gives us. Perry is purely ideas, and if he's less involved, that leaves it to the more pragmatic, logistical of us, who sit there and say, 'Okay, what are we going to do?' It affected us immensely." Next year, he and Perry vowed together, would be different. In the meantime, there was nothing to do but get on with this year's.

Lollapalooza '93 followed its immediate predecessor both in terms of its sheer magnitude and in the weight of criticism that descended upon the final billing. Even after the original dream of concentrating on mainstream artists whose careers nevertheless retained a glimmering of alternative credibility—

the likes of Sting, who opted instead to open for the Grateful Dead, Neil Young, and the re-formed Velvet Underground—had been discarded, still Lollapalooza read like a corporate-rock menu, and a very formulated one at that.

(What would become Young's seemingly annual dalliance with the Lollapalooza wish list finally ended in 1995 when, according to Perry, the singer simply priced himself out of contention. "Neil is a great guy, but my aim is to deliver a good show for a certain amount of money." He would deliver a good show as well, with or without Neil Young.)

Alice in Chains maintained the previous year's Seattle connection; Arrested Development was even more of a token rap act than either of their predecessors; Front 242 stepped into Ministry's well-worn industrial booties; and Fishbone, of course, was after the Red Hot Chili Peppers' crown.

The only real surprise was the inclusion of Babes in Toyland, and that wasn't too much of a surprise, really, not after Anthony Kiedis's highly publicized complaints about L7's treatment the previous year. Babes in Toyland were girls, and they rocked as well—or at least, they would for half the tour. Pioneering what has since become another Lollapalooza tradition, the lowest-billed bands would play through only part of the tour. Midway into the outing, Babes in Toyland would be replaced by Tool, an aggressive Soundgarden-esque rock band—managed by Ted Gardner.

Once again, of course, there was some suggestion that Porno for Pyros themselves would be on the bill, but Peter DiStefano was swift to scotch them. "I don't think we deserve to play. I want us to *earn* the right to get up there with the bigger bands." Porno for Pyros were in Europe for much of that year's Lollapalooza and that in itself only emphasized the distance between Perry and his baby.

The United States Secret Service had seen a lot of counterfeit bills over the last few years. The ready availability of color photocopiers made the production of such things cheaper and easier than it ever was in the past—just four years before, in

1989, the Secret Service made its largest-ever seizure of counterfeit notes, which had simply been run off on a laser copier in Phoenix. The ever-greater volume of cash that changed hands on the high street every day meant that it could be weeks, even months, before a high-quality reproduction was even detected.

Somehow, though, the agents who stood talking with the manager of a Miami Denny's restaurant doubted that they had suddenly stumbled upon another major forgery ring. For a start, the hundred-dollar bill that they'd been called in to investigate didn't even attempt to reproduce the manifold security devices with which genuine Federal Reserve notes are peppered. It didn't feel right either, but even more damning, it didn't look right. Even at his most abandoned, Benjamin Franklin never wore a ring through his nose.

It hadn't even crossed Perry's mind that he might be breaking the law when he printed up the sackful of imitation hundred-dollar bills that he intended distributing to his audience on Porno for Pyros' spring tour, 1994. Such novelties turned up all the time in gift stores and mail-order offers, carrying everything from the Statue of Liberty to the faces of Disney characters. Alice Cooper even gave away a free billion-dollar bill with his *Billion Dollar Babies* album. Each of Perry's bills even carried his face instead of Franklin's. Nobody could ever confuse the two.

Or could they?

The bill that wound up in the Miami office of the Secret Service had passed into circulation late that same evening, handed on, presumably, by one of the concert-goers who hit Denny's on their way home from the Porno for Pyros show.

The penalties for counterfeiting American currency are harsh. The manufacturing of fake or altered bills bears anything up to a five-thousand-dollar fine, and a fifteen-year prison sentence. Simply distributing them carries a similar punishment. And although nobody at the agency believed that these bills were intended to deceive, and a few agents even thought the whole affair was rather amusing, that wasn't the point.

A warning went out to local stores and merchants to carefully inspect any hundred-dollar bills that they might be offered, and to contact the Secret Service if they came upon any suspicious ones. Then, the following evening, before the concert at the Bayfront Amphitheater, the Miami police and federal agents swooped, counted, and then confiscated Perry's funny money. No charges were filed.

Porno for Pyros had swung back into intermittent action early in the new year, sharing a bill with Alice in Chains, Primus, and Tool at the Hollywood Palladium on January 7, 1994. The show was a benefit for Norwood Fisher, raising funds to help him fight the kidnapping charges that were preferred after he allegedly attempted abducting a former bandmate who he claimed was suffering from mental problems. Subsequently, Norwood was acquitted of all charges.

Again, it was not a satisfying show. Rousing sets from Tool and Primus gave way to an almost incoherent Porno for Pyros outing, characterized almost from the outset by the catcalls and bellows for the headlining Alice, which ricocheted from the floor. While Alice in Chains was no better, probably even worse as they meandered through a brief unplugged set, that was no compensation for Perry. Then, with the Miami banknote business following so swiftly on the heels of one of the worst shows he'd ever played, it was with considerable relief that he watched the media spotlight turn back toward Lollapalooza.

After the debacle of the previous year's outing, Perry was determined that the two-month Lollapalooza IV, which would be kicking off in Las Vegas on July 7, 1994, would return to every ideal he had imbibed its prototype with.

"Perry's more involved this year than he's ever been," John Rubeli, the second-stage organizer, told *Alternative Press*. "It's kind of like the President gathering around all his Vice Presidents [and] saying, 'This is how I want things to go.'"

For months the grapevine had buzzed with the news that Nirvana were set to headline the tour, for a staggering $100,000 a night. It was a fascinating scenario. Since their emergence with the *Nevermind* album, less than three short years before, the Seattle group had become synonymous with the same "Generation X" culture as Lollapalooza was targeted toward. It was a synonym Kurt Cobain fought furiously to escape—furiously, desperately, and increasingly hopelessly.

In early March, at the conclusion of Nirvana's latest European tour, a comatose Cobain was rushed to a Rome hospital suffering, the official statement insisted, from an inadvertent overdose of alcohol and painkillers. He returned home to Seattle shortly after, and at the end of March 1994 checked himself into rehab, the Exodus Recovery Center, in Marina del Rey, one of Los Angeles's southern suburbs.

His wife, singer Courtney Love, was in Los Angeles at the same time, preparing for the media blitz that was gearing up around her own band's new album, Hole's *Live Through This*. She was one of the few people who knew the truth about the Rome incident—that it was in fact a suicide attempt, but Kurt was in the center now. She prayed that he'd be allright.

Two days later, Cobain disappeared, checking himself out of the center and, as far as anyone could tell, simply vanishing from the face of the planet. For the next five days, Love telephoned everybody she could think of, in the hope that one of them may have seen Kurt. Nobody had.

"Courtney called me . . . and asked me if he was at my house," Perry told *Spin*. "He ran away from rehab, and she thought he might be heading my way."

"If he should turn up . . . talk to him? Try and make him understand . . ." Love's voice was weak with worry, and Perry promised he would try. He and Cobain were never close to each other, but from what Love told him, "I guess he respected my work, so she thought that he would listen to advice."

What advice could Perry have offered him, though? What advice could anyone have offered him? "Fame goes away," Perry knew from his own recent experiences. "Bro, let me tell you, it goes away quick."

The fame that engulfed Cobain went beyond simple pop stardom, beyond even the megastardom that rock 'n' roll so capriciously gives and then snatches away. No longer the property of the music press alone, Cobain was more than a star; like Frank Sinatra or Elvis Presley, he was an icon, the symbol of the nineties' disaffected youth. Even in total isolation he would have remained one. It was that, more than anything, that he could not bear to live with, the knowledge that whatever he did, he would always be Kurt Cobain.

Nirvana's withdrawal from the Lollapalooza lineup was announced by the band's own Gold Mountain management company, the same day Perry received Courtney Love's phone call. It was only later that Perry would acknowledge that while everyone around him was keen, Cobain himself never actually agreed to do Lollapalooza. It was other people entirely who suggested that the official denial was only issued now in the hope that Cobain's disappearance was somehow connected to that reluctance, and that with the pressure off him, he would quietly resurface.

The ruse didn't work. Two days later, Cobain's body was discovered in a room above the garage of his plush Seattle home.

Perry was devastated. "It makes me sick that he did that. They were working [him too] hard, I guess, and the kid didn't know what to do, how to say 'Fuck off.'"

Lollapalooza made no attempt to replace Nirvana, even within the provisional running order. The recently revitalized funkmeister George Clinton was originally approached to take over as the show's headliner (for a cut-price $25,000 a night); when he declined the offer, Smashing Pumpkins, the Chicago outfit that led the explosion of bands following Nirvana out of the trap, was pushed into the headline position instead, topping the bill over the most esoteric clutch of acts since the original Lollapalooza: Clinton, the Beastie Boys, the Breeders, A Tribe Called Quest, Nick Cave and the Bad Seeds, Green Day and the Boredoms (who split the opening slot between them), and, finally fulfilling Anthony Kiedis's dream, L7.

True to their determined vows of the previous year, too, the original organization team—Perry, Ted Gardner, Marc Geiger (now an executive at Rick Rubin's label, American), and Don Muller and Peter Grosslight, from the William Morris Agency—was back in place, doing its level best to rekindle its original dream, to reaffirm Lollapalooza, as Geiger succinctly put it, "as the beacon for all things alternative."

The team operated out of a basement in the William Morris Agency's Beverly Hills headquarters. Over at American, Heidi Robinson, Jane's Addiction's old publicist who worked alongside Geiger at the label, set about administering the plethora of tour propaganda that would be mailed out to journalists over the next six months. On every front, Lollapalooza '94 exploded with energy.

In the past, Perry had loudly proclaimed that the music was only a fraction of what Lollapalooza was really all about. His boasts had sounded hollow in the past, but this year there really was a truckload of diversions littering "the Mindfield."

Regular press releases, each one stamped with a photograph of a wide-grinning Perry, documented the developments as they happened. Once the tour got under way, a daily tour newspaper, *Teeth*, would continue the service.

A Revival tent was set up for spoken-word forums and off-the-cuff performances; and amidst all the poets and performance artists who were invited to literally walk in from the crowd, there were a few surprises: in Los Angeles, when poet Michael McClure joined former Doors keyboard player Ray Manzarek on the tiny stage; in San Francisco, where Angelo Moore of Fishbone jammed with members of the Beastie Boys; and in Miami, on August 15, when Perry blew in breathless from Woodstock, and hammered out an unannounced four-song acoustic set.

Cameras representing a visual dating service would roam the festival site, inviting people—a total of 2,583 by tour's end—to introduce themselves on a giant video wall.

There would be a Rain Room, with a constant temperature of fifty degrees, to cool off in, and a lavish interactive exhibit of computer technology and virtual reality, the Electric Carnival, which was set up with a $2 million grant from Microsoft co-founder Paul Allen. The exhibit was Perry's idea. "You can't beat nature," he said, "but it can't hurt to have some manmade fun." According to Marc Geiger, this spectacle was only the beginning.

"Hopefully, we can get wilder and more adventurous over time," he told *The New York Times.* "We still have to consider the economics, because we're still playing certain big places and we have to sell tickets. The more Lollapalooza can sell tickets on its own, the more adventurous we can become." He admitted his ambition was to have Lollapalooza "sell fifteen thousand or twenty thousand tickets without [us] announcing any acts of any consequence. Then we can really get crazy." Even so, Perry added, "we'll be mixing the known with the unknown and getting away with it."

Ticket sales were encouraging from the start. Although one date, in Utah, was canceled, other shows sold quickly. Even in the face of widespread cynicism regarding the site itself, the mid-river Randall's Island, the two New York City dates sold 43,000 tickets in one weekend. By June 14, all 50,000 tickets were sold, a full sixty days before the show.

Denver, Chicago, Detroit, Toronto, Atlanta, Dallas —the SOLD OUT signs went up even faster than Lollapalooza '94 could add fresh dates, which was happening constantly. Shows now stretched into early September, a forty-three-date outing adding up to the longest Lollapalooza yet. Ultimately, there would be a total paid attendance of more than 900,000 people, at twenty-eight dollars a ticket. A little less than one dollar apiece, a total of over $850,000 would be donated to charity.

However, memories of the previous year's festival, and, in particular, Perry's virtual absence from the event, remained vivid, even among the bands whose presence on the second stage Perry apparently paid special attention to.

"I saw Perry Farrell on TV looking so *crazy!*" Luscious Jackson's vocalist, Jill Cunniff, remarked.

"Oh, he's a *freak,*" drummer Kate Schellenbach responded.

"And he's the guy who organizes the whole thing?" keyboardist Vivian Trimble asked. "Does he still?"

The same questions were asked on the Internet network through which Electric Carnival–goers suddenly found themselves able to communicate with a few of the performers, when Lollapalooza reached Denver on July 9. But it was Nick Cave, the most surprising turn on the bill, and, as it transpired, the one Perry had been trying to bring on board for four years now, who gave the most inspiring responses.

He painstakingly answered every question he received, about his creative processes and his hopes for the tour. Then, at the end of the session he turned to *Details* journalist Gavin Edwards and complained, "Not one of them really took advantage of the direct access that we've given them."

Edwards looked surprised. "What do you mean?"

"Nobody ever wants to know how big my dick is."

Lollapalooza would also be one of the subjects addressed on July 25, when Perry debuted Warner Brothers' new Cybertalk interactive talk show via the America On-Line computer network.

It was not the first event of its kind. In recent months several other Warner Brothers acts, Depeche Mode, New Order, Lou Reed, and the recently erupting Green Day included, had all attempted interactive press conferences, going one-on-one with their audience. It was, said Jeff Gold, Warner Brothers' senior VP of creative services, "the next logical step" to an already existing relationship with the public; Warner Brothers had gone on-line to the public several months previously. Giving the public the opportunity to communicate directly with the artists was indeed an innovation. It wasn't one that Perry himself necessarily needed.

* * *

Even with the apparent downward turn in his critical reception, even with Porno for Pyros having patently failed to simply pick up at the same point Jane's Addiction fell away, Perry Farrell continues to stand alone among the artists of his generation—the living artists anyway, for Kurt Cobain possessed that same sharp ability—in that the communication he offers his listeners comes from the gut, not from the mouth.

So what if a lot of what he says is hype; even if a lot of what is written in this book, drawn as it is from his own pronouncements, is also hype? The people to whom Perry addresses himself are not concerned with fact or fiction anyway. They believe, as Perry believes, in a truth above truth, and a law beyond the law. The gospel according to Perry Farrell—to rework an analogy that has all too frequently, and all too often, facetiously, been applied to his words—is above all else to be true to yourself. "Everyone is born an angel and dies a slave," Perry once remarked. "I want everybody to try and die angels."

As a child, he chose his heroes carefully, beginning with the boxer Cassius Clay. The greatest fighter of his generation, Clay won his first world heavyweight championship in 1964 in Perry's hometown, Miami, when he knocked out the defending champion, Sonny Liston. He repeated the feat in 1965, then confirmed his supremacy by demolishing Floyd Patterson, himself an eight-time champion, later in the year. By March 1967 Clay had won ten championship bouts, and equally important, won the admiration of the world with his sheer arrogance. He was the greatest, and he never missed the opportunity to remind people of the fact. Then everything went sour.

Refusing the U.S. Army's offer of an expenses-paid trip to fight in Vietnam, Clay was stripped of his title. It would be another seven years before he returned to the ring, as an Islamic convert named Muhammad Ali. Between 1974 and his retirement in 1979, he won thirteen more championship fights.

"Look what he did," Perry marvels. "In the sixties, in the midst of the war, he objected to joining the army, he changed his name and his religion, he said 'I am the greatest.'"

"The man burned himself up. He made everything look so easy. Something that's so difficult, taking shots to the face. And every time he did, he would open his mouth and eyes real wide and shake his head, 'No no no.' And now he can hardly even speak. Because he made it look so easy, but those shots really took their toll on him.

"I can relate to the guy, but he also scares me because I don't want to end up like him. Because I'm the kind of guy who can take the shots and shake my head and say, 'It don't hurt, look look look,' and do my windmill with my right hand and punch you with my left, and then move my feet real fast.

"I just feel sometimes that if people have that flamboyance, they burn fast. They burn themselves up fast. It's unavoidable. Yeah, a lot happens in my life, and maybe I'll burn out fast as well.

"But I'm gonna leave behind something good, I know it."

From "Jane Says" to "Pets," Psi Com to Porno for Pyros, and, towering above the modern musical landscape, Lollapalooza, some would say he already has.

ACKNOWLEDGMENTS

Now that it's all over, I'd like to thank everybody who helped see this book through to completion: Tony Secunda, who put the deal together; Jo-Ann Greene, who schemed the original dream; Rob Cherry, Joe Banks, and Jason Pettigrew, my editors at *Alternative Press* magazine, for pointing me in directions I might otherwise have missed completely; Gaye Black; Marion Breeze, Liz Coldwell; Barb East; Bobby Gale; K-Mart (not the store!); Geoff Monmouth; Ella Mueller; Chris Nickson; Orifice; Julian Paul; Howard Parr; Brian Perera; Lisa Ridley; Frankie Secunda; Tim Smith; Snarleyyow the Cat Fiend; Tim Stegall; Triple X; and all at St. Martin's Press. Cheers also to the many people who, for reasons of their own, spoke only under condition of anonymity. Their own recollections, and the factual wrongs they righted, made all the difference!

I would also like to acknowledge the many other sources I consulted during my research, singling out a handful as being of especial value: *Route 666—The Road to Nirvana*, by Gina Arnold (St. Martin's Press, 1994); *Babes in Toyland*, by Neal Karlen (Times Books, 1994); *Ramones: An American Band*, by Jim Bessman (St. Martin's Press, 1993); and *Appetite for Destruction*, by Danny Sugarman (St. Martin's Press, 1991).

Elsewhere, issues of *Alternative Press, American Music Press, BAM, Billboard, B-Side, Calgary Herald, Details, Detour, The Face, Goldmine, Hypno, Ice, Interview, Island Ear, Keyboard World*, the *Los Angeles Times*, the *Los Angeles Weekly, Melody Maker, Musician*, the *New Musical Express, People, Propaganda, Pulse, Record Mirror, Rolling Stone, Select, Smash Hits, Sounds, Spin*, and *Stanza* all proved invaluable.

Finally, the biggest bouquet goes to Amy, who put up with a lot, then came back for more.

Perry Farrell